GROUNDED

First published in 2010 by Blueimprint
Text copyright © 2010 by the Contributors

All rights reserved. No part of this publication may be reproduced, stored in a retrieval system, or transmitted, in any form or by any means, electronic, mechanical, photocopying, recording or otherwise, without the written permission of the publisher. The publisher does not have any control over and does not assume any responsibility for author or third-party websites or their content.

Library and Archives Canada Cataloguing in Publication

    Grounded : the work of Phillips Farevaag Smallenberg / edited by Kelty McKinnon ; with contributions by Michael Van Valkenburgh ... [et al.].

ISBN 978-1-897476-20-8

    1. Phillips Farevaag Smallenberg (Firm). 2. Landscape architectural firms--Canada. 3. Landscape architecture.
4. City planning. I. Van Valkenburgh, Michael II. McKinnon, Kelty III. Phillips Farevaag Smallenberg (Firm)

SB469.386.C3G76 2010   712.0971   C2010-901340-9

We gratefully acknowledge for their financial support of our publishing program the Canada Council for the Arts, the BC Arts Council, and the Government of Canada through the Book Publishing Industry Development Program (BPIDP).

 Canada Council for the Arts   Conseil des Arts du Canada

Book design by Pablo Mandel / CircularStudio.com

10 9 8 7 6 5 4 3 2 1

Printed in China

COVER   Washington Mutual Centre Roof Garden. Seattle, WA.

PAGES 4–5   Wall Centre. Vancouver, BC.

PAGES 6–7   Constructed stormwater pond at Glenlyon Foreshore Park. Burnaby, BC.

GROUNDED
THE WORK OF PHILLIPS FAREVAAG SMALLENBERG

Edited by Kelty McKinnon

With contributions by
**Michael Van Valkenburgh
Ken Greenberg
Jacqueline Hucker
Dr. Eduard Koegel
Bruce Kuwabara
Kelty McKinnon
Douglas Paterson
Julian Smith**

Contents

8 **Foreword**
by Michael Van Valkenburgh

11 **Introduction**
by Kelty McKinnon

19 **Landscape into Urbanism**
The evolving role of landscape architecture in contemporary city-building
by Bruce Kuwabara

67 **Dynamic Alliances**
A collaborative design process
by Ken Greenberg

87 **Place, Body, Memory**
Placemaking in a global world
by Douglas Paterson

131 **Interview**

157 **Cultural Landscapes**
Architecture and landscape in the 21st century
by Julian Smith

183 **Global Acculturation**
Urbanism in contemporary China
by Dr. Eduard Koegel

211 **Elysian Fields**
Nature in the service of commemoration
by Jacqueline Hucker

243 **SuperNatural**
The burden of wilderness
by Kelty McKinnon

274 PFS Partners
276 Staff
278 Contributors
280 Project Credits
284 Image Credits
285 Book Credits

Foreword

by Michael Van Valkenburgh

The emergence of landscape architecture as a distinct and separate professional discipline is relatively recent, occurring in the middle of the 19th century as American cities began to address the practical environmental and social challenges resulting from rapid growth and industrialization. During this era of professional luminaries such as Frederick Law Olmsted and Charles Eliot, landscape architecture was practiced as a publicly-oriented profession with strong ties to progressive political efforts to promote social values, environmental health and overall quality of life. Somewhere within the 20th century, however, the urban leadership role of landscape became vastly reduced as professionals seemed more concerned with the aesthetics of architectural Modernism than they did with exploring the core materials and experiences that were inherent within and unique to their own medium. Brilliant exceptions, such as Richard Haag, Ian McHarg and Lawrence Halprin, transcended this tendency, but the general condition of the profession was that of a caboose at the end of the design train.

Phillips Farevaag Smallenberg is the kind of practice that restores my faith in the idea that the 21st century will find the core social and environmental leadership values of the discipline restored. I first met them and grew to admire their work through our collaboration on the design of the Lower Don Lands mixed-use neighbourhood planning project in Toronto. This abandoned industrial port facility was in many ways an ideal meeting ground for two firms with a shared faith in the power of landscape thinking to catalyze integrated social, ecological and infrastructural transformations.

PFS has a masterful command of the communicative power of the landscape. In a practice that is very rooted in place, even as it expands around the globe, the landscapes designed by PFS, whether they are wholly urban or partly natural, emerge as centres of multidimensional experience and demonstrate a resourceful approach to the pragmatics of integrated design thinking. Similarly in their planning work, the landscape becomes the element that unifies the infrastructural pragmatics, environmentally positive strategies and the disparate social uses of the city: live, work, play, etc. This represents an important paradigm shift from architecture-based urban design to something that better approaches the fluid associations and shifting contexts that are the core subject of the emerging field of landscape urbanism. PFS is not alone in advancing this cause, but they are important pioneers in promoting a fundamental paradigm shift in the way that we design and build cities. I admire their present achievements while I look forward to their future work.

Introduction

by Kelty McKinnon

5th and Madison. Seattle, WA.

How we define and conceptualize 'ground' discloses much about how we understand and relate to landscape. The eminent figure-ground diagram, for instance, has been used since the Renaissance to comprehend the scale and pattern of urban structure. In this representation, space is a rigid dialectic. Ground becomes the antithesis to form—a white space that is invisible, inert and immaterial. Without architecture, landscape is illegible—its spatial qualities dependent on its circumscription. The optical illusion of black contrasted with white reinforces the dichotomy. As demonstrated by Rubin's vase (the famous double image of a black vase and two white faces), the eye is only able to perceive either figure or ground at any one time, never simultaneously. One occludes the other.

A more recent architectural fascination with facades and surfaces ushered ground from void to two dimensions, and reconceptualized it as flat, autonomous and purely visual. Like architecture, ground was defined as a skin, conceptually (and often literally) separated from subsurface physicality, and reliant on surface pattern and materiality for its spatial effects. But the conceptual frenzy over thin horizontality separated ground from its rich subsurface realities, limiting it to a thin stylistic canvas.

But an attention to surfaces need not mean lack of depth. Ground is sectionally deep with multidimensional effects. Within the soil are plants, animals, insects, bacteria and fungi; artifacts, infrastructure and architecture. Subsurface water gathers and flows in lakes, rivers and pipes. Electricity, gas, sewage, hydro and communications pass through the ground, as do trains, people and information. And ground is home to multiple physical, chemical, biological and anthropogenic histories encrypted in its horizons. These histories become visible above grade, in plant species that respond to particular soils, subsequent insect and animal life, and land uses made possible by underlying soil structure. Subsurface and aboveground conditions are tightly interconnected with reciprocal effects. Thus ground is so much more than just sectional lines and planar surfaces. It is both material and process, space and time. And when we think about its multispatial flows, ground is anything but an immaterial void. The lines dividing above and below, form and space, architecture and landscape, culture and nature become blurred and difficult to pinpoint. Ground is a spatial practice.

The complex and mutable definition of ground is what interests Phillips Farevaag Smallenberg. Nearing its third decade of practice, PFS is first to see the folly of attempting to define a unified and consistent approach to their work. Instead they embrace dynamic process, where the specifics of site, client, community, technologies and conversations feed into unique and unrepeatable methodologies and outcomes. But over time, a series of conceptual attitudes to landscape and urban design have emerged. With this first published collection of projects and essays, we invited seven practitioners and academics to write an essay on current issues in contemporary landscape architecture and urban design. What results is a cross section, a kind of core sample, of perspectives that grounds PFS to particular practices—from contemporary city-building and placemaking, to collaborative practice, critical global consultation, historical intervention, commemoration and the formation of new relationships to nature.

Bruce Kuwabara's essay *Landscape into Urbanism* identifies landscape architecture as a prime generating force in contemporary city-building. In the process of creating cities with vibrant public realm, landscape is repositioned "to engage with, rather than detach from the city" by aligning with urban networks and infrastructure. The ways in which landscape can intensify the urban are exemplified in several civic projects in suburban contexts: British Columbia's Richmond City Hall, Ontario's Vaughan City Hall and Civic Precinct, and Washington's Bellevue City Hall; in projects along Toronto's Waterfront including the Toronto Harbourfront Competition, Sherbourne Park, and the West Don Lands Public Realm Plan; and in the Ravine House North Garden, a private landscape in Toronto.

In *Dynamic Alliances*, Ken Greenberg discusses a lateral and collaborative model of urban design inspired by a new understanding of cities as ecological entities that are dynamic, diverse and perpetually unfinished. Through the joint efforts of multidisciplinary teams that share diverse knowledge and experience, flexible frameworks are devised that allow for innovation, organic growth, change and surprise. Rather than predicting fixed master plans, these

frameworks anticipate and guide long-term transformations. Two new community projects: Ottawa's Rockcliffe Redevelopment and Toronto's East Bayfront Precinct Plan; and a master plan for the new University of British Columbia Okanagan campus (UBCO) in the Interior of British Columbia describe this methodology in action.

In *Place, Body, Memory*, Douglas Paterson explores a variety of perspectives on meaningful placemaking in a world under siege by global capitalism. He argues for new ways to embody the local without denying the global by focusing on the particular: particular ecologies, climates and people. He describes how several of PFS's projects "respect the past, enlarge the present and point to the future": a public cloister in downtown Vancouver, Cathedral Place; Washington Mutual Centre Roof Garden in Seattle; a historic civic cemetery in Vancouver, Mountain View Cemetery Masonic Area Redevelopment; a major Vancouver park, Hastings Park Restoration Plan; and a Landscape Plan for Canada's seat of democracy, Parliament Hill, in Ottawa.

Julian Smith's essay, *Cultural Landscapes*, heralds a paradigm shift in the way environments are theorized and worked with. A Modernist obsession with building—objects (and zoning tools that map space into discrete parcels) is giving way to a focus on experience, ritual, relationships and landscape. He uses the term 'cultural landscape' to stress the interconnected qualities of culture and environment and further defines the term by describing four collaborative projects dealing with complex historic sites: Ottawa's Confederation Square; a Landscape Design and Management Plan for the Canadian governor general's residential grounds at Rideau Hall; the Canadian Embassy in Rome, Villa Grazioli; and a Management Plan for a 567 hectare historic research farm in Ottawa, the Central Experimental Farm.

China's recent rapid urbanization is grounded in Dr. Eduard Koegel's *Global Acculturation* to a historic framework that describes the development of Chinese urbanism, political and economic reforms and reciprocal global influences. While the physical environment in China has radically transformed, so too has social behaviour, with a resulting demand for public space. Koegel describes the multiple and often conflicting roles that landscape plays and calls for an ecologically, socially and politically sustainable approach to new developments in China. He critiques several of PFS's initiatives in China: two new communities, Zhuzhou's Hui Tian Ran CityPark Master Plan and Changsha's Golden Ox Mountain; a suburban residential development in Shanghai, Blue Mountain; an urban apartment complex and streetscape in Chengdu, Metropolitan Apartments; a CMHC (Canadian Mortgage and Housing Corporation) commissioned study, the Shanghai Sustainable Community Standard; and a cultural master plan for the mausoleum of one of China's five legendary emperors, the Shouqiu Shaohao Historic Site in Qufu.

Jacqueline Hucker's *Elysian Fields* traces the radical effects of 18th century Romanticism on the public perception of both death and nature, and argues that the "primordial wilderness of the new world" became intertwined with the immanence of God. This transcendental perspective of nature, combined with the tremendous loss of soldiers' lives in World War I coalesced to forge a powerful sense of Canadian nationalism. She describes the power of landscape in expressing the solemnity of commemoration in four national memorials and monuments: Vimy Memorial, Canada's First World War memorial at Vimy Ridge in France; the Tomb of the Unknown Soldier at the National War Memorial in Ottawa's Confederation Square; the Canadian Police and Peace Officers' Memorial on Parliament Hill in Ottawa; and the Canadian Veterans' Memorial in Queen's Park, Toronto.

In my essay *SuperNatural*, I look to legendary British Columbian painter Emily Carr for strategies with which to approach landscape in an environment overly influenced by its surrounding spectacular scenic wilderness. Vancouver's setting of mountain, sea and rainforest has established an expectation for all landscapes to be calibrated (and secondary) to the image of wild nature. Carr's paintings and writings depart from this scenographic view of landscape and hint at a methodology that promotes emergence, multiplicity and open-endedness. Intertwined with nature and culture, her work is embedded in the land, emphasizing process and movement as much as form. These strategies are explicated in three projects: a public seawall promenade in Vancouver's Coal Harbour Marina Neighbourhood Phase One; Vancouver's Langara College Library; and a Master Plan and Cultural Resources Interpretation

LEFT North Vancouver Library. North Vancouver, BC.
RIGHT Richmond Olympic Oval. Richmond, BC.

Management Plan for a park in the District of North Vancouver, Cates Park / Whey-ah-Wichen.

An interview with founding partners Chris Phillips, Marta Farevaag and Greg Smallenberg rounds out the essays to discuss the great diversity of project sites, scales and approaches taken in the last two decades. The interview reveals the evolution that the firm has gone through and the formation of larger conceptual attitudes that have developed over hundreds of projects and collaborations. What emerges is commentary on the state of landscape architecture, planning and urban design in Vancouver, Canada and the world.

This core sample of ideas collectively reinforces a general theoretical shift from object to field in architecture, landscape and urban design, and demonstrates that ground is no simple substrate. The heterogeneous landscapes of PFS do not seek a stable state, but a generative engagement with natural and cultural flows to intensify the urban. Motivated by the desire to ground landscape to place, process, research, global realities, historic interpretation and future potentials, PFS's work shows that when ground becomes grounded it moves from object to action, greatly enriching the territory for improvisation.

5th and Madison. Seattle, WA.

Essays

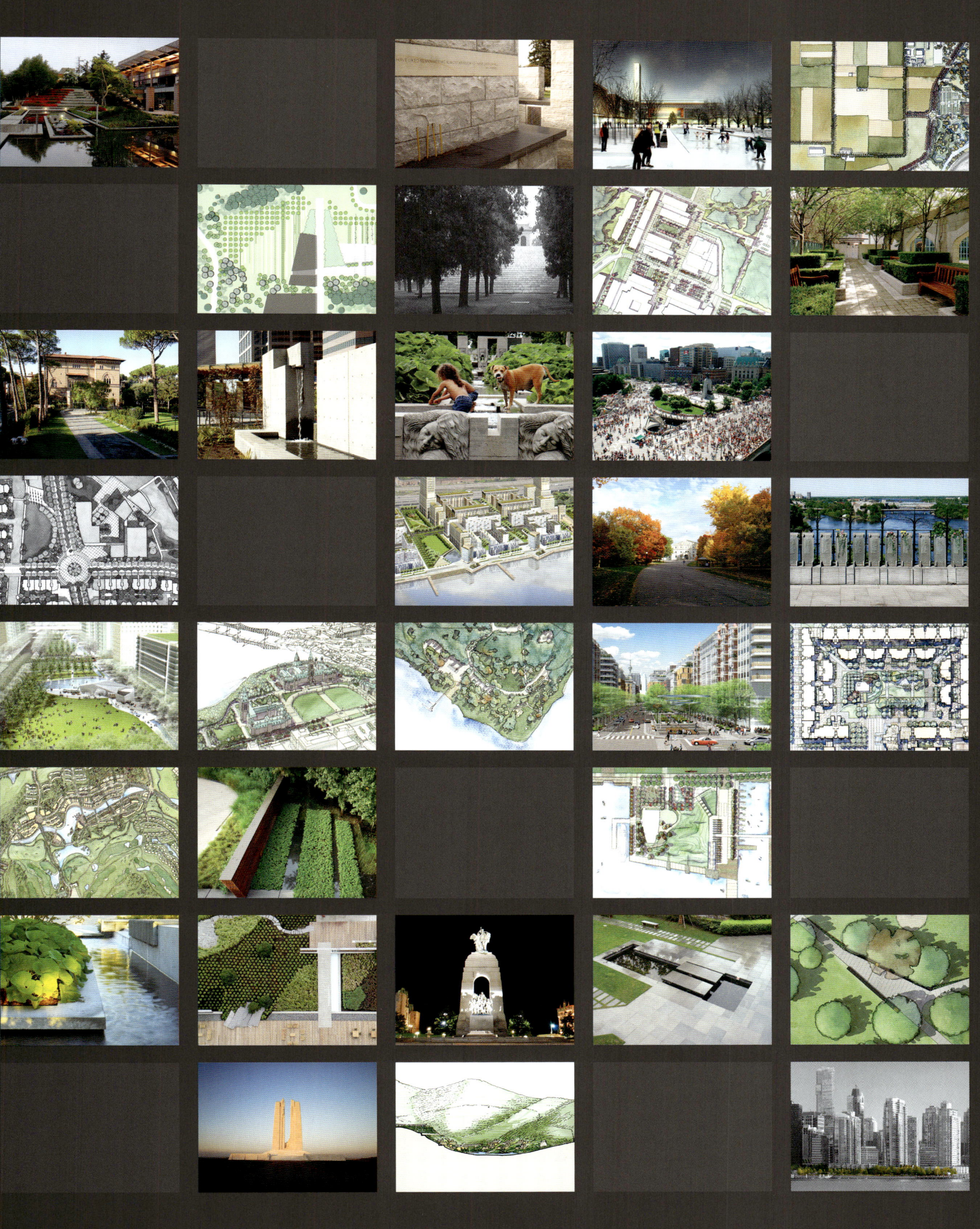

Landscape Urbanism repositions landscape to engage with rather than detach from the city. In this sense it is a 21st century counterpoint to the Garden City movement of the 19th century which involved the introduction of public parks into city cores to offer citizens reprieve from the oppressiveness and smog of the industrialized city. Landscape architecture has evolved as a generative force for reinventing cities as supportive, healthy live/work communities that operate within the framework of a connected, vibrant public realm.

Landscape into Urbanism
The evolving role of landscape architecture in contemporary city-building

by Bruce Kuwabara

The contemporary city is dynamic, constantly evolving its physical layers and processes. In urban design, each design move implies a position with respect to the complex conditions of the public realm. At the broadest level, the contemporary city is a post-industrial, knowledge-based centre with open, tolerant societies that drive local, national and global economies. Its challenges are population growth, urban sprawl and the formation of communities.

The relatively recent global explosion of urban populations has necessitated a paradigm shift in the processes of 21st century city-building. For the first time in the history of civilization, more people live in cities than in rural areas.[1] The challenges of the contemporary city are most effectively being addressed by interdisciplinary teams of local and international talent and expertise comprised of urban planners, architects, engineers and landscape architects. These global teams are applying integrated design processes to resolve often competing public and private sector interests related to infrastructure, housing, transportation, community services, public and commercial space, energy and the environment.[2]

Through these initiatives and processes, the discipline of landscape architecture has evolved as a generative force for reinventing cities as supportive, healthy live/work communities that operate within the framework of a connected, vibrant public realm. And it is firms such as Phillips Farevaag Smallenberg (PFS) that are effectively expanding the role of landscape architects to be advocates and creators of the shaping of spaces between built form into engaging public spaces, or the 'spaces of appearance'.[3]

Landscape Urbanism

The term 'Landscape Urbanism' was coined by Charles Waldheim in the early 1990s to describe the emerging approach to urban planning and landscape architecture that promotes the integration of environmental sciences, technologies and economics. It also describes a process that repositions landscape to engage with rather than detach from the city. In this sense Landscape Urbanism is a 21st century counterpoint to the Garden City movement of the 19th century which involved the introduction of public parks into city cores to offer citizens reprieve from the oppressiveness and smog of the industrialized city.

As a process-based activity characterized by inclusive, critical and interdisciplinary methodologies and teams, Landscape Urbanism strategically addresses the realities of our urbanizing planet. City-building initiatives are therefore shifting from individual buildings to connected, livable public spaces and social destinations.

To date, projects of Landscape Urbanism have been characterized by the re-purposing of abandoned industrial, military or transportation sites and structures into popular park-like destinations to improve civic identity. Examples include Chicago's Millennium Park built over active railroad tracks and a surface parking lot; Seattle's Olympic Sculpture Park by Weiss/Manfredi Architecture, built over the barrier of existing transportation infrastructure; and Manhattan's High Line by Diller Scofidio and Renfro, modeled after the Promenade Plantée in Paris, which transforms a raised transportation structure into an elevated park.

Effective practices of Landscape Urbanism must negotiate and facilitate complex public processes and communications conducted in real-time, mediated public forums as well as digital portals. These encompass: community management groups, planning and building authorities, environmental agencies, social programming, official plans and zoning by-laws, community approvals processes, street and park design requirements, transportation systems, fire and life safety codes, waste management, loading and servicing, wayfinding and signage, lighting standards, building code and accessibility requirements, sustainable systems, stormwater management, environmental remediation, maintenance and operations, implementation management systems and public art.

The aesthetics and processes of Landscape Urbanism express succession and the celebration of civic life. Ultimately a livable civic community is predicated on a walkable, connected and accessible public realm. Landscape Urbanism offers a sustainable strategy for making vibrant public places out of continuous networks of urban infrastructure that also combine recovered natural systems and abandoned industrial sites.

It is within the context of the contemporary city and the framework of Landscape Urbanism that a landscape firm such as PFS is evolving a greater and more dynamic role in city-building in the 21st century.

PAGE 18   Sherbourne Park South. Toronto, ON.
THIS PAGE   Sherbourne Park South – skating rink and pavilion. Toronto, ON.

Bruce Kuwabara   Landscape into Urbanism

Collaboration and Leading with Landscape

It is one thing to design a garden, park or tract of land surrounding a major building as a set piece. It is another to design landscape at an urban scale in the public domain. It was, however, in the private domain where I first encountered the urban landscapes of PFS in three condominium towers in downtown Vancouver (two by James Cheng and one by Bing Thom). All were exemplary in terms of how the landscape surrounding each tower responded to and integrated with the broader urban and natural setting of the city. It was this work that catalyzed the first collaboration between PFS and Kuwabara Payne McKenna Blumberg Architects (KPMB), on Richmond City Hall.

I have observed an exponential evolution of PFS's focus from landscape architecture to city-building. While PFS has always addressed both the public and private realms, they also consider the civic contributions of even the most private landscapes, something few landscape architecture firms in Canada have achieved.[4] Since our collaboration on Richmond City Hall, PFS has grown from an excellent knowledge-based firm known for their reinterpretation of traditional landscape strategies with West Coast sensibilities, to a dynamic, engaged practice of integrated thinkers influencing a range of projects. These projects include civic places in suburban contexts (Richmond City Hall, Vaughan City Hall and Civic Precinct, Bellevue City Hall), urban landscapes in the public realm (Toronto Harbourfront Competition, Sherbourne Park, the West Don Lands Public Realm Plan), and the occasional garden in the private realm (Ravine House North Garden).

The knowledge of historic landscape design and urban planning, ecological processes and practical built experience is fundamental to meaningful practice. PFS has consistently expanded and integrated the science and technologies of large-scale sustainable infrastructure and servicing and the art of city-building into their projects while imaginatively and effectively evolving its core talent to contribute strong analytical and intuitive skills to amplify the geography, typology and culture of placemaking.

As a collaborator, PFS shapes sustainable social and natural systems to reinforce architectural form and to position landscape as intrinsic to the creation of livable, beautiful cities. As leaders, PFS applies integrated thinking, bringing together landscape and city-building, contemporary models and precedents and international experience. Increasingly, PFS is handling large-scale urban precincts, campuses and community projects consistent with the tenets of Landscape Urbanism. In this sense PFS has effectively expanded the role of landscape architecture in Canada to a more generative shaping of the public realm.

 Richmond City Hall

 Vaughan Civic Precinct

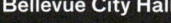 Bellevue City Hall

  West Don Lands

 Sherbourne Park

 Toronto Harbourfront Competition

The civic gardens at Richmond City Hall symbolize the coming of age of a metropolitan suburb as a mature city with a character and imagery of its own.

Civic Space in Suburban Contexts

In the course of its practice, PFS has played an integral role in the making of a series of highly civic-minded spaces located in the midst of disjointed suburban contexts. I have selected the following three examples of collaboration with KPMB to demonstrate how PFS repositions landscape architecture to catalyze civic engagement.

Richmond City Hall
Richmond, BC

Located south of Vancouver on the Fraser River delta, Richmond was founded as a farming and fishing community. It is now one of British Columbia's fastest developing municipalities. Perceived as a suburb of Vancouver, Richmond's long-term vision was to reassert itself as a viable urban centre.[5] Designed by KPMB Architects in association with Hotson Bakker, the project creates a civic heart within Richmond's suburban context of big box shopping malls, suburban neighbourhoods and high-rise condominium towers. It also established a benchmark in healthy workplace and sustainable environmental design in Canada.

Conceived of as an ensemble of three buildings, the composition is oriented to the southeast to optimize visual connectivity with Brighouse Park. PFS, as part of the consultant team, developed the landscape to merge seamlessly with the architecture, and to reinforce the concept of a civic plaza. Combining artificial topography, terraced platforms, concrete walls and steps, loops of public movement, and water in the form of cascades and pools, the design engages the street and the pedestrian by providing spaces for both large civic gatherings and intimate respite. A coalition of hard and soft elements creates an abstract network of landforms and vegetation that symbolically refers to Richmond's indigenous terrain.

In conjunction with the City of Richmond's mandate to use low-maintenance, low-impact landscaping, PFS strategically retained heritage tree groupings and utilized high-quality soils and indigenous, low-maintenance vegetation.

Richmond City Hall demonstrates how PFS calibrates abstract, Modernist patternmaking with natural materials, processes, plantings and contextual references to reinforce the role of landscape in civic placemaking.

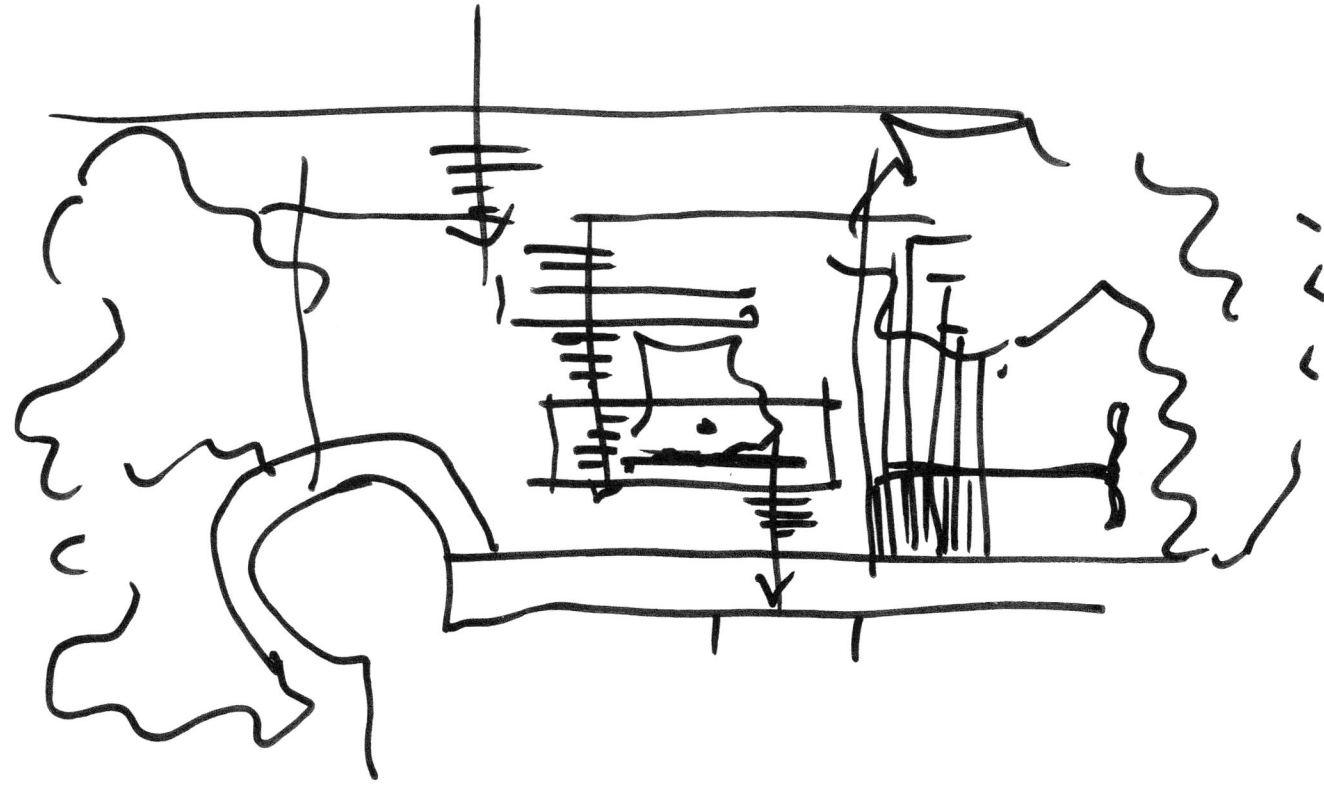

OPPOSITE PAGE TOP Cascading water edge along the south court. Terraced grading, berms and landscape treatments are used to compensate for a high water table that resulted in a finished floor height 1.5 metres above street level. BOTTOM LEFT AND RIGHT Civic gardens in the south court. The city of Richmond is located on Lulu Island, completely surrounded by the Fraser River on its way from mountain to sea. This geography is abstracted as an island in the pond fed by a rapidly flowing river. THIS PAGE Conceptual sketch of connectivity between street and city hall at south court. Richmond's rapid development as a suburb relied heavily on the language of West Coast Modernism. A contemporary modern design language is used to express this heritage and its principles of simple forms and connectivity between indoor and outdoor spaces.

Bruce Kuwabara Landscape into Urbanism

THIS PAGE LEFT View from the south court to terraced birch hillock. The city is protected from flooding by dykes – bold and distinctive landforms along its water's edge. At City Hall, the dykes are expressed as berms used to screen service areas, including waste, storage and the entrance to underground parking. RIGHT Massings of red flowering Japanese azaleas celebrate Richmond's acidic bog cranberry farms and multicultural Asian population. OPPOSITE PAGE TOP 'River to sea' metaphor. BOTTOM LEFT While there was initial skepticism from the City about the need for both indoor and outdoor civic space to host community events and gatherings, subsequent booking requests have exceeded expectation. Indoor and outdoor public spaces are closely linked, expressing the spirit of West Coast Modern design. BOTTOM RIGHT Birch grove at north forecourt. The remnant birch and shore pine forest with salal understory is unique to the region. The planting design stresses these native plant associations throughout the site.

Bruce Kuwabara   Landscape into Urbanism   29

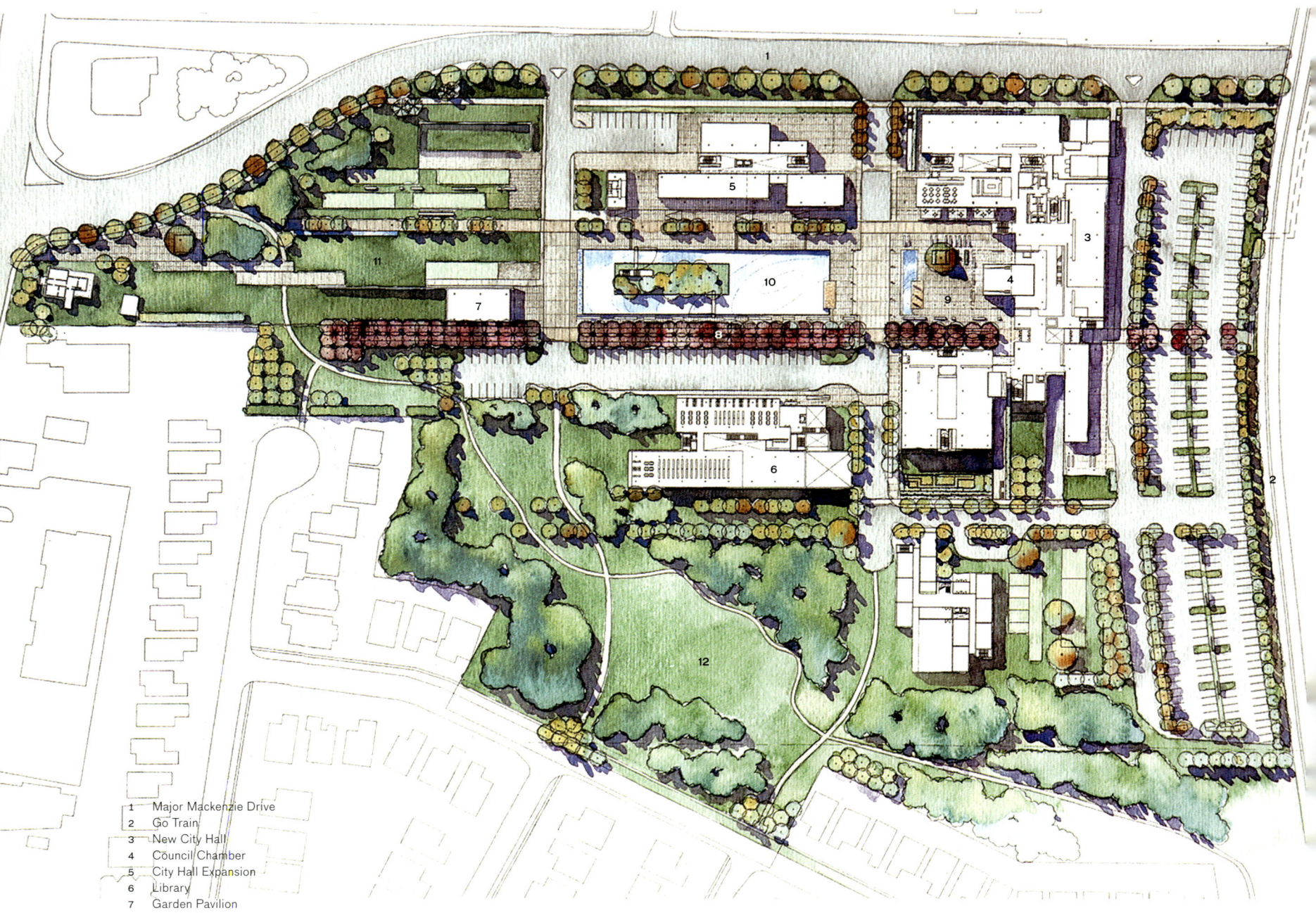

1 Major Mackenzie Drive
2 Go Train
3 New City Hall
4 Council Chamber
5 City Hall Expansion
6 Library
7 Garden Pavilion
8 Maple Allée
9 Civic Square
10 Reflecting Pool/Skating Rink
11 The Green
12 John W. Gamble Park

LEFT Vaughan Civic Centre Competition rendered site plan.
RIGHT Competition presentation model.

Vaughan City Hall and Civic Precinct
Vaughan, ON

Originally an agriculturally-oriented hinterland located at the northern edge of metropolitan Toronto, the city of Vaughan evolved in the absence of a clear civic vision. Rapid suburbanization contributed to the dissolution of the area's rural farmland communities as well as its regional architectural artifacts.[6] Pastoral landscapes and villages were consumed by generic spaces of consumerism (shopping malls and big box retail), residential living (subdivisions and 'monster homes'), and work (monolithic corporate headquarters) connected via high speed transport networks (highways and heavily trafficked four lane streets).

In 2003, the City organized an invited design competition for a new civic centre and a master plan for the development of a 10 hectare site bounded by high speed vehicular routes and residential subdivisions. The City called for proposals that would set the tone and standard for the development of Vaughan into the 21st century and establish a formal civic identity and centre for the city.

As one of four invited firms, KPMB engaged PFS to join its competition team, resulting in the winning scheme: a civic landscape composed of a series of low-rise buildings organized around a central rectangular civic square. The buildings' outdoor spaces are organized to align with the underlying concession grid system that once characterized the rural environment. The ordering system also draws on the clarity of Ontario town planning where City Hall, Civic Square, Market and Cenotaph formally define an identifiable civic precinct, as well as European traditions of the square or piazza for gathering and celebration.

PFS amplified the contextual, heritage and sustainability mandates of the City of Vaughan into the landscape strategy, reversing the suburban pattern of clearing out natural features and creating an interconnected terrain between built forms. The broader landscape strategy was inspired by campus planning and landscape systems to create a ground plane highly integrated with the architecture and building interiors to catalyze a dynamic public life, inside-out and outside-in.

The civic centre landscape strategy is comprised of four primary landscape zones: the Green, the Pool, the Civic Square and John W. Gamble Park. Each of these zones is connected by a number

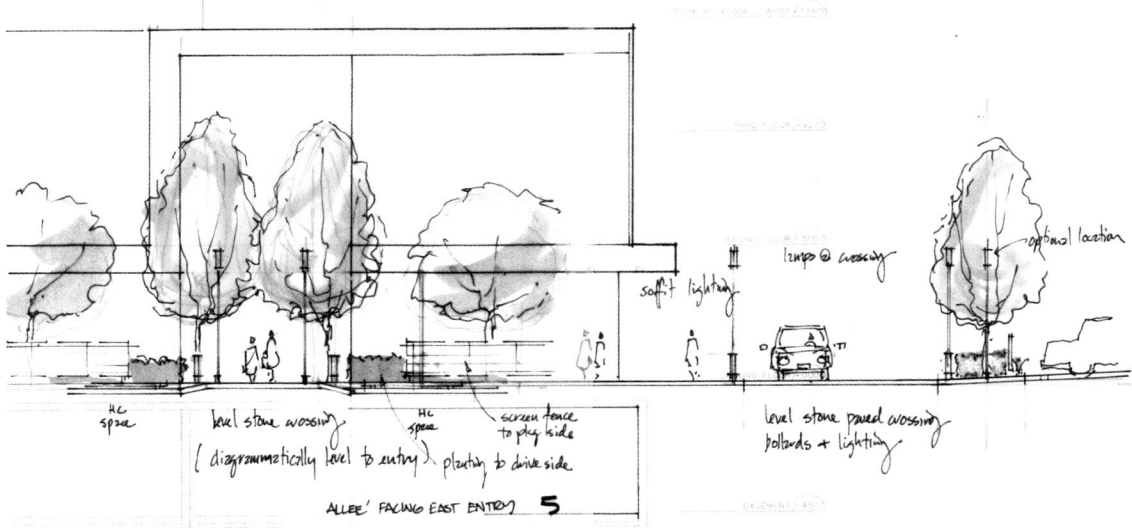

of supporting spaces and elements. The Green, a composition of open spaces defined by a series of strong east-west lines, recollects the agricultural and topographical legacy of the concession grid. Integrated into the grid are recreational and leisure-related gardens animated by a children's water play area, a Japanese garden, bocce courts, barbeque grills and ample seating opportunities. Plantings are curated to harmonize with the changing seasons.

The Civic Square, the main outdoor public space of the overall landscape, is closely linked to the program of the City Hall building. The council chamber overlooks the Square and is connected at grade with a glazed multipurpose room. The Reflecting Pool/Skating Rink ensures the Civic Square is animated throughout the Canadian seasons. It is graded gently from east to west, emerging from below surrounding grades at its eastern edge and gradually rising until it falls in a cascade at its western edge.

The Green, the Pool and the Civic Square are linked by a long axial walkway and maple allée—an organizing spine that anchors the south edge of the civic precinct and leads to the main entrance of City Hall. John W. Gamble Park, an existing park to the south, is integrated into the civic 'campus' and rejuvenated to improve neighbourhood amenities.

PFS also specified native and geographically adapted vegetation to achieve a seamless composition of architecture, landscape and sustainable design. They developed innovative strategies for stormwater management including biofiltration swales in the parking lots, a retention pond and a cistern for groundwater collection to be used for landscape irrigation.

Ultimately, the Vaughan City Hall and Civic Precinct project demonstrates the imaginative and collaborative contributions of PFS in placemaking, and their ability to realize sustainable mandates while creating urban oases in the midst of edge city conditions.

TOP LEFT AND RIGHT Phase One study sections.
BOTTOM Competition rendering of skating rink and civic forecourt beyond.

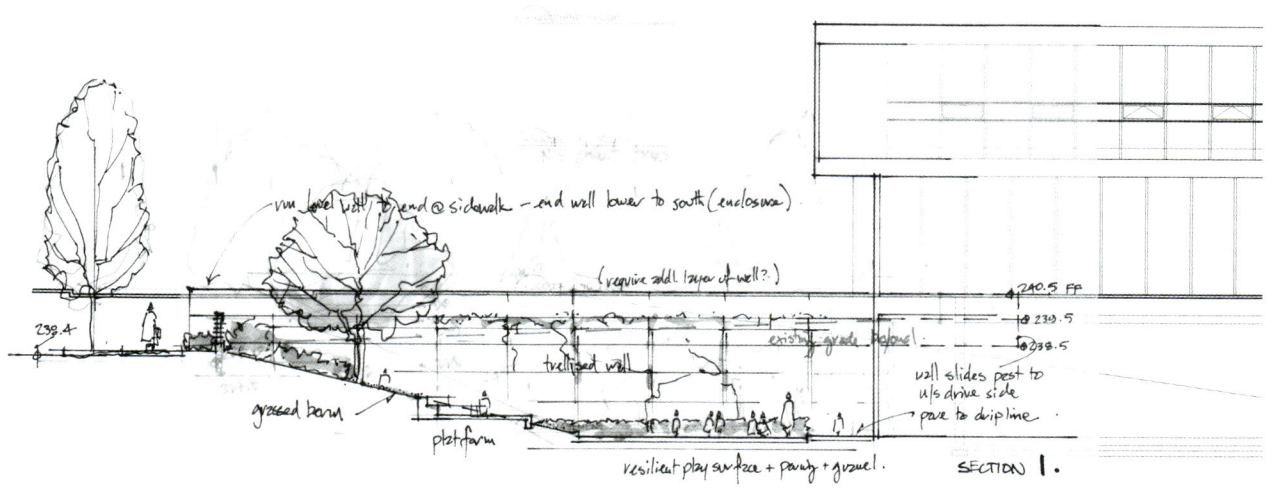

Bruce Kuwabara Landscape into Urbanism

LEFT A cascading waterfall provides acoustic interest between cast-in-place walls at the edge of the civic lawn. The three-metre drop symbolizes the difference in water level that permits access from the Port of Bellevue to Puget Sound. RIGHT Conceptual sketch of the lower water feature demonstrating the intended relationship of building to water.
PAGES 35–36 Water court with floating glass spheres. Sandwiched between Lakes Washington and Sammamish, Bellevue is fully surrounded by water. The pedestrian bridge across the lower water feature subtly echoes the bridges that connect Bellevue to its environs.

Bellevue City Hall
Bellevue, WA

Bellevue City Hall involved the adaptive reuse of an outdated office building into an inviting civic destination. PFS was engaged by architects SRG Partnership to strengthen City Hall's connection to its distinctive urban and natural context. PFS drew on the bold contrast between the indigenous geography and Modernist man-made forms evident in the city of Bellevue, a city bracketed by Lakes Washington and Sammamish.

The design strategy is anchored to the simple gesture of a new diagonal axial walkway that intercepts the expanded lobby of the existing building, directly connecting it to the street and outdoor civic plaza. The axis defines the edge of the civic space—a ceremonial lawn flanked by a bosque of honey locust trees, a restaurant pavilion, a terraced water feature and long linear steps for seating. The use of water is a civic and symbolic gesture that invigorates the arrival sequence. The axis is punctuated at key points with three public art installations: *Root* and *Longboat/Reed/Rookery*, by Seattle artist Dan Corson, and *Compass* by Vancouver artist Alan Storey.

THIS PAGE TOP LEFT The existing building extends into the landscape at two levels. Water is used to dramatize the extension. TOP RIGHT The public walkway connects NE 44th Street to the new city hall. BOTTOM RIGHT Detail of entry trellis with seating. OPPOSITE PAGE Rendered site plan emphasizing the strong contrast between Bellevue's natural terrain and its relentless suburban grid. The building atrium reaches out diagonally to the city and frames the new civic open space.

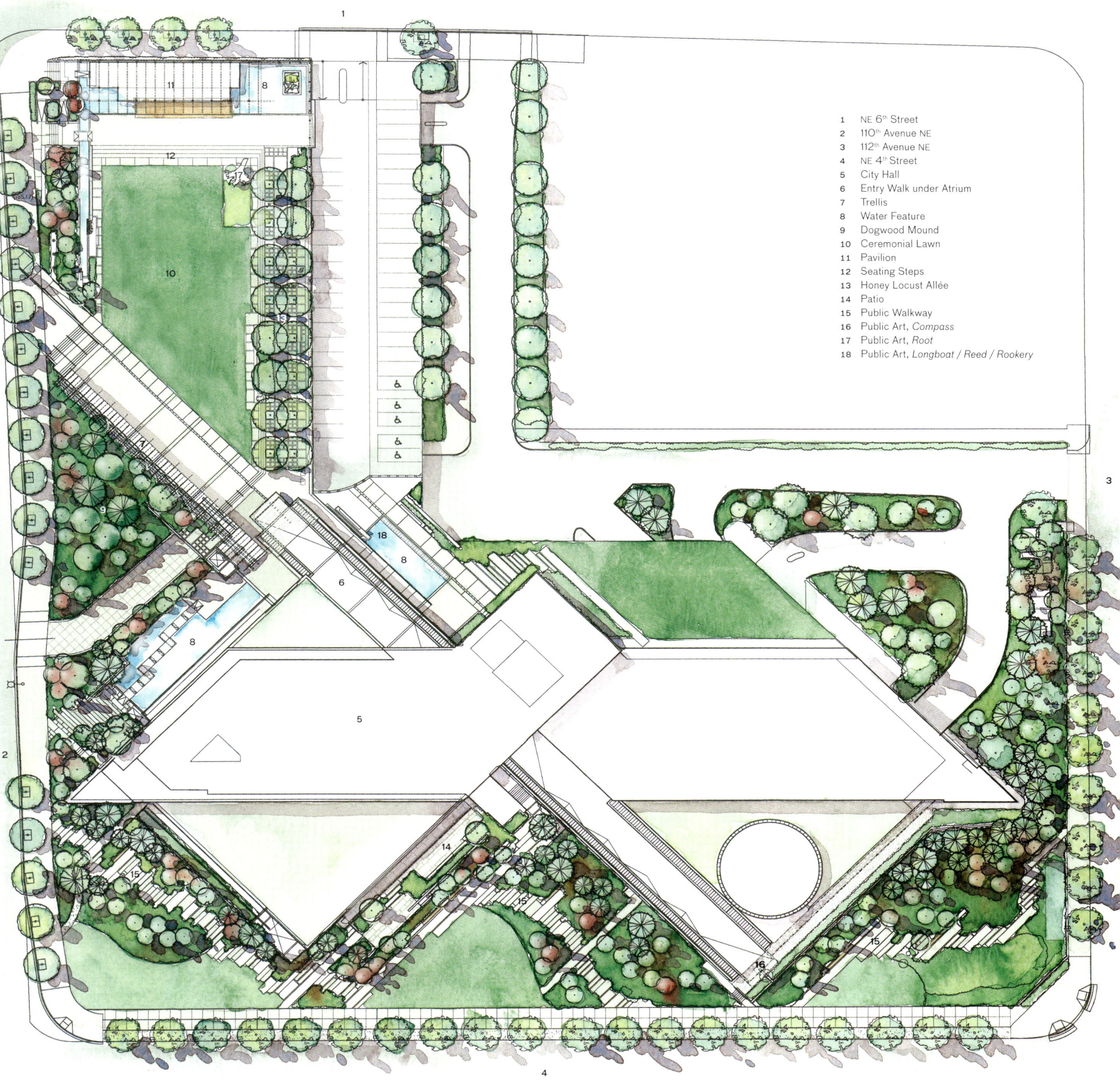

1. NE 6th Street
2. 110th Avenue NE
3. 112th Avenue NE
4. NE 4th Street
5. City Hall
6. Entry Walk under Atrium
7. Trellis
8. Water Feature
9. Dogwood Mound
10. Ceremonial Lawn
11. Pavilion
12. Seating Steps
13. Honey Locust Allée
14. Patio
15. Public Walkway
16. Public Art, *Compass*
17. Public Art, *Root*
18. Public Art, *Longboat / Reed / Rookery*

Bruce Kuwabara Landscape into Urbanism

THIS PAGE Comprehensive competition concept plan.
OPPOSITE PAGE TOP Pre-competition aerial photo of Maple Leaf Quay.
BOTTOM Aerial perspective of concept for Maple Leaf Quay.

1   Lake Ontario
2   Gardiner Expressway
3   Lakeshore Boulevard
4   Queen's Quay Boulevard
5   Spadina Avenue
6   Harbourfront Pier (Continuous)
7   Western Gate
8   Air Park
9   Harbourfront Community Gardens
10 Norwegian Air Force Memorial Walk
11 Existing Norway Park
12 Canada Malting Silos
13 Circus School in the Seaway Queen
14 Garrison Creek Ecological Gardens
15 Existing Music Garden
16 Bird Park
17 Existing Spadina Quay Wetland
18 Spadina Avenue Slip
19 Peter Street Slip
20 Peter Street Basin
21 Maple Leaf East Quay – The Confluence
22 Skateboard 'Street' Course
23 Pumphouse Park
24 Cafe and Climbing Wall
25 Reese Street Slip
26 John Street Cultural Corridor
27 New Media Sculpture Garden
28 The City Link
29 SkyDome
30 CN Tower
31 Simcoe Street Slip

Toronto Harbourfront Competition
Toronto, ON

The Toronto Harbourfront Competition, conducted in 2003, was one of the City's preliminary steps toward the renewal of its waterfront. The objective was to transform a 40.5 hectare precinct of lake and land into a major civic destination for citizens and tourists. PFS's team, which included KPMB and Julian Smith, was one of three finalists invited to advance a conceptual harbourfront park and open space design.

The scheme, dubbed 'Urban Confluence', created a dense landscape fabric that played off the openness of the harbour and John Graves Simcoe's historic military grid pattern. Simcoe's grid established the innate urban order of Toronto as a framework of south facing green spaces with related public/institutional buildings. The PFS team proposed a colossal green which effectively re-oriented the SkyDome, the city's major sports and recreation arena, to appear as a south facing cultural building. By extending the green south to Lake Ontario and north to the John Street Cultural Corridor, PFS responded to the long held dream to reconnect the city back to the waterfront.

The competition also required a more detailed design scheme for Maple Leaf Quay West. PFS conceptualized an undulating green that played off a highly programmed multipurpose community building designed by KPMB. This building was a contemporary interpretation of the linear pier buildings historically found along the waterfront, now programmed as a public amenity housing the canoe and rowing club, community gathering space, food services and washroom facilities. Architecture and landscape were fused together topographically and programmatically. At the same time PFS demonstrated their ability to merge aesthetics with performance by integrating stormwater filtration into a series of water features that resonated with the rise and fall of the topography and Lake Ontario.

Leading with Landscape – Toronto Waterfront
The city of Toronto is undergoing an unprecedented urban renaissance involving the simultaneous revitalization of academic campuses (University of Toronto and Ryerson University), cultural institutions (Gardiner Museum, Canada's National Ballet School, the Royal Conservatory of Music, the Art Gallery of Ontario and the Royal Ontario Museum), healthcare institutions (Centre for Addiction and Mental Health and Bridgepoint Health), the Railway Lands, low income residential neighbourhoods (Regent Park), and mixed-use neighbourhoods and parklands on Toronto's Central Waterfront (East Bayfront, the West Don Lands and the Lower Don Lands).

Since 2003, PFS has been working as a consultant and designer to develop strategies for the systems and networks that weave public realm into Toronto's previously neglected waterfront. As chair of the Waterfront Toronto Design Review Panel, I have reviewed many of PFS's projects, observing that they have increasingly moved into the domain of Landscape Urbanism, generating vital contributions to the making of continuous, sustainable and vibrant public realms.

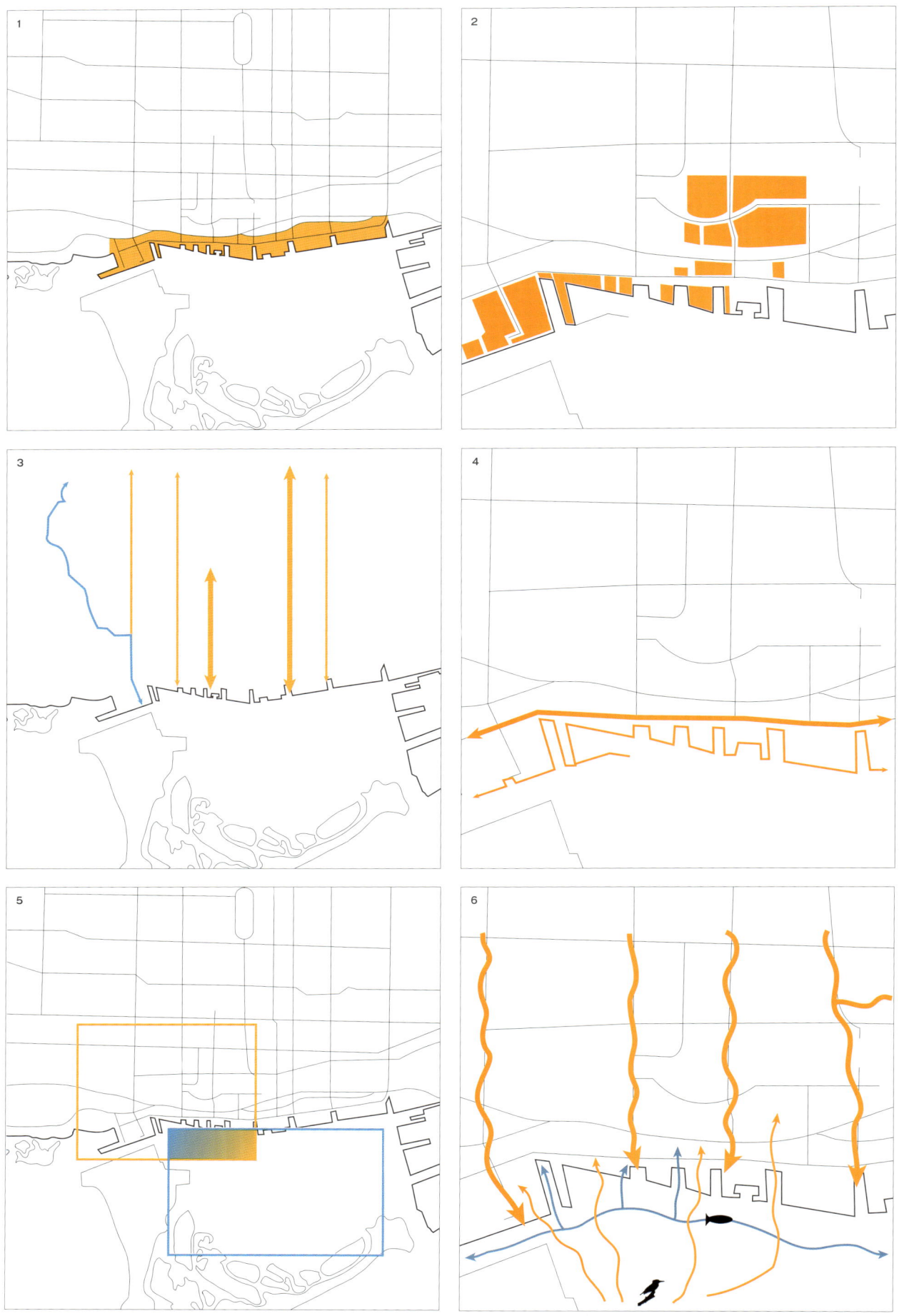

Mediating Scales: The Colossal and the Patch

(1–2) Harbourfront is the interface between the vastness of Lake Ontario and Canada's largest city. Rather than perceive its immense scale as a constraint, the opportunity existed for a grand gesture that could express Toronto's status as a world-class city recognizable in the global milieu. Concurrent to the colossal is the patchy, accretive condition of the existing Harbourfront site. In landscape ecology, the patch is a way of describing and understanding an organism's spatial domain in terms of composition and structure. Patches are dynamic and occur on a variety of spatial and temporal scales, often simultaneously. Each site along the Harbourfront holds a unique relationship to water and city, and a unique history that is at once cultural and material. Expanding tourism and residential development places even greater pressure on Harbourfront to become a social, cultural and recreational centre for downtown Toronto. This patchy condition was interpreted as an opportunity to promote a multitude of diverse experiences while stitching them together within larger scaled systems. Layers of program and material were used to merge various scales of public and private space without destroying the unique qualities of each urban patch.

Making Connections: Conduits and Threads

(3–4) The existing site of Harbourfront is largely disconnected from the city it seeks to express. Expansive rail and vehicular corridors combine with large buildings on immense city blocks to create a vast physical and psychological barrier, severing downtown Toronto from Lake Ontario. Accepting these infrastructural conditions, a series of bold north-south 'Conduits' were proposed that would simultaneously extend the city fabric to the water and pull Harbourfront Park north into the downtown core. Maximizing views both to and from the lake and entry and exit points would increase the permeability of Harbourfront's edges. As a counterpoint, a system of horizontal 'Threads'—an improved Queen's Quay Boulevard and a continuous pier along the edge of slip and quay—were designed to sew the heterogeneous collection of waterfront patches into a coherent 'place' that would register on the collective mental map of Torontonians.

Hybrid Ecologies: Incorporating Flows

(5–6) Facing both the Toronto Islands and the downtown core, Harbourfront mediates between the natural and the urbane. Hybrid ecologies were proposed that interpreted the everyday workings of the lake and city as ecological process, weaving together natural, infrastructural and cultural flows. A remnant of an industrial era that is now obsolete, the abrupt edge condition of Harbourfront currently polarizes nature and city by minimizing exchange between land and water. A more complex edge would reveal a new kind of 'working landscape' where human and ecological process could intertwine and mutually support one another. Slowing, storing and cleansing stormwater; creating habitat for fish, birds and insects; and creating zones of protective vegetative cover would create a newly interpreted littoral edge that is transitional, complex and gradual. Adding three-dimensional complexity to the edge through program, material and design would also intensify the relationship between land and lake, integrating the physical presence of water into the life of the city. Waterfront traffic, pedestrians, bicycles, joggers and information would intermingle with the passage of stormwater, plants and animals. Extending the notion of flows, the incidental and accretive growth of Harbourfront was interpreted as an ecology of time and process, where the project site would be developed incrementally in a design flexible to spontaneity and change.

Historical, Geometric and Cultural Stratigraphy

(7–8) An archaeological approach to the project site yielded three kinds of stratigraphies that were collectively historical, geometric and cultural. First, a vertical stratigraphy dug deep, revealing a robust palette of materials: the bedrock, earth and vegetation of the historical lake bed; the wood of early settlement piers, piles and sailing vessels; the concrete of piers, grain silos parking lots and the Gardiner; the steel of derricks, train tracks, tramways, bridges and cars; and glass—the new layer of translucent construction that emphasizes permeability and light. Second, a lateral stratigraphy emphasized the shifting edge condition that has transformed the lake edge from an undulating escarpment to an increasingly geometric crenellation of slip and quay. Finally, historical, poetic and personal experiences have peppered the many sites of Harbourfront to create an accumulated mental stratigraphy. The collection of narratives was interpreted to form temporal and permanent depositions that revealed the many stories of the waterfront. Flexible spaces were designed to allow for these mental stratigraphies to reveal themselves in diverse ways.

LEFT AND RIGHT Conceptual diagrams and descriptions analyzing the particular conditions of the harbourfront that set the approach for 'The Confluence' competition proposal.

Bruce Kuwabara   Landscape into Urbanism   43

1 Queen's Quay Boulevard
2 Harbourfront Pier (Continuous)
3 Flour Gardens
4 Reading Room
5 Dining Room
6 Peter Street Overlook
7 Entrance Plaza
8 Park Kiosk, Washrooms
9 Cafe Terrace
10 Ephemeral Grove
11 Existing Firehall
12 Undulating Green
13 Illuminated Glass Walls
14 Littoral Notches
15 Water Wedge
16 Maple Leaf Ridge
17 Kayak Rack
18 Relocated Nautical Centre (Temporary)
19 Boardwalk
20 Maple Leaf Pier
21 Floating Dock and Gardens
22 Rees Street Overlook

OPPOSITE PAGE TOP Rendered site plan of Maple Leaf Quay. BOTTOM Section showing Phase One building strategy – community pier building and undulating green. THIS PAGE MIDDLE LEFT Aerial perspective showing open space connection strategies to the city and the relationship with the SkyDome. MIDDLE RIGHT KPMB's proposed community pier building.

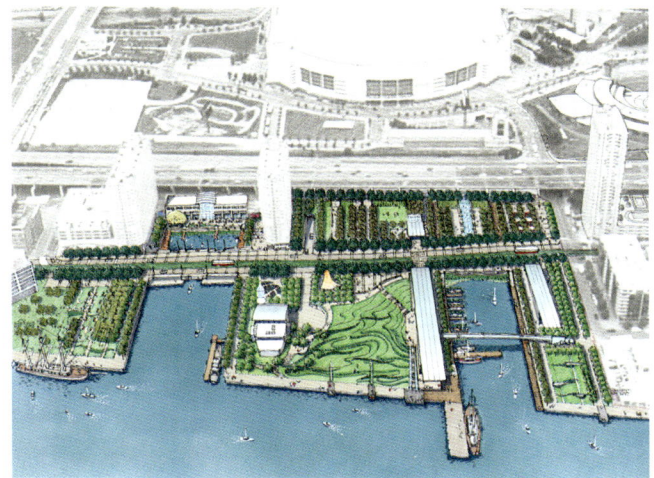

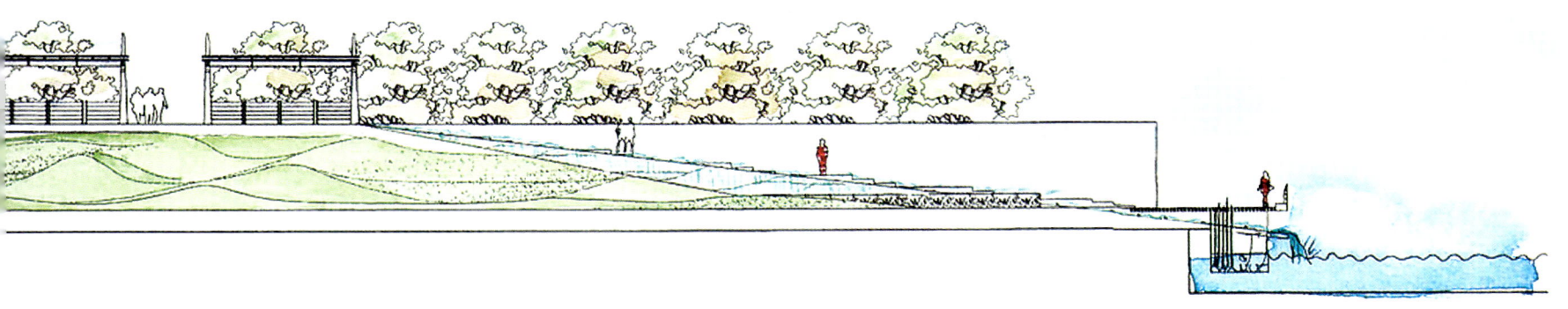

Bruce Kuwabara Landscape into Urbanism   45

Sherbourne Park
Toronto, ON

PFS was responsible for the East Bayfront Public Realm Plan, a component of the East Bayfront Precinct Plan led by Koetter Kim and Associates (KKA), and designed Sherbourne Park within the Precinct Plan framework. Located in the heart of the West 8 and du Toit Allsopp Hillier (DTAH) Central Waterfront Competition winning scheme, Sherbourne Park is conceived of as a major amenity linking city and lake, and functioning as both small neighbourhood park and grand civic destination. The north side of the park, north of Queen's Quay Boulevard, is designed for smaller gatherings and informal children's play while the south side is designed as a great civic green.

PFS abstracted the iconic Ontario lake-edge landscape into three spatial typologies: the Green, the Woods and the Water. The 'Green' references the natural clearing often found on the lakeshore, and is translated into a great urban green 'room' south of Queen's Quay Boulevard and next to Lake Ontario. Within the Green is a sculptural park pavilion designed by Teeple Architects. The 'Woods' are represented by a grand bosque of red maple trees that crosses Queen's Quay Boulevard and binds the north and south parks together. It is bracketed by a red oak allée along Sherbourne Street Promenade to the west and an American beech allée to the east that facilitate access to Lake Ontario. The 'Water' is a multipurpose central pond offering cooling water jets in the summer and skating in the winter, and intersected by a lineal water sluice that connects the north park with the south green and Lake Ontario.

The KKA/PFS plan for East Bayfront included a preliminary strategy, refined by others in subsequent stages, to capture all of the stormwater in East Bayfront for detention and filtration. Most of East Bayfront's stormwater will be dispensed into Sherbourne Park and purified via biofiltration and UV filtration before being passed into Lake Ontario. The stormwater narrative is the primary organizing feature of the Park and describes the journey and transformation of stormwater from the sky to the ground and ultimately to the lake.

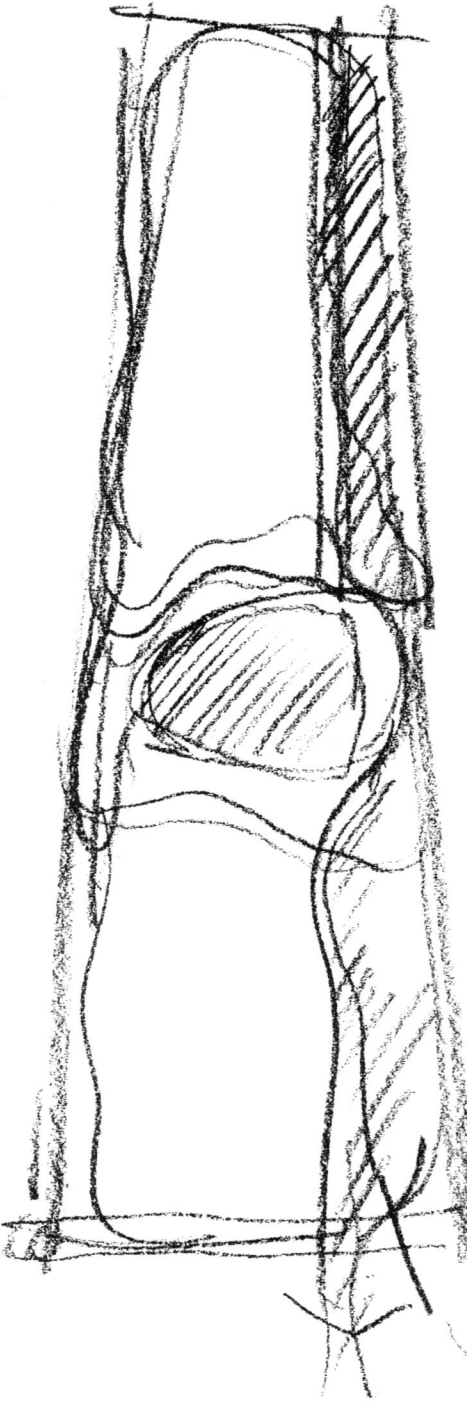

LEFT Generative sketch. RIGHT Rendered view over South Sherbourne Park to North Sherbourne Park.

Bruce Kuwabara   Landscape into Urbanism

THIS PAGE LEFT Ontario's lake-edge landscape abstracted into three typologies: The Woods, The Water and The Green. RIGHT Conceptual diagram of three landscape zones combined: The Woods, The Water and The Green. OPPOSITE PAGE LEFT Rendered site plan. RIGHT COLUMN Early model studies.

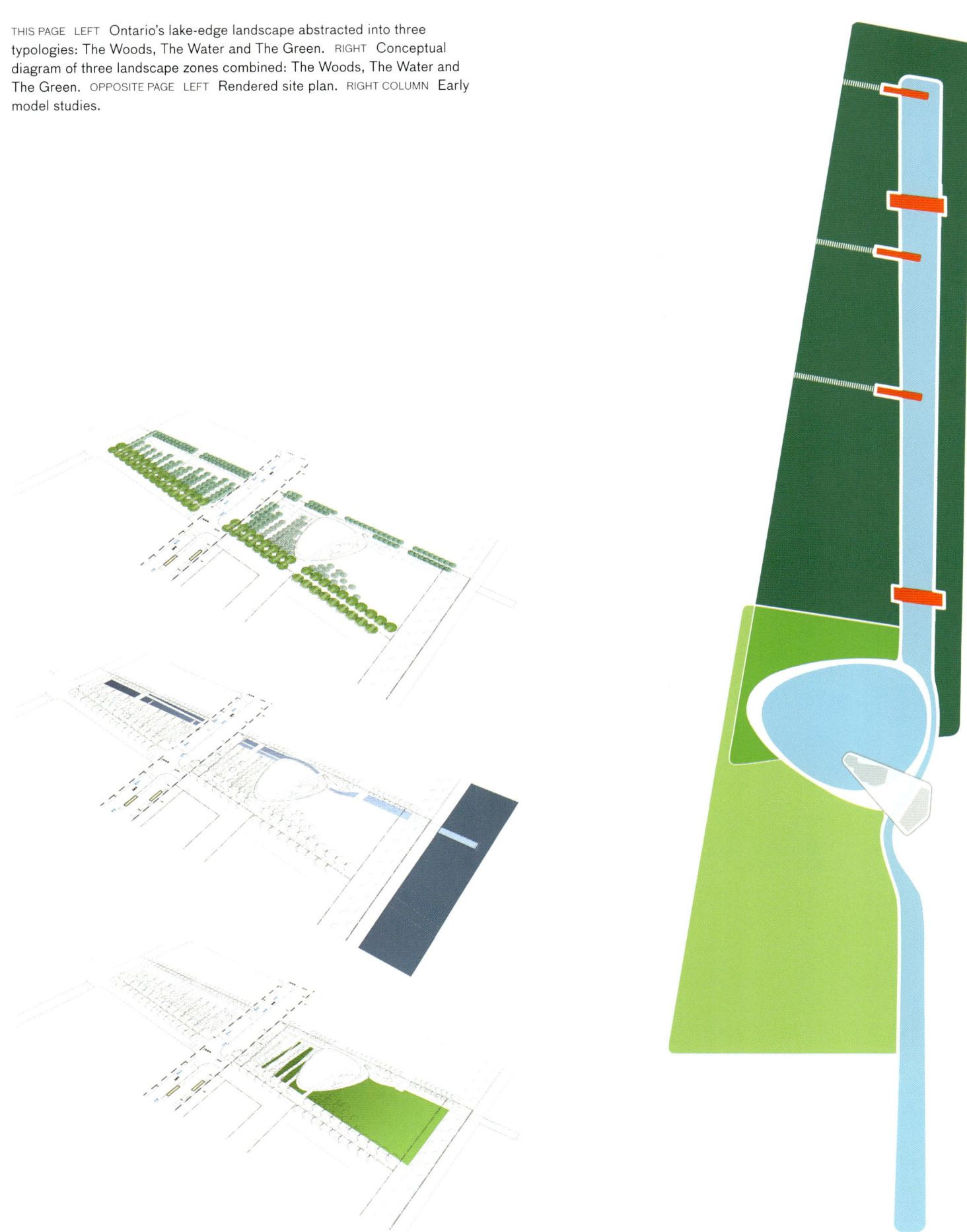

1 Lake Ontario
2 Queen's Quay Boulevard
3 Gardiner Expressway (above)
4 Lakeshore Boulevard
5 Sherbourne Street
6 North Sherbourne
7 South Sherbourne
8 Sherbourne Promenade
9 Eastern Walkway
10 The Woods
11 The Water
12 The Green
13 Water Sluice
14 Channel Crossings
15 Public Art, *Light Showers*
16 Pavilion

Bruce Kuwabara   Landscape into Urbanism

THIS PAGE Rendered view looking north from Queen's Quay Boulevard along water channel and Jill Anholt's public art installation, *Light Showers*. Water ascends through the sculpture to depict the idea of stormwater collection and UV purification. The purified water then flows down an illuminated metal scrim to pass through a series of biofiltration beds before being fed into a raised multipurpose pool. Cleansed water is then displayed in a succession of pools before discharging into the lake.
OPPOSITE PAGE TOP RIGHT Model of Anholt's *Light Showers*. MIDDLE RIGHT Rendered view looking south of Queen's Quay Boulevard towards the park pavilion. BOTTOM RIGHT Rendered view of playground and stormwater channel in North Sherbourne Park.

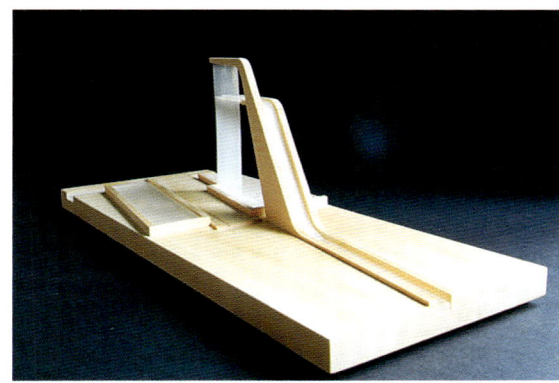

Bruce Kuwabara Landscape into Urbanism 51

1 Don River
2 Don River Park
3 Distillery District
4 District Energy
5 Cherry Street
6 New Streetcar Line
7 Streetcar Turnaround
8 Front Street
9 Mill Street
10 Bayview Avenue
11 Eastern Avenue
12 Adelaide Street
13 King Street East
14 St. Lawrence Street
15 River Street
16 Local Street
17 Lane

OPPOSITE PAGE Comprehensive public realm precinct plan showing the relationship of Cherry Street, Mill Street and Front Street to Don River Park.
THIS PAGE Rendered plan of Front Street. Its asymmetric configuration increases the space allocated to the public realm while doubling the number of street trees in the right-of-way, contributing significantly to the City's goal of 30% to 40% average canopy coverage throughout the neighbourhood.
PAGES 54–55 Rendering of westward view from Don River Park down Front Street East. A central allée forms a grand promenade along which a series of outdoor rooms are organized. Each block is allocated a programmable pavilion, a play space, feature tree plantings and gardens, public art and spaces for active and passive gathering.

West Don Lands Public Realm Plan
Toronto, ON

Waterfront Toronto was established in 2001 to lead the renewal of the city's lakefront as a sustainable, vibrant series of mixed-use neighbourhoods interspersed with a variety of public parks and networks of movement along the shoreline. As the design lead in an interdisciplinary team led by The Planning Partnership (TPP) for the design of the West Don Lands' public realm, PFS reworked public streets to leverage the habitability of the public realm and privilege the pedestrian.

Front Street East, one of the city's original east-west streets, is reconfigured into an asymmetrical street with a thickened, active landscape along the northern edge. The street becomes a green finger that pulls Don River Park, designed by Michael Van Valkenburgh Associates (MVVA), into the heart of the West Don Lands community. The asymmetric layout allocates more space to the pedestrian and maximizes tree canopy growth due to its enhanced solar exposure and greater soil volumes. The result is a highly programmed greenway that promotes adjacent building activity, allowing restaurants, cafes and markets to extend into the park.

The Cherry Street corridor links the West Don Lands to waterfront communities being developed to the south including the Lower Don Lands, for which PFS worked with MVVA on the design of the public realm. PFS's design builds on the Toronto Transit Commission's Environmental Assessment, developed by DTAH, by integrating transit into the pedestrian realm, by reducing the perceived distance that pedestrians have to cross traffic, and by integrating north-bound passenger loading on the eastern sidewalk.

Mill Street is reconceived as an ecological corridor that incorporates dedicated bicycle lanes, street trees, stormwater treatment, public art and new material conditions into a relatively narrow existing right-of-way.

Bruce Kuwabara Landscape into Urbanism

LEFT Rendering of 'shared-street' concept. Curbs and signage are removed to merge the street and sidewalk into one continuous pedestrian realm.
RIGHT Southward view of Cherry Street's enhanced public realm near Front Street. The streetcar is accommodated in its own right-of-way on the east side of the street and a median buffer between tracks and road allow another row of street trees to narrow the perceived width of the street.

LEFT Cantilevered landscape wall enclosing the North Garden.
RIGHT Black tulip field in spring.   PAGES 60–61 Il Giardino Segreto.

Ravine House North Garden
Toronto, ON

The Ravine House North Garden is an example of PFS's conceptualization of landscape in the private realm. Designed by KPMB, the Ravine House was conceptualized to bring the civic-scale into a single family residence intended for both domestic life and public events.

Located in the picturesque 19th century Rosedale neighbourhood northeast of downtown Toronto, the house sits at the edge of one of the city's ancient ravine systems.[7] Sited on a deep half-acre lot with a heavily treed ravine on one side and a Georgian revival residence on the other, the Ravine House was built on the splayed footprint of a pre-existing 1950s bungalow. As a result, it occupies a small percentage of the half-acre site to minimize its impact on the ecosystem and topography of the ravine.

While the house was completed in 2001, there has been an ongoing collaboration between the architects and the owner to evolve and refine the relationship of the building to its natural setting. The tip of the site, visible from the street, remained problematic because of excess stormwater from the large cantilevered roof above and the site's limited exposure to natural light.

In 2007, KPMB invited Greg Smallenberg to consult on this portion of the landscape. Following an analysis of the themes of the house and its landscape, Smallenberg proposed the creation of a *giardino segreto*, or 'secret garden'. The garden would unfold in stages, concealed behind a long, horizontally-slatted illuminated fence—an extension of the existing fence that encloses the site. KPMB then refined the form and materiality of Smallenberg's concept. A series of polished black granite bands and a double stepped retaining wall extends the views from the interior of the house out to the forested valley. Low evergreen plantings and seasonal black tulips are integrated for visual and seasonal diversity. By thinning out the existing trees, the spatial extension of the interior was magnified, reinforcing the relationships of inside to outside, art to nature.

Smallenberg's reinterpretation of this particular section of the site clarified the house's relationship between public and private, resolving the deeper connection between the domestic scale of the house to the more expansive scale of the ravine system.

OPPOSITE PAGE TOP AND BOTTOM Entry drive and forecourt defined by layered planting and garden wall. THIS PAGE TOP Evening in the North Garden. BOTTOM Illuminated landscape wall and polished granite band cutting through plant massings.

Conclusion

The strategic deployment of landscape to reshape and reframe contemporary urban conditions for placemaking is fundamental to the practice of PFS. Their attention to materials, constructed details and plantings fuse performance and aesthetics, and is balanced against their ability to generate complex formal ordering systems through open-ended processes. Global influences are negotiated against local conditions of climate, indigenous materials, vegetation, the physical, social and economic context, as well as financial and temporal constraints.

It is one thing to have a thesis, an idea and a master plan. It is another to implement concepts into tangible, effective and dimensional exemplars that set standards for quality and change. And it is precisely the ability of PFS to work at multiple scales and across disciplines—cultural, environmental, urban and economic— that situates PFS as active contributors to reinventing civic life in Canada, and increasingly as practitioners of Landscape Urbanism at a global scale.

Notes

1. Arthur Lubow, "Inside the Mega-Megalopolis," *The New York Times Magazine,* June 6, 2008: 47, 62. In 1900 10% of the world's population lived in cities; in 2008 50% live in cities; and by 2050 the predicted estimate is 75% of the world will be urban dwellers. In Canada, for example, the ratio of urban to rural dwellers is sobering: 80% of the population now lives in cities, and less than 20% lives in rural areas.
2. See Roger Martin's *The Opposable Mind: How Successful Leaders Win Through Integrative Thinking* (Boston: Harvard Business School Press, 2007). Martin demonstrates how integrative thinking has been successfully used to generate creative solutions out of the tension of opposing models. While Martin's focus is in the world of business, his book offers insights to understanding integrative design processes and teams.
3. The term 'space of appearance' is borrowed from George Baird's book of the same title (Cambridge: MIT Press, 1995) which in turn comes from a passage in Hannah Arendt's *The Human Condition* (Chicago: University of Chicago Press, 1998): "Action and speech create a space between the participants which can find its proper location almost any time and anywhere. It is the space of appearance in the widest sense of the word, namely, the space where I appear to others as others appear to me, where men exist not merely like other living or inanimate things but make their appearance explicitly." In other words, space—civic or social, public or private, inside or out—is only as vibrant and active as the presence of the people who occupy it.
4. See also the works of du Toit Allsopp Hillier and NIPPaysage Landscape Architects.
5. After World War II, the population of Richmond grew rapidly and farmland was subdivided for housing without the foresight of long-term planning. In 1949 a Town Plan was passed that divided Richmond into family dwelling, industrial, business and commercial and rural districts. However, this partitioning into classified districts consequently undermined the development of a strong civic core.
6. Vaughan was originally a rural township interspersed by four communities: Thornhill, Woodbridge, Kleinberg and Maple. In twenty years, the population of Vaughan increased by 276%, from 65,058 in 1986 to 238,866 in 2006. City of Vaughan *Population Growth* PDF file (Vaughan, ON: Economic and Technology Development Department, City of Vaughan, 2009).
7. In the late 18th century, Toronto was surveyed as a ten block orthogonal grid of small units. Since then, its innate geography as a rising terrain carved of deep valleys, ravines and watersheds has been deceptively developed, and subsequently perceived, as a flat terrain.

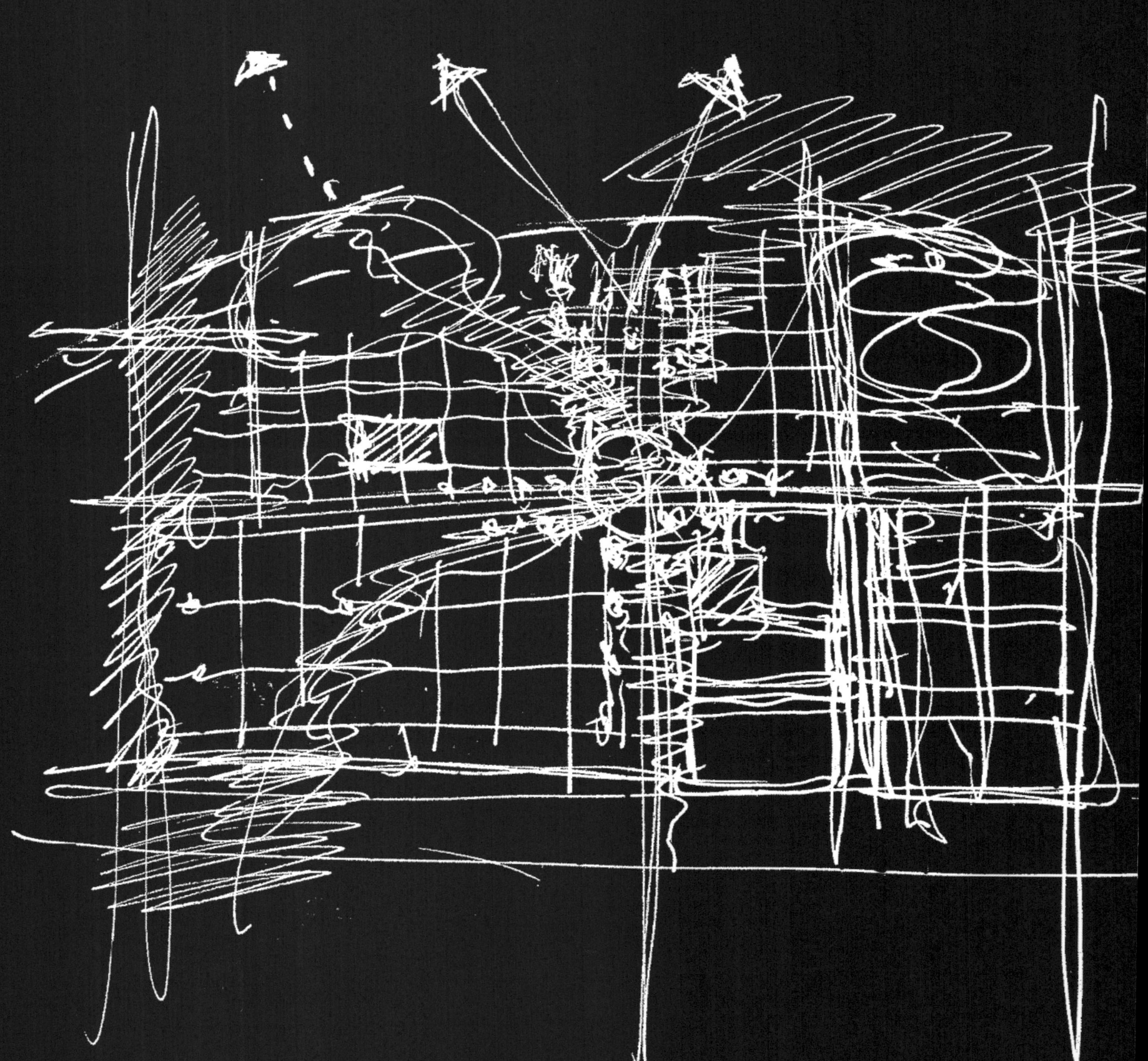

Dynamic Alliances
A collaborative design process

by Ken Greenberg

Shared Leadership

Successful urban design for complex and evolving environments can no longer be the hegemony of a single profession. The traditional preoccupation with the integration of the work of architects, planners and landscape architects has effectively been subsumed within a much larger dynamic enterprise with fluid boundaries and the sharing of leadership. Necessity has created new and dynamic alliances with various branches of engineering, economics, environmental sciences, and arts, culture and social partners among others. This broad fusion of different kinds of expertise and knowledge, based on the need to know and an expanded perception of opportunity, is not compromising but enabling.

Such teamwork demands an extended dialogue in real time. Methodologies and working styles are emerging which are much less hierarchical—iterative rather than linear—and supported by an explosion in communications technology which permits and facilitates rapid information sharing. With multiple stakeholder participation, trial solutions develop rapidly in which many complex variables are layered and morphed. In North American and European contexts, this work is increasingly done in highly public and contested conditions with the acknowledged right and need for affected communities to be at the table.

It is now also clear that shared and overlapping leadership needs to extend well beyond the initial act of creation of an urban design plan, well into its implementation and ultimately into the stewardship of the places created. In political terms this generally means time frames which extend over multiple administrations. It also implies long-term relationships with a shift in leadership as projects evolve and mature. The reality of this evolving and complex process raises significant issues in terms of assigning urban design credit. As much as the media's pressure for star power singles out individuals for identification, this is most often an erroneous and misleading description of what really occurs.

City/Nature/Sustainability

Perhaps more rapidly than we realize, we are witnessing the force majeure dissolution of the false dichotomy, both professional and conceptual, that divides the city from the natural world. Like many powerful and timely impulses, this reconciliation has had many sources: scientific, cultural and aesthetic. It is a simultaneous realization motivated by a sense of crisis as the scientific community calls attention to the appalling degradation, dangerous consequences and undeniable fragility of human life on the planet.

This change in consciousness was anticipated and fostered by inspired practitioners and writers including Ian McHarg (*Design with Nature*), Anne Whiston Spirn (*The Granite Garden*), and Michael Hough (*City Form and Natural Process*). Their ideas fostered new ways of thinking, beyond conventional mitigation of impacts on nature, to a creative synthesis working with natural process that suggests a new and expanded role for landscape architects working on urban projects.

As the imperative to modify our self destructive practices begins to suggest forms of development which are inherently more environmentally sustainable, cities are the crucibles where solutions are found to problems that are otherwise intractable. The environmental thrust is gaining traction and broad popular appeal as a common ground which cuts across class, cultural and political lines and is rapidly pushing urban design into new areas of investigation. In ways both superficial and profound this desire for 'greener' solutions is resulting in lower impact lifestyles and new design approaches at the level of city districts as well as individual buildings and landscapes. It augurs a greater mix and proximity of daily life activities such as living, working, shopping, culture, recreation and leisure; increased walkability, cycling, transit and less car dependency; and improved waste management and treatment, new approaches to storm and waste water management, use of alternative resources and lower energy consumption.

This seismic shift in goals and priorities is also producing a cultural predisposition to a new form of coexistence, the intertwining of city and nature and an altered sense of place. And as this transformed perspective takes hold we can also look forward to a change in the image and use of urban places and a greater integration with natural settings. Renewed places reflecting these approaches will become more rooted and specific, with the underlying layers of nature

PAGE 66 Generative sketch of Rockcliffe Master Plan. Ottawa, ON.
THIS PAGE Rendered aerial view of East Bayfront Community as imagined in the Precinct Plan. Toronto, ON.

Ken Greenberg   Dynamic Alliances

revealed, incorporated and better appreciated. In the words of Betsy Barlow Rogers, the former Executive Director of the Central Park Conservancy, "As the city becomes more park-like, the park becomes more city-like."

There are a number of extremely powerful corollaries to this increased environmental and ecological consciousness. An increased understanding of the complexities of succession and interdependence in nature can be directly linked to a much greater awareness of the dynamic and evolving character of cities, too, as perpetually unfinished human creations. Additionally, there is a deeper understanding that diverse and changing environments having a greater mix and complexity of land use and a broad range of population (cultural, economic and age cohort served by full life cycle housing options and forms) contribute to a richer and more inherently sustainable urban society and culture. A second and related corollary is that the need to cope with this increased complexity clearly demands new and expanded professional alliances.

The Embrace of Indeterminacy

Once we accept cities as complex, multigenerational and inherently unfinished artifacts of human creation we are forced to confront our limitations as urban designers operating at one point in time. Experience is showing that overly prescriptive templates do not hold up well as market forces, changing programs and new needs come into play. What are needed instead are flexible frameworks that allow for innovation, hybridization, organic growth, change and surprise. While this shift is challenging to the kind of risk-averse planning which aspires to an illusionary level of end state predictability, its inherent pragmatism has the potential to liberate design and harness many levels of creativity and initiative by others. Urban design becomes more like improvisational jazz, providing a structure that sets up solo opportunities, and less like composed classical scores (even avant garde ones). Applying Stewart Brand's terminology, we are learning "how cities learn."[1] Rather than producing finite products, urban design is increasingly about the anticipation and guidance of long-term transformations without fixed destinations, and the mediation between values, goals and outcomes.

Consistent with this open-ended stance, the true test for urban design is to achieve coherence and build relationships, but at the same time to leave ample room for the emergence of new ideas, market and social innovations, and expanded creativity. By not predetermining outcomes, the whole array of design disciplines including architecture, landscape architecture, engineering, industrial design, graphic design and lighting design that will then materialize the plan is left with much more latitude for additional levels of creativity in the translation.

PFS Projects: Variable Roles

In the following projects, Ottawa's Rockcliffe Redevelopment, Toronto's East Bayfront Precinct Plan, and Kelowna's University of British Columbia Okanagan Master Plan, Phillips Farevaag Smallenberg (PFS) played a variety of roles on different teams and projects, and brought particular knowledge, intuitions, skills and sets of priorities to the table. In these projects they sometimes lead and sometimes support, but they always represent a unique and identifiable point of view.

Rockcliffe Redevelopment

UBC Okanagan

East Bayfront

TOP Computer study model of Rockcliffe's massing and open space. Green fingers create portals to the river between which dense, compact urban blocks are formed. BOTTOM Aerial photo of existing conditions of the decommissioned Canadian Forces Base Rockcliffe.

Rockcliffe Redevelopment
Ottawa, ON

Canada Lands Company is an arm's length, self-financing Canadian Crown Corporation charged with disposing of surplus government property to bring optimal value to Canadian taxpayers. One such property is the 130 hectare former Rockcliffe Airforce Base, five kilometres east of Parliament Hill in Ottawa, Canada's capital city.

Located along the Ottawa River, and surrounded by existing neighbourhoods and institutions, the former base[2] is the largest remaining redevelopment site inside the Ottawa Greenbelt.[3] Several years ago, Canada Lands committed to make Rockcliffe a flagship community for a series of similar infill projects in major Canadian cities. The goal was to set a new benchmark for sustainable and financially successful development, combining creativity, innovation and design excellence, and emphasizing responsible stormwater control, reduced energy consumption, improved waste management, regeneration of natural features and orientation away from the automobile.

Work on the Rockcliffe community design plan demanded the formation of a complex multidisciplinary consultant team.[4] At the same time it required the ability to be highly efficient and focused. To deal quickly with an enormous number of interrelated variables, an open-ended 'framework' was developed that was capable of continuously learning and responding to new information and feedback. In practical terms, this meant working through a series of structured 'iterations' that became progressively more refined and complete as knowledge was gathered along the way, and as they were continuously tested from multiple standpoints.

A resulting sequence of plan diagrams illustrated this process and provided a model for the type of integrated, flexible thinking required to shape contemporary cities and neighbourhoods. The drawings produced reflected the contributions of different team members to an intensive, evolving exploration of the site and expressed the layering of objectives, needs and perceptions over a period of several months.

In this process, all the balls were in the air from the start. But there was also a relatively complete concept at each stage, based on an ever-increasing level of knowledge and understanding. Periodically all contributing parties would come together to explore interrelationships and opportunities for lateral thinking. But the goal of each iteration was to address a sequence of issues at a higher level of precision, as specific technical input was acquired to push initial concepts toward greater refinement.

Throughout the process, the Canada Lands client group was a key participant. The City of Ottawa, through its Technical Advisory Committee[5] and the National Capital Commission (NCC)[6] also provided critical input.

Natural Infrastructure

The team's first step was to arrive at a number of 'breakthrough' linking ideas which could simultaneously address multiple objectives. The first was simply to take advantage of conditions on the site and of larger planning concepts for the region, such as the National Capital Commission Greenbelt established in 1950 by Jacques Gréber, the capital's master planner.

The Ottawa Greenbelt features 100 kilometres of trails for hiking, jogging and cross country skiing, which combine with the city's extensive network of bike paths to reinforce Ottawa's image as an active, healthy place to live. The Rockcliffe site abutted this greenbelt trail network along the Ottawa River. It also already possessed a mature landscape including a densely wooded escarpment overlooking the river; areas of rolling, open lands with scattered trees; and two protected forests—the National Research Council's Woods North and the Montfort Hospital Woods.

From the outset the team emphasized continuity with this existing 'green infrastructure'. Such a strategy would create vital connections within the city and region, as well as generate a memorable context for the Rockcliffe development. In laying out residential streets and arteries, some primary goals were to link the community to the bike paths and hiking trails that wind through the surrounding green space, to connect to the bike network along the Rockcliffe Parkway, and to afford spectacular views of the river, Parliament Hill and the Gatineau Hills.

Rather than adhering to minimal planning norms for green space, a bold effort to preserve and expand access to natural features of the site became the fundamental structuring idea of the master plan. This meant integrating built spaces with a network of internal

LEFT Generative sketch of interwoven open space corridors as the driver of Rockcliffe's urban form. RIGHT Rockcliffe's master plan framework was designed as a living instrument capable of absorbing change and responding to evolving needs. A vibrant mixed-use community is concentrated along the High Street and public transit corridor, providing retail, work, transit and amenity within a five-minute walk of every residence.

greenways that could facilitate landscape regeneration, stormwater management, and wildlife and pedestrian connections among the Montfort Woods,[7] the National Research Council (NRC)[8] campus, the National Capital Commission (NCC) parkland along the Ottawa River and beyond.

This strategy also meant planning to build more densely in a reduced development area—a requirement that was addressed by a series of compact mixed-use urban villages, each with a distinct character, mix and range of building types and uses.

Community Forms

The area's settlement history dates back to the early 1800s. The plan set out to preserve and celebrate the site's rich native and military heritage by drawing these features into integrated relationships with new development. Should the project move forward, this will eventually include a strategy for relocating, rehabilitating or recycling materials from 469 remaining military family dwellings.

One of the most significant aspects of sustainable planning for the Rockcliffe Redevelopment is the integration of a true mix of uses, allowing people to live, work, play, shop and have access to a full variety of community amenities. Opportunities for synergistic relationships were explored with the adjoining NRC campus and other nearby institutions (including Montfort Hospital, the Canada Aviation Museum[9] and several federal agencies). Minimum targets for employment on the site were set, with the expectation that these could be exceeded.

The plan also provides for a strong retail presence on a pedestrian oriented high street and around a market square that occupies the base's former parade ground. This retail space would serve not only the site's residents and employees but surrounding communities as well. Housing on the site would provide a great variety of form, tenure, income level and lifestyle options. The overall goal was to mirror the assortment of use and form typical of the diverse Greens Creek Sector in which Rockcliffe is located.

A transportation strategy was also developed to effectively connect Rockcliffe's new population to the surrounding city. This strategy de-emphasizes the automobile in favour of an assortment of alternatives. First and foremost, people are encouraged to walk within and among the new villages. An extensive network of bike lanes and off-street multi-use trails weave through greenways, connecting to communities to the south and west and improving access to the river and the regional trail system leading to downtown Ottawa. A new transit spine is also identified that would run through the heart of the community and link to the regional bus transitway. Its stops would be key neighbourhood focal points. Other planned transportation strategies include traffic demand management, controls over parking supply and emphasis on shared parking areas.

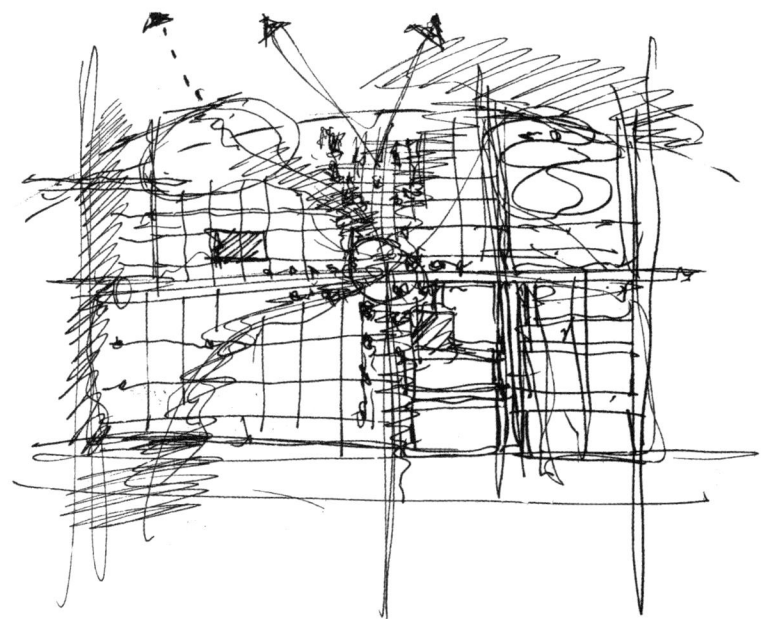

1 Ottawa River
2 Rockcliffe Parkway
3 Aviation Parkway
4 Montreal Road
5 Codd's Road
6 Centre Town
7 Market Square (Former Parade Ground)
8 Hilltown
9 Forest Houses
10 Research City
11 Montreal Road Gateway Development
12 South Village
13 West Village
14 North Village
15 School
16 School and Community Centre
17 Museum
18 Wetlands
19 Recreational Fields
20 Urban Park
21 Rockcliffe Airport
22 Canadian Aviation Museum
23 NRC Campus
24 NRC Forest (Woods North)
25 Montfort Hospital
26 Montfort Hospital Woods

LEFT Program, built form and landscape study for a major community gathering space overlooking the Ottawa River. Rockcliffe's prime location is given over to the public realm. RIGHT Study of porous and transitional relationship between greenways and tight urban grid. Existing habitat and wildlife corridors, natural drainage patterns, biological regeneration and green infill determine where the green network is located.

A Public Infrastructure

For any undertaking of this scale, a master plan can only serve as a 'framework'—a living instrument capable of absorbing change and interpretation. Over time, some elements will remain fixed while others will evolve. Through this process, if it indeed moves forward at some point in the future, the Rockcliffe plan will need to remain accountable to original commitments, while remaining flexible enough to accommodate unexpected market-driven opportunities. Such flexibility has been the great lesson of large-scale planning in recent decades.

To reconcile this dilemma, the plan proposes a design for the public realm that is both more explicit and more detailed than that for a conventional development. In essence, the public realm plan embodies Rockcliffe's 'big idea'. The greenway network will provide its essential connecting web and structuring framework.

The public realm specified in the plan does not just comprise a utilitarian network of streets and park reserves. It includes preliminary park designs: locations for trails, gardens, constructed wetlands and regeneration areas; an array of hardscapes and softscapes; a rich hierarchy of street types; specific ways of integrating transit; and a mixture of public facilities and programs.

These features are ultimately the guarantors of what could make Rockcliffe distinctive, and they are intimately tied to the successful implementation of sustainability strategies. They are what Canada Lands Company was encouraged by the design team to commission and build as the master developer, in order to establish the fundamental DNA and character of the development.

In summary, then, the Rockcliffe plan focuses on weaving together found assets (both built and green), new networks for movement, a synergistic mix of uses, and appropriately scaled built form. But in time, should this project move forward, the ultimate test of the iterative process that produced it will be its ability to encourage the formation of attractive, active places: the high street, the market square, sidewalks, trails, parks and neighbourhood gathering spaces. When inhabited, it is these spaces that will create the basis for real community.

1   Hemlock Road Extension
2   Museum
3   Pier
4   Urban Park
5   The Orchard
6   Escarpment
7   The Meadow
8   Hilltown
9   Montfort Woods
10 Wetlands
11 West Village
12 South Village

Ken Greenberg   Dynamic Alliances

East Bayfront Precinct Plan – Public Realm and Streetscape
Toronto, ON

The East Bayfront Precinct Plan is one of a series of planning initiatives that has been taken on by Waterfront Toronto. This agency was created by the federal, provincial and municipal governments with a mandate

> To put Toronto at the forefront of global cities in the 21st century by transforming the waterfront into beautiful, sustainable new communities, parks and public spaces, fostering economic growth in knowledge based, creative industries and ultimately redefining how the city, province and country are perceived by the world.

Centrally located south of the Gardiner Expressway between Jarvis and Cherry Streets and along Lake Ontario in Toronto's Inner Harbour, East Bayfront is one of Waterfront Toronto's key early initiatives. Much of the land on which this new neighbourhood will take shape is vacant and underutilized. The lands are under both public and private ownership. Immediate adjacencies include the Redpath Sugar Company facilities to the west, the Gardiner Expressway and CN tracks to the north and the Keating Channel and the mouth of the Don River to the east.

Setting a New Standard

The East Bayfront community, when it is complete, is intended to set a new standard for city development and community building in downtown Toronto. Over a relatively short period of time it is expected to incorporate several exciting new cultural institutions, market and non-market housing, highly energized retail streets, offices, studios, a primary school, daycare, community facilities, parks, open spaces and a vital public waterfront. It will be home to upwards of 9,000 residents in a variety of neighbourhoods and building types. Generally it will build out as a series of discrete high-density, mid-rise, street-focused developments each with a unique character but all guided by the design intentions of the community plan. It will be a 'green' community, well supported by public transit, pedestrian and bicycle routes.

This project required the close collaboration of a multidisciplinary team led by Koetter Kim and Associates (KKA). PFS's particular responsibility within this team was to lead the planning, design and

LEFT Presentation sketch showing a reconfigured Queen's Quay Boulevard with a strong double row of street trees, generous sidewalks and the greening of the TTC tramway. RIGHT The East Bayfront Master Plan envisions one of the largest urban developments in Canada.

1 Lake Ontario
2 Queen's Quay Boulevard
3 Lakeshore Boulevard
4 Jarvis Street
5 Jarvis Slip
6 Stormwater Catchment
7 Sherbourne Street
8 Sherbourne Park
9 Waterfront Promenade
10 Parliament Street
11 Parliament Slip

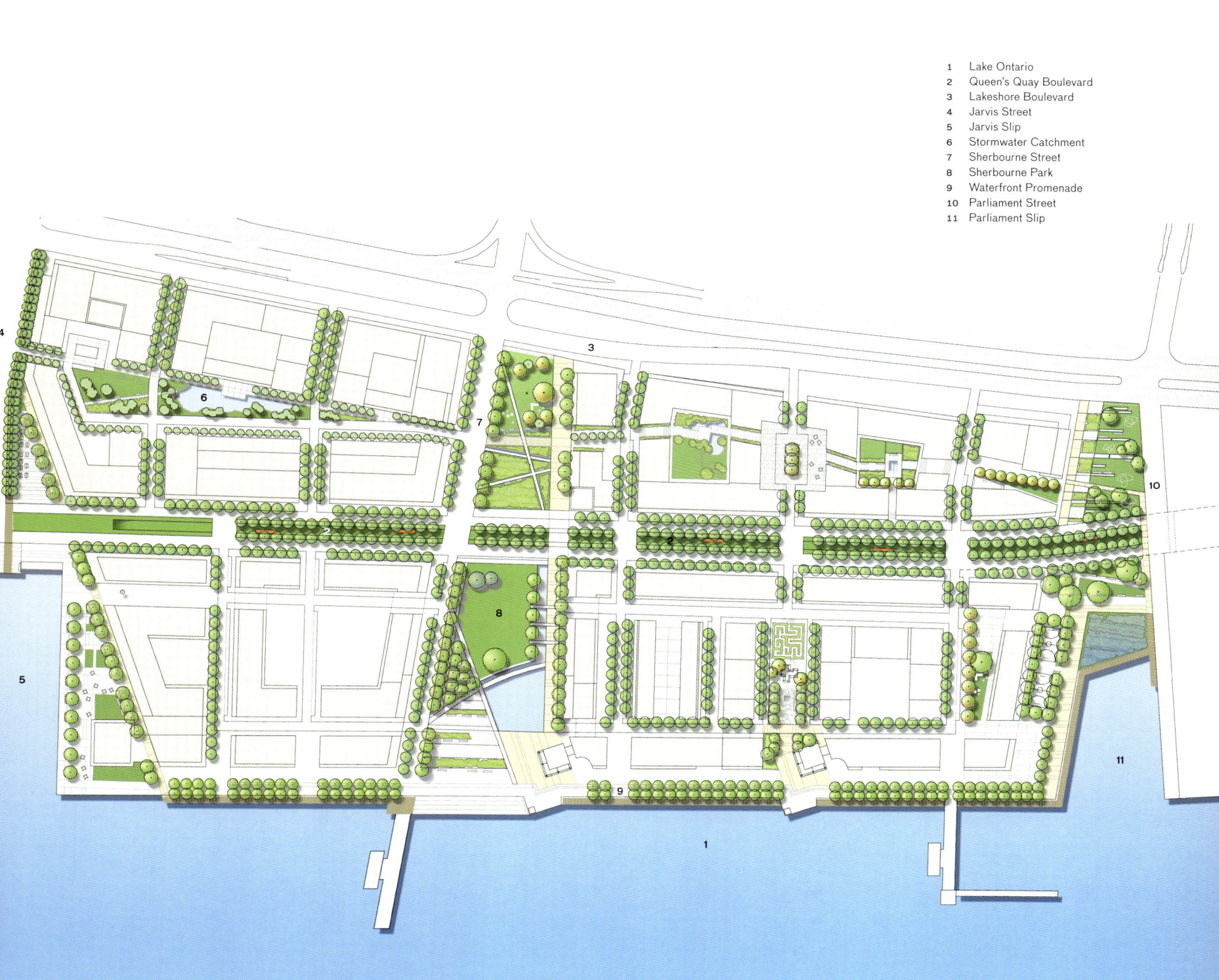

OPPOSITE PAGE TOP Early sketch of Sherbourne Park looking north. BOTTOM Rendered aerial perspective of East Bayfront illustrating 2005 Precinct Plan intentions. THIS PAGE Early sketch of Silo Park east of Parliament Slip.

conceptual program development of all public realm components of the project including parks, outdoor facilities for a school and daycare and waterfront edges. PFS worked closely with the team to develop comprehensive sustainability strategies including stormwater capture and use, incorporation of green roofs into building planning and the use of native planting within the public realm.

Unfettered Access to the Water's Edge in a Clearly Defined Public Realm

Torontonians have been looking for a new attitude to redevelopment along their waterfront for decades. They want communities that emphasize the public realm through great streets and open spaces with unfettered access and good connectivity to the water's edge. Most of all they want a more beautiful and livable city. The East Bayfront Plan focused on all these ambitions and the public's perception of the potential of landscape architecture has been greatly heightened through the extensive public consultation component of the project. Landscape played a central role in a series of townhall-type engagements and well-attended public forums.

In the planning, PFS helped to establish four primary open spaces that each connect directly to the waterfront and create a much needed porosity between the city and Lake Ontario. Jarvis Slip (now Sugar Beach, designed by Claude Cormier), Aitkens Place, the head of Parliament Slip and Sherbourne Park together are intended to provide the necessary north-south linkages. The East Bayfront Plan also recognized the need for a kinder, more pedestrian responsive Queen's Quay Boulevard—the primary east west corridor through the new community. The KKA/PFS design created a reasonably scaled road section, given Queen's Quay Boulevard's trafffic demands, and illustrated a strong streetscape of trees and a green transit corridor to mitigate what would continue to be a primary artery. The plan also developed the initial ideas for a continuous waterfront promenade that would knit the primary open spaces of East Bayfront together as a composition of neighbourhood open spaces.

The creation of the East Bayfront Precinct Plan presented an opportunity to shape this key component of Waterfront Toronto's comprehensive plan for the Central Bayfront and became the catalyst for city-wide support and ongoing public interest in the whole of Toronto's lakeshore. It has initiated a new attitude towards waterfront community building in Toronto that, until now, has been met with understandable skepticism in the aftermath of the 'wall of condos' created in earlier years to the west. Developed within an atmosphere of multijurisdictional review, the design team needed to address a wide variety of often competing interests. In the end, the plan has successfully incorporated new ways of thinking about parks, streets and sidewalks. It has dealt with stormwater in inventive ways, created a bold new waterfront with meaningful open spaces rooted in the site's history and achieved a new level of environmental integrity. In this team setting landscape architecture played a central role in the formation of the plan, demonstrating the profession's indispensable contribution to the creation of new communities.

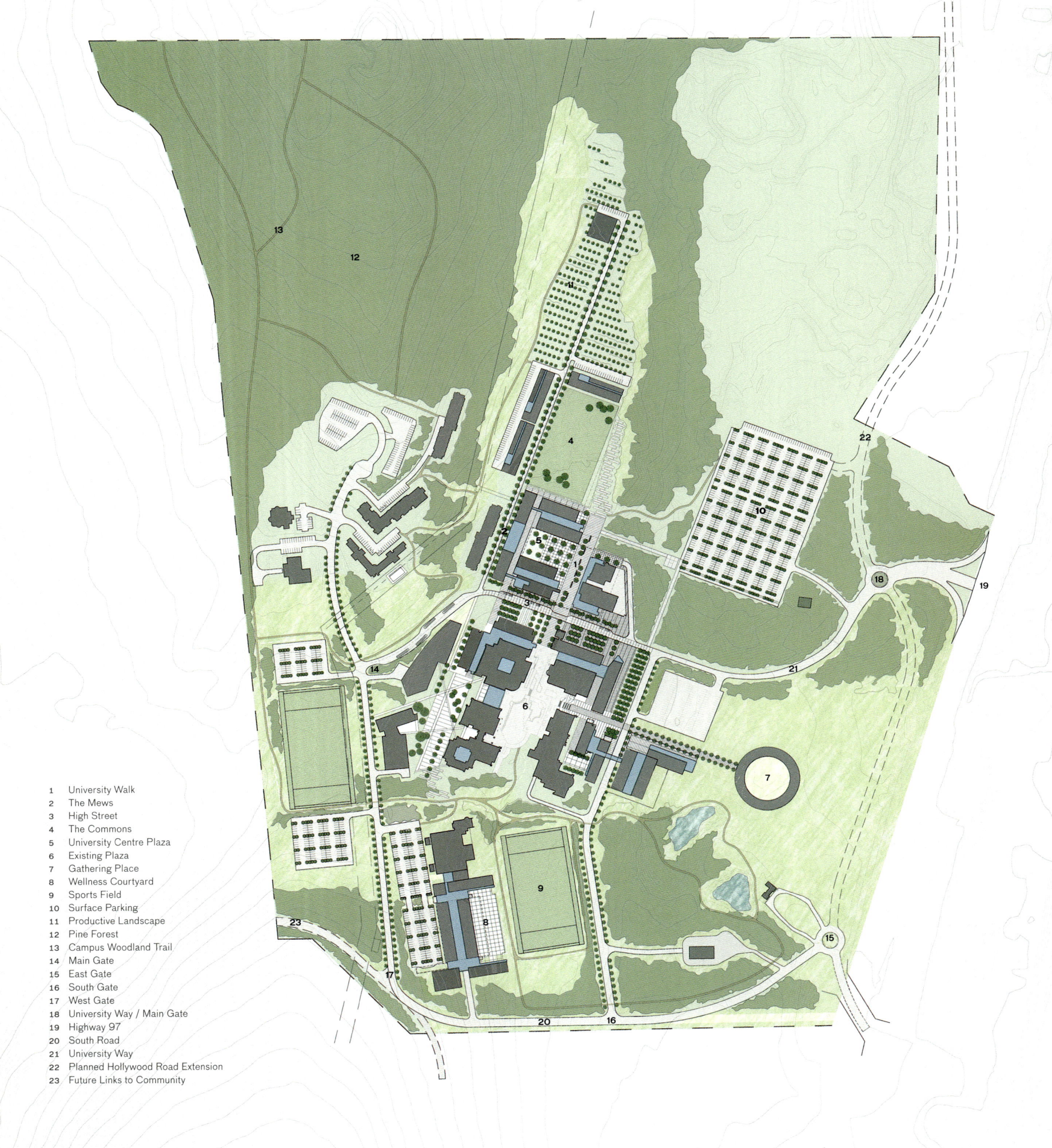

1 University Walk
2 The Mews
3 High Street
4 The Commons
5 University Centre Plaza
6 Existing Plaza
7 Gathering Place
8 Wellness Courtyard
9 Sports Field
10 Surface Parking
11 Productive Landscape
12 Pine Forest
13 Campus Woodland Trail
14 Main Gate
15 East Gate
16 South Gate
17 West Gate
18 University Way / Main Gate
19 Highway 97
20 South Road
21 University Way
22 Planned Hollywood Road Extension
23 Future Links to Community

LEFT UBCO Campus Master Plan. RIGHT Landscape precinct diagram.

The University of British Columbia Okanagan (UBCO) Master Plan
Kelowna, BC

The UBCO Master Plan was initiated to create a new UBC campus in the Interior of British Columbia. This is the first significant expansion of UBC's presence outside of Vancouver and is intended to respond to a growing interest from students outside of BC's Lower Mainland. This includes residents who are looking for a university closer to home as well as to national and international students looking for a relatively small campus within a unique and beautiful Canadian setting.

The master plan has been informed by a new and exciting academic plan, emphasizing new forms of learning within an environment that fosters social and academic mixing in a setting with wide-ranging opportunities for communication and recreation. The diverse curriculum includes traditional liberal arts offerings as well as an emphasis on computer sciences, engineering, business, education, health and wellness, indigenous studies, and visual and performing arts.

The 100 hectare campus site is located within a typical Okanagan landscape mix of grassland and ponderosa pine. The site is bracketed by agricultural lands to the west and south, a new residential community and golf course to the north, and the main highway and airport to the east. The site was partially occupied by a community college that left behind a small grouping of buildings along with a network of roads and services that were rationalized within the new UBCO Plan.

Landscape as Organizing Frame

PFS was the prime consultant, working closely with KPMB, responsible for coordinating the multidisciplinary team in developing a landscape-driven physical plan that integrated well with the intentions of the Academic Plan. The Academic Plan emphasized sustainable site planning strategies and celebrated the remarkable surrounding environment. All planning and design decisions were filtered through a landscape lens. A plan was collaboratively developed that integrated building and site physically and programmatically, to create new campus connections that structured buildings and open spaces.

A physical form evolved that will allow an aggressive building program to unfold quickly to provide for studies and housing that will soon accommodate a student body of approximately 7,500 students.

All of this was achieved with an acute sensitivity to surrounding terrain and vegetation, emphasizing key views to the iconic Okanagan landscape and developing 'green strategies' that include ground sourced heating and cooling, LEED® responsive building types, sustainable landscapes and meaningful, well positioned open spaces and recreational facilities throughout the campus. The plan also acknowledged First Nations as the stewards of this land and integrates this awareness into a symbolic welcome at the entry to the campus.

The UBCO Plan and the process undertaken to complete it drew considerable interest throughout the Okanagan region due to the anticipated effects a new university would have on the city of Kelowna and the surrounding area. Due to significant public exposure, the perception of landscape as the underlying framework for complex, large-scale projects was reinforced in the public eye as well as within the government and the ranks of the university administration.

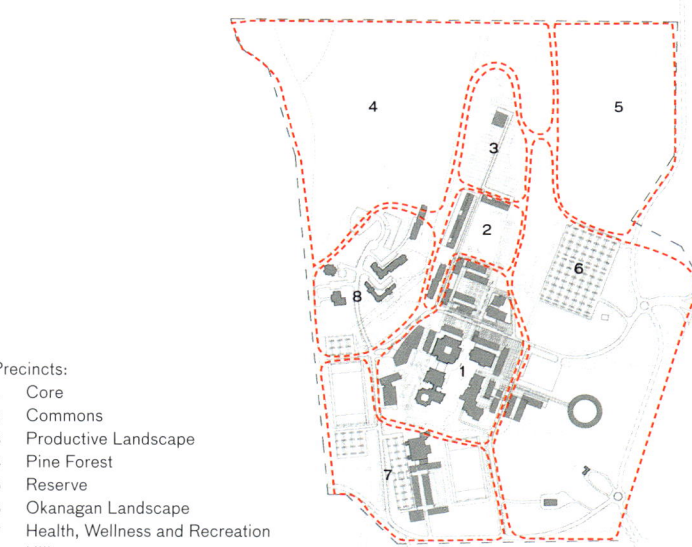

Precincts:
1. Core
2. Commons
3. Productive Landscape
4. Pine Forest
5. Reserve
6. Okanagan Landscape
7. Health, Wellness and Recreation
8. Hilltown

TOP Computer study model of Rockcliffe's massing and open space. Green fingers create portals to the river between which dense, compact urban blocks are formed. BOTTOM Aerial photo of existing conditions of the decommissioned Canadian Forces Base Rockcliffe.

Rockcliffe Redevelopment
Ottawa, ON

Canada Lands Company is an arm's length, self-financing Canadian Crown Corporation charged with disposing of surplus government property to bring optimal value to Canadian taxpayers. One such property is the 130 hectare former Rockcliffe Airforce Base, five kilometres east of Parliament Hill in Ottawa, Canada's capital city.

Located along the Ottawa River, and surrounded by existing neighbourhoods and institutions, the former base[2] is the largest remaining redevelopment site inside the Ottawa Greenbelt.[3] Several years ago, Canada Lands committed to make Rockcliffe a flagship community for a series of similar infill projects in major Canadian cities. The goal was to set a new benchmark for sustainable and financially successful development, combining creativity, innovation and design excellence, and emphasizing responsible stormwater control, reduced energy consumption, improved waste management, regeneration of natural features and orientation away from the automobile.

Work on the Rockcliffe community design plan demanded the formation of a complex multidisciplinary consultant team.[4] At the same time it required the ability to be highly efficient and focused. To deal quickly with an enormous number of interrelated variables, an open-ended 'framework' was developed that was capable of continuously learning and responding to new information and feedback. In practical terms, this meant working through a series of structured 'iterations' that became progressively more refined and complete as knowledge was gathered along the way, and as they were continuously tested from multiple standpoints.

A resulting sequence of plan diagrams illustrated this process and provided a model for the type of integrated, flexible thinking required to shape contemporary cities and neighbourhoods. The drawings produced reflected the contributions of different team members to an intensive, evolving exploration of the site and expressed the layering of objectives, needs and perceptions over a period of several months.

In this process, all the balls were in the air from the start. But there was also a relatively complete concept at each stage, based on an ever-increasing level of knowledge and understanding. Periodically all contributing parties would come together to explore inter-relationships and opportunities for lateral thinking. But the goal of each iteration was to address a sequence of issues at a higher level of precision, as specific technical input was acquired to push initial concepts toward greater refinement.

Throughout the process, the Canada Lands client group was a key participant. The City of Ottawa, through its Technical Advisory Committee[5] and the National Capital Commission (NCC)[6] also provided critical input.

Natural Infrastructure

The team's first step was to arrive at a number of 'breakthrough' linking ideas which could simultaneously address multiple objectives. The first was simply to take advantage of conditions on the site and of larger planning concepts for the region, such as the National Capital Commission Greenbelt established in 1950 by Jacques Gréber, the capital's master planner.

The Ottawa Greenbelt features 100 kilometres of trails for hiking, jogging and cross country skiing, which combine with the city's extensive network of bike paths to reinforce Ottawa's image as an active, healthy place to live. The Rockcliffe site abutted this greenbelt trail network along the Ottawa River. It also already possessed a mature landscape including a densely wooded escarpment overlooking the river; areas of rolling, open lands with scattered trees; and two protected forests—the National Research Council's Woods North and the Montfort Hospital Woods.

From the outset the team emphasized continuity with this existing 'green infrastructure'. Such a strategy would create vital connections within the city and region, as well as generate a memorable context for the Rockcliffe development. In laying out residential streets and arteries, some primary goals were to link the community to the bike paths and hiking trails that wind through the surrounding green space, to connect to the bike network along the Rockcliffe Parkway, and to afford spectacular views of the river, Parliament Hill and the Gatineau Hills.

Rather than adhering to minimal planning norms for green space, a bold effort to preserve and expand access to natural features of the site became the fundamental structuring idea of the master plan. This meant integrating built spaces with a network of internal

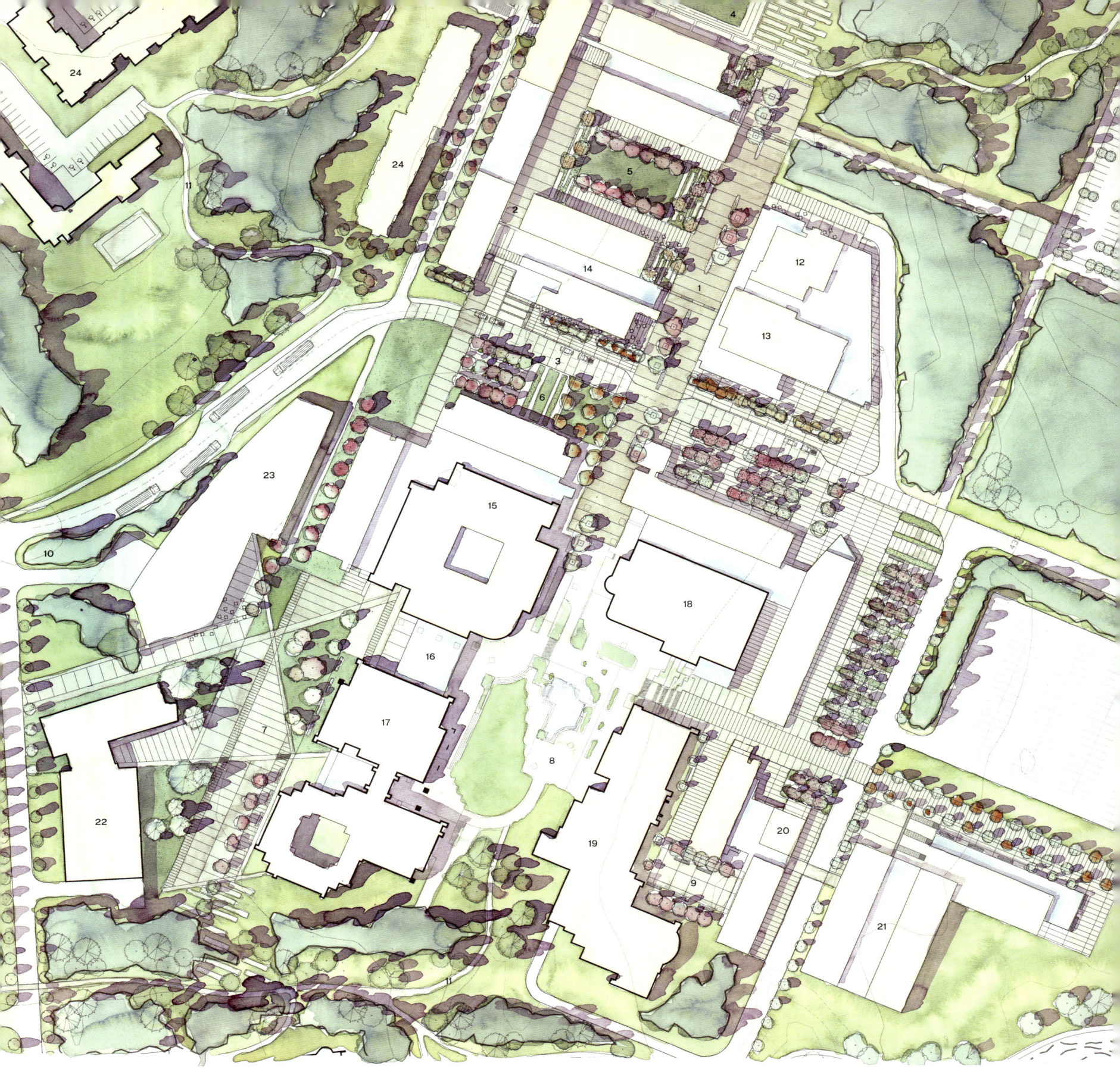

1. University Walk
2. The Mews
3. High Street
4. The Commons
5. University Centre Plaza
6. Urban Rooms
7. Arts and Science Courtyard
8. Existing Plaza
9. Engineering and Management Courtyard
10. Main Gate
11. Campus Trail
12. Lecture Theatre
13. Drama Theatre
14. University Centre
15. Multipurpose
16. Irving K. Barber Atrium
17. Creative Studies
18. Learning Commons
19. Cafeteria / University Club / Academic
20. Management
21. Engineering
22. Fine Arts / Creative Studies
23. Cinematheque / Academic
24. Dormitories

Notes

[1] Stewart Brand is author of *How Buildings Learn: What Happens After They're Built* (New York: Viking, 1994).
[2] The operational facilities of Rockcliffe Airforce Base were vacated in 1985.
[3] The Ottawa Greenbelt, established in 1956 by Jacques Gréber, is a 14,950 hectare crescent of land within the present day boundaries of Ottawa in which real estate development is strictly controlled.
[4] The Rockcliffe consultant team was assembled in April 2006.
[5] The City of Ottawa Technical Advisory Committee is a public advisory committee with broad neighbourhood and stakeholder representation.
[6] The National Capital Commission (NCC) is a Crown corporation that was created by Parliament in 1959 as the steward of federal lands and buildings in the National Capital region.
[7] The Montfort Woods is a natural woodlot of maple trees to the southeast of the project area.
[8] The National Research Council (NRC) is Canada's premier science and technology research organization, and an immediate neighbour east of the project area.
[9] The Canada Aviation Museum is Canada's premier aeronautical collection housed in a facility due north of the project area.

Rendered plan of the central precinct showing the existing quadrangle redefined by carefully structured new open spaces and buildings.

Ultimately, to think, live and act locally is to explicitly focus on the particular: particular ecologies, climates and people with particular memories embodied in the local. This specificity of place cannot be over emphasized. The making of good place involves a conscious effort—a full commitment that takes great pleasure in the endless possibilities that the immediate world has to offer. In current times, the responsibility and imagination of the designer play a critical role in bringing place back to our attention. The places we make must be joyful if we are to continue to see them, to tend them and to make them central to our lives and our thinking.

Place, Body, Memory
Placemaking in a global world

by Douglas Paterson

The word 'Place' conjures substantially different and invariably conflicting reactions within the design and academic communities as well as within society at large. For some, place is the essence of being situated in the world—of being phenomenally earth-bound. As the philosopher Edward Casey recently asserted, "To live is to live locally, and to know is first of all to know the place that one is in."[1] In this view the world unfolds from the place in which one stands, grows, loves, lives and dies. It evokes images not only of delightful villages and small cities created by societies over time in various parts of the world, but it also recognizes the great achievements of our built world from Delphi to Angkor Wat, from Prague to Varanasi. It is explicated by terms such as genius loci, topos, topophilia, homesickness and pride of place. These views of place open up new, imaginative possibilities for dwelling and making in the world.

For others however, the idea of place is fundamentally fascist, representing one way that those in power have aggressively thrust their dominant views upon 'others' in their society. Consider the references to a 'glorious homeland' that so dominated the rhetoric and actions of Nazi Germany. In a similar but less severe vein, many of the current critics of New Urbanism in North America accuse its proponents of holding an overly simplistic and nostalgic view of historic lifestyles—a contrived image of an idealized society pushed on people who have had little or no association with that history whatsoever. Some of these critics instead embrace the restless and placeless suburban sprawl of current North American society as a normal and acceptable product of our times. The disneyfication of society, the emergence of Las Vegas as a model for urbanism and the touristic branding of every place worldwide are ultimately seen as natural, often unproblematic outcomes of current capitalistic intentions.

These opposing positions (of either a full immersion in or a rejection of 'Place') warrant recognition and resolution or, at the very least, a stated presence in any discussion of place. There is, however, a third perspective on place that is equally significant and perhaps even more problematic. For many, place is incidental—simply not au courant or part of contemporary discourse. Consider comments made by Jane Amidon in her book *Radical Landscapes*:

"No longer is the idea of context an implication of local proximity. Materials, arrangements and forms that constitute a space may refer to and be taken from geographically, ecologically and culturally far flung sources."[2] From this perspective, it would seem that we can play with whatever toys are available in whatever ways we choose. Place becomes a silent backdrop. Yet the irony in this position is that the very idea of the radical involves a return to roots (inherent in the term 'radicans'), a return that must involve a recognition of place.

While the idea of place may be loved, feared, distrusted or simply ignored, it is apparent that places of every sort—rural and urban landscapes around the world—are struggling and fundamentally transforming under the assault of rampant globalization and capitalism. If history is indeed dead, as is often claimed, then the destruction of place, as one of our most significant vessels of individual and collective memory, sounds history's ultimate death toll. The uncertain turmoil that percolates around the idea of place needs to be made use of as a way to rethink the nature of place in these times. The essence of this need was captured by French phenomenologist-philosopher Paul Ricoeur in his oft-quoted challenge to the world, "how [do we] become modern and...return to sources; how [do we] revive an old, dormant civilization and take part in modern civilization?"[3] This challenge became central to the emergence of 'critical regionalism' which suggested a way of resisting the onslaught of globalization while seeking new ways to embody the local that abandon associations with fascist, kitschy or overly sentimental past practices.

Critical regionalism, particularly as presented in the writings of Kenneth Frampton and his oft-cited paper "Towards a Critical Regionalism: Six Points for an Architecture of Resistance",[4] called for an abandonment of the avant-garde. In the current media-dominated world, the 'shock of the new', he argued, is immediately and ineffectually reduced to little more than novelty that is quickly consumed and discarded. Instead, Frampton argued for an arrière-garde, a position which "distances itself equally from the Enlightenment myth of progress and from the reactionary, unrealistic impulse to return to the architectonic forms of the pre-industrial past." He also called for, among other forms of resistance, an emphasis on context, topography

PAGE 86 Hastings Park's Italian Rain Gardens. Vancouver, BC. Fountain detail developed by artist Ken Clarke. THIS PAGE Children at play in the Italian Rain Gardens at Hastings Park. Vancouver, BC.

and climate over culture, and an emphasis on the tactile over the visual and scenographic. But Frampton's writings, although widely read and received, remain too abstract. A more straightforward yet equally critical explanation is necessary.

Ultimately, to think, live and act locally is to explicitly focus on the particular: particular ecologies, climates and people with particular memories embodied in the local. The works we create respect a past, enlarge the present and point to a future in which we and our works will also be remembered. Seen in this manner, place and placemaking offer not only a critique of the global but, as art critic Lucy Lippard suggests, also offer "tantalizing glimpses of new ways to enter everyday life."[5] And place is the home where our children's early understandings of self and life merge, the setting where special life activities and events unfold, the scene that captures our artistic imagination, the environment that teaches us how to be good stewards and the ground which receives our body at the end of its journey. Place is, along with love, the parent of poetry. And place is the inspiration for what Randolph Hester calls "an ecological democracy."[6] Place is one of the truly central concerns of any time, but particularly so in these times of global shifts, cultural unrest and impending ecological collapse.

This importance of particularness, this specificity of place, cannot be overemphasized. Each locale has its own genius loci—its own topos, ecology, people, heritage, senses of wonder and ways of being. Each locale liberates the body to explore and delight, or be constricted and rejected. Each can host an endless array of wonderful memories or deny one's presence. The making of good place involves a conscious effort, a full commitment that takes great pleasure in the endless possibilities that the immediate world has to offer. In current times, the responsibility and imagination of the designer play a critical role in bringing place back to our attention. The places we make must be joyful if we are to continue to see them, to tend them and ultimately to make them central to our lives and our thinking. Perhaps Douglas Kelbaugh's description of the five fundamental attitudes required of a critical regionalist says it best. They include, he argues, a "Love of Place, Love of Nature, Love of History, Love of Craft and a Love of Limits."[7]

For place to assume its rightful role in the making of the world, it must be regarded critically in a way that exceeds any limited notions of resistance and in a way that is imaginative about future possibilities. If place is central to making, as is being suggested here, then it must be hugely robust to offer endless ways in which to envision a more tangible world.

If place is by definition contextual, so too is good design. As cognitive scientist and designer John Seely Brown has so eloquently described, "When you come to honour the context you let the world do more of the work for you."[8] The range of contextual possibilities is endless. The work of Phillips Farevaag Smallenberg (PFS) continually seeks to describe that context, its appropriateness and the best ways to bring it into form—to give love to that context. The following five projects demonstrate these ideas: Cathedral Place, an urban space in downtown Vancouver; Washington Mutual Centre Roof Garden in Seattle; Hastings Park Restoration Plan, a major city park in Vancouver; Mountain View Cemetery Masonic Area Redevelopment, a revitalized old city cemetery in Vancouver; and Parliament Hill Landscape Plan for Canada's seat of democracy in Ottawa.

Mountain View Cemetery

Cathedral Place

Hastings Park

Parliament Hill

Washington Mutual Centre
Roof Garden

TOP Generative sketch showing connectivity of cloister to the greater urban fabric. BOTTOM View over the green towards the Bill Reid Gallery.

Cathedral Place
Vancouver, BC

Cathedral Place, a retail-office complex in downtown Vancouver designed in association with Paul Merrick Architects and advisor Cornelia Oberlander, realizes the contextual in a site plan that both reflects and gathers the surrounding city and situates one meaningfully within the downtown core. The project distinctly reflects the spirit of Christopher Alexander's theories of urban design when he asserts that

> the entrances, the main circulation, the main division of the building into parts, its interior open spaces, its daylight and the movement within the building, are all coherent and consistent with the position of the building in the street and in the neighbourhood.[9]

The lobby of Cathedral Place extends the sense of the vestibule of an adjacent church while accommodating commercial activities along busy Georgia Street. The hallway leading from the lobby to the Bill Reid Gallery merges into an allée of trees that traverses a cloister. At the end of this indoor-outdoor corridor is the gallery's entry. The cloister provides a quiet urban retreat from the noise of the city. On one side, a folly in the form of a second storey 'corridor' suggests a physical connection between the main tower and the gallery, while effectively mediating the scale of a looming bank building located across the street. In contrast, on the other side of the cloister, major views open to the city beyond. Here the cloister is closed only at the scale of the body but the mind remains free to roam, this openness further providing a powerful sense of being located in both the greater and the immediate urban fabric. And for those coming and going through the main entrance to the Hotel Vancouver across Georgia Street, a small pavilion located on axis with the hotel's entrance marks one corner of the cloister and serves as a delightful invitation to enter the space.

The project is not without its faults, mainly resulting from the usual undue worries of risk managers and conservative market analysts. A mid-block passage was not completed, limiting movement to and through the cloister and reducing the visitor's cognitive understanding of the site; and one edge of the tower framing the cloister became slated for a credit union rather than a restaurant at the market analyst's insistence, thus sealing the base of the tower off from the cloister. The project has also been controversial. Some have been offended by the complex's post-modern style, by the way its roof mimics that of the nearby Hotel Vancouver and by its various exuberant architectural and landscape architectural details. In the project's fundamental urban contextual responses however, Cathedral Place is a piece of urban design at its very best and most critical. It argues against the current object-focused ways in which buildings and public spaces are planned in the city, and demonstrates a more complete approach to 'building', or a 'seeking of topos', in the urban fabric.

LEFT Pergola and edge seating. RIGHT The inner cloister adjacent to Christ Church Cathedral.

Washington Mutual Centre Roof Garden
Seattle, WA

In smaller spaces, we find design moves that reflect the fact that little things can mean a lot. The Washington Mutual Roof Garden offers a 17th floor Pacific Northwest Coast oasis in the middle of downtown Seattle. The stone, wood, trees and groundcovers of the garden define the regional landscape in an appropriately abstract manner—there is no frivolous attempt to mimic but rather an intention to capture the elemental scale and materiality of the region. The powerful, luring connections between indoor lounge and outdoor garden further express the casual nature of Seattle living. And wherever one sits in the garden or lounge, the detailed views of the garden set against the distant views of Puget Sound give a sense of being well-located in both the city and region. Our innate need to experience both the intimate and the infinite together is carefully satisfied.

The bank's personality and intentions are also given form in the garden. A large glass-beaded abacus, an ancient device for counting, screens undesirable views while reflecting the most basic act of 'accounting for' that all banks must execute. The screen is a delightful reminder of that duty. In addition, the garden also contains a linear 'Change Garden', a repository for spare change that is donated to several Seattle charitable organizations. The Change Garden serves as a reminder of the need for good corporate citizenship and for commitment to a particular people and community, especially when juxtaposed against current corporate crises.

At the end of the day, one inhabits this particular place in a particular city—this roof garden in Seattle—with a particular sense of pleasure in and obligation to the place. This is the very essence of good placemaking. As Daniel Weil has noted,

> To do design as problem solving is one thing, but to do good design is quite another. I cannot say that what I do is good design, but I hope that it is about actually 'putting in' for other people to be able to see and understand something else. And that's how I think good design is defined—that other people will use it as a tool to understand and to go further.[10]

LEFT Rather than meet the City of Seattle's minimum open space requirements, the garden's usable area was enlarged threefold to provide decks and pathways that showcase views across Puget Sound. RIGHT Boldly patterned native plantings play off the architectural linearity of decks, walkways and screens.

LEFT The roof garden mirrored in building glazing. The garden's ecological attributes, including urban heat island effect reduction, stormwater retention and native and drought-tolerant planting, demonstrate that sustainable function can also be social, symbolic, practical and contemporary.
RIGHT Plantings include drought-tolerant species such as feather grass and shore pine, which evoke the windswept plateaus and shorelines of the state of Washington.

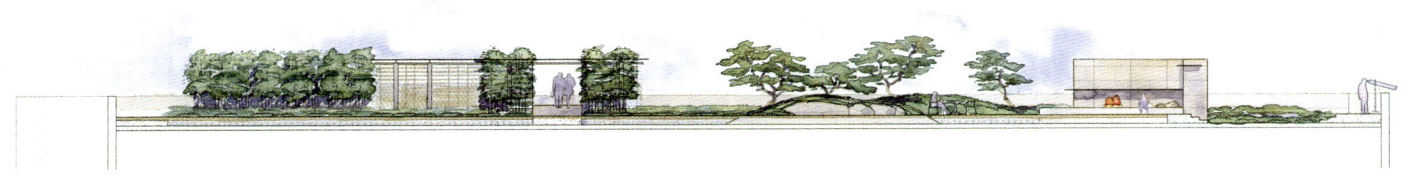

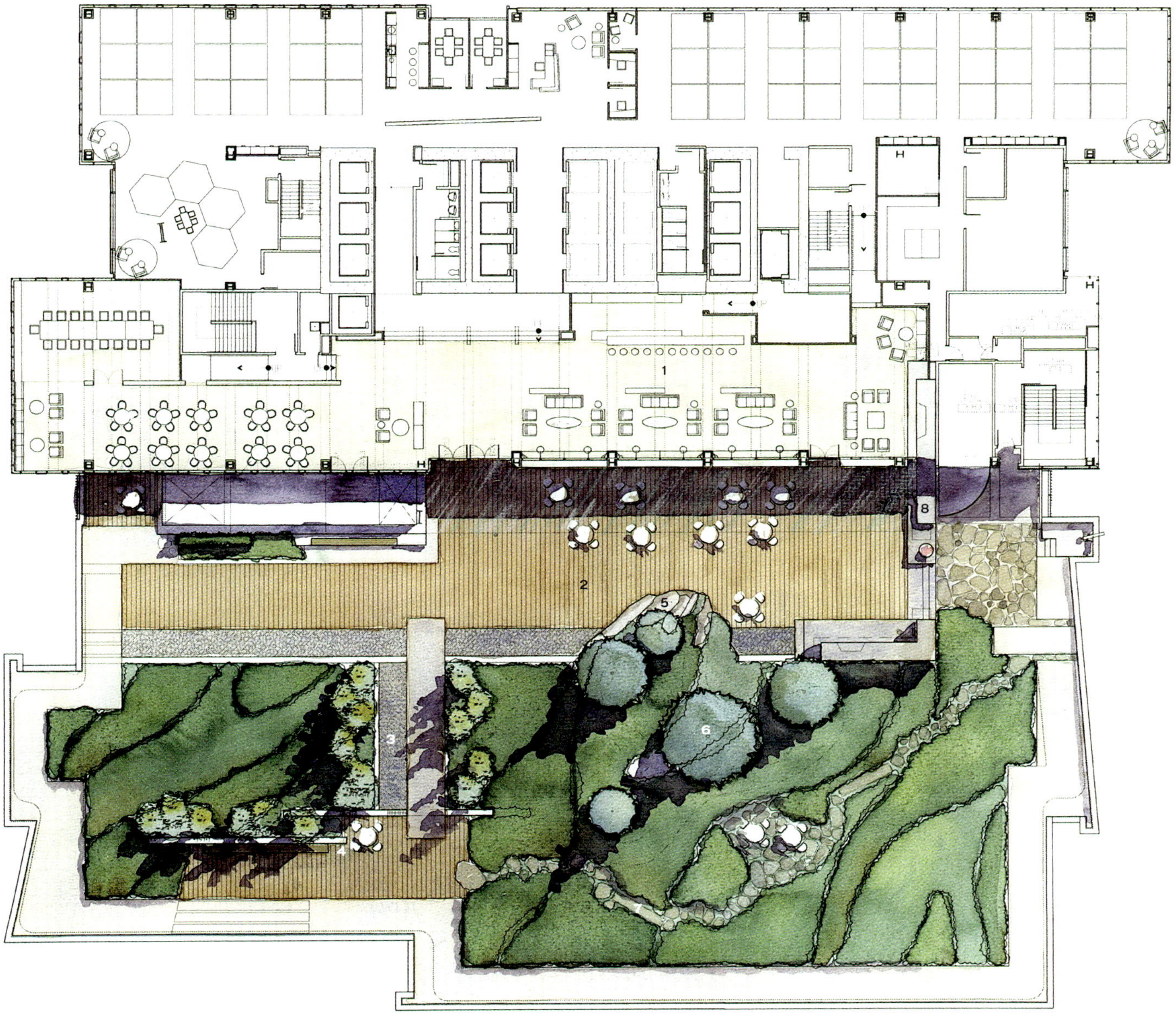

1 Cafeteria
2 Outdoor Dining Terrace
3 Change Garden
4 Glass Abacus
5 Slab Outcrop
6 Shore Pine Grove
7 Garden Walk
8 Outdoor Fireplace

OPPOSITE PAGE TOP The 17th floor green roof is also the vital social space and civic heart of the bank's downtown campus. Reflective surfaces visually expand the space and create alternative views. BOTTOM A turquoise-beaded abacus is integrated into the screen wall. Its individually fabricated glass beads slide on stainless steel rods. THIS PAGE Presentation plan and section.

Douglas Paterson Place, Body, Memory 101

THIS PAGE TOP The Change Garden is a receptacle for spare change collected for donation to charity. The garden represents the bank's role as a prominent corporate citizen in the local community. BOTTOM The boulder outcropping was mocked-up off-site, numbered and craned into place. It evokes the windswept rocky headlands of the Pacific shoreline while serving as a bench for lunches and an informal podium for evening social events. OPPOSITE PAGE The 17th floor garden is one of Seattle's largest green roofs.

Existing monuments and daylighted historical curbs in Cemetery Green.

Mountain View Cemetery
Masonic Area Redevelopment
Vancouver, BC

How we regard death as well as life says a great deal about who we are. In much of our sterile, ritual-free world death has become something to be shunned, sanitized and relegated to the distant corners of our cities and regions. Death has become privatized and corporatized and is no longer a central civic concern. Only our older city cemeteries, our necropolises, serve as reminders of our collective human passions, heroic deeds, sufferings and tragedies; and of the subtle similarities and differences in who we ultimately see ourselves as being and what we believe in at the end of life. Despite our fears of death, the great necropolises of the world continually draw us to them to explore and contemplate. However, many of these older cemeteries are at capacity, over-burdened and struggling to maintain their sense of dignity and relevance. Finding a renewed sense of place for these worlds of the dead becomes paramount to representing the full power of life in the city.

Begun in 1897, Mountain View Cemetery is Vancouver's oldest cemetery, now housing some 96,000 souls. It covers 42 hectares, descending north from the top of a ridge and offering commanding views of the North Shore mountains. The last gravesite was sold in 1986. The cemetery gradually became run-down due to a lack of funding. There seemed to be a general feeling that the upkeep of old cemeteries was an undue burden on municipal taxes. In the mid-1990s a private firm made a bid to take over the control and management of the cemetery. A group of caring and dynamic City staff, however, had a different vision. With Council's permission they hired a consortium of firms led by Philips Wuori Long, including Pechet and Robb Art and Architecture, Lees + Associates and Harris Hudema Consulting, to examine the design, planning, character, operations and financial possibilities for upgrading the cemetery and extending its life as a central feature in the city. The consultants undertook an exhaustive analysis of the cemetery that led first to a Council-approved vision plan before then proceeding to a more formal master plan in 2000.

The master plan was notable at several levels. First it defined the identity of twelve distinct zones within the cemetery such as veterans, religious and ethnic cemeteries. By thickening the edge of the cemetery and linking it to various city greenways, the plan strengthened the presence of the cemetery in the larger urban fabric. A strong north-south spine, Mountain View Way, was introduced through the middle of the site to structure and gather together the various zones and site entrances. Along this spine the plan called for a powerful centre for the cemetery that included a Celebration Hall, an Administrative Centre, an Operations Centre, a Cemetery Green and an outdoor Community Memorial. Finally, by intensifying other edges and developing a variety of memorials for different citizen needs, the master plan provided new space for the interment of as many as 75,000 new souls, adding another 75 years to the active life of the cemetery (cremations now account for some 75% of all interments in the city). These new interment sites provide the funds needed to reenergize and improve the cemetery as a special place within the city.

The detailed design for the first major upgrade in the cemetery, including the Masonic cemetery and the nearby administrative-celebration complex, were given to PFS, Lees + Associates, and Birmingham & Wood Architects. Their work furthers the spirit of the master plan and the making of good place. The sense of place emerges first in the extensive healing of what was already there: revealing and protecting old granite edges, improving the conditions for tree growth and adding new trees to reinforce the spaces formed by the existing trees. Rather than using the industry catalogue standard, the columbaria, family vessels and ossuaries are collaboratively designed to express a sense of elegant individuality and community. Openings in the columbaria wall frame and draw attention to nearby monuments. The placing of family vessels on plinths along Mountain View Way adds to a sense of the ceremonial and somber while new fountains delight and calm. Ten thousand spring bulbs become part of a larger landscape of native plants, berries and flowers that can be cut for use on the interments by cemetery visitors, reminding them that this place cares for them in their times of mourning.

The cemetery is slowly reinserting itself into the life of the city. The initiation of a children's memorial garden and the Night for All Souls ceremony each October have furthered the healing process, bringing more people to the cemetery and to a renewed understanding of the many dimensions of life and death within the city.

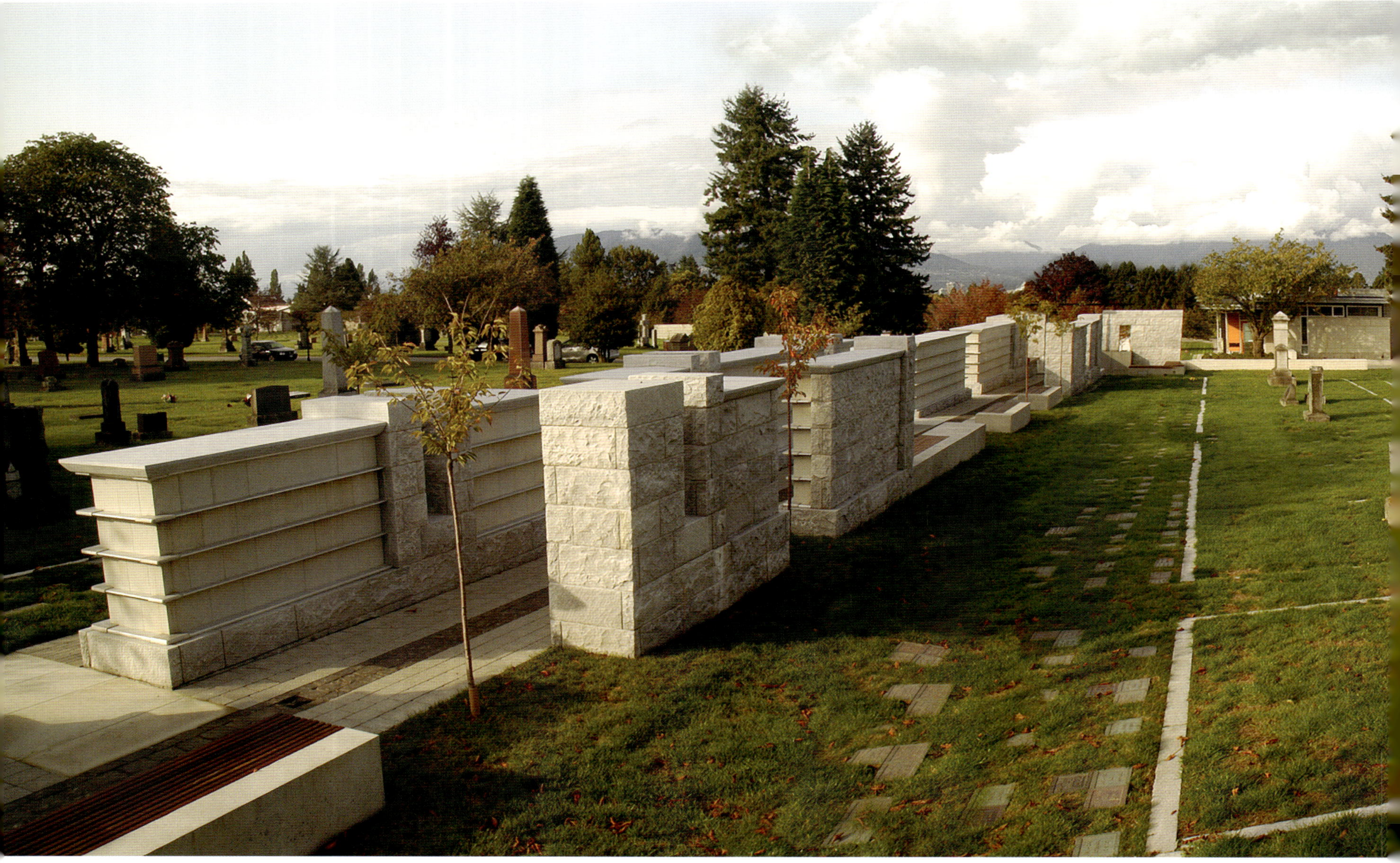

7'-9"
8'-0"
3'-0"
RAIN WATER SPOUT
POLISHED INNER CASEMENT (STONE) WITH INNER CONCRETE COMPARTMENTS TO HOLD URNS
CONCRETE OUTER CASE W/ IVY & TRELLIS STRUCTURE
4'-8"
CENTRAL
1'-2"
PAVED WALKWAY
3'-0"
5'-0"
6'-0"
1'-6"
3'-0"
12'-6"

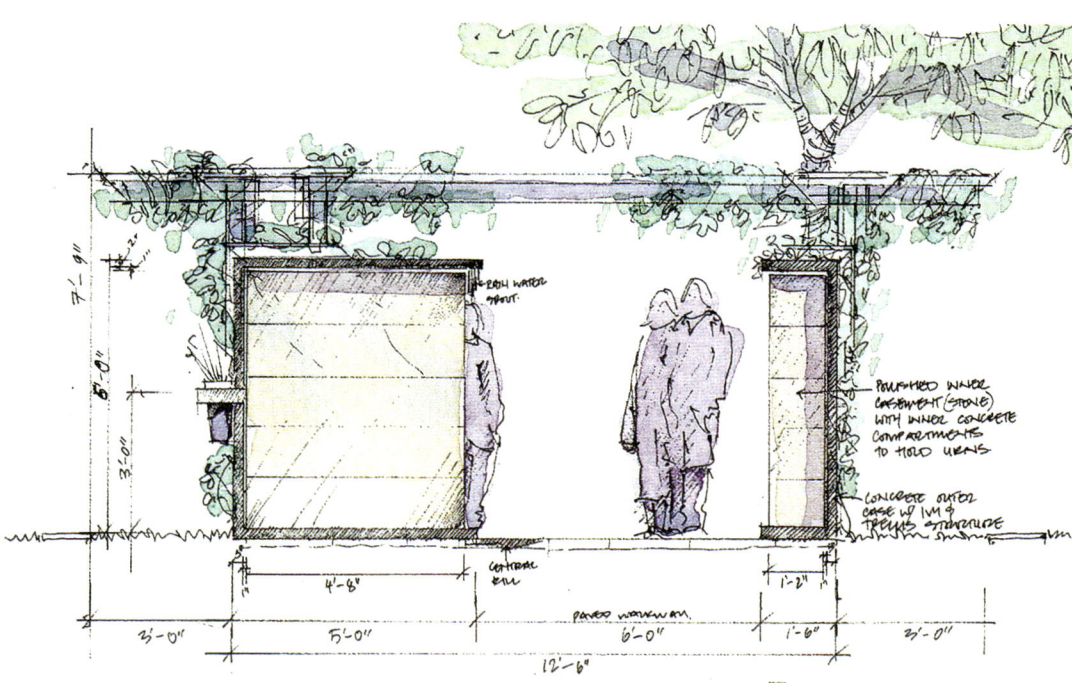

TOP Mountain View Way and Cemetery Green featuring columbaria walls, cremation borders, daylighted historical curbs and existing monuments.
BOTTOM Study sketch illustrating single and double loaded columbaria walls.

THIS PAGE TOP Masonic East water feature. BOTTOM Cemetery necessarium featuring bronze faucet and basalt basin. OPPOSITE PAGE TOP Openings in columbaria wall aligned with existing historical monuments. BOTTOM Columbaria window framing view across cemetery green.

Douglas Paterson Place, Body, Memory

LEFT Rendered site plan of Phase One – Masonic Area Improvements.
RIGHT Central Pathway with basalt and andesite mosaic.
PAGES 112–113 Incense necessarium featuring basalt counter and incense basin, granite walls and andesite inscription stones.

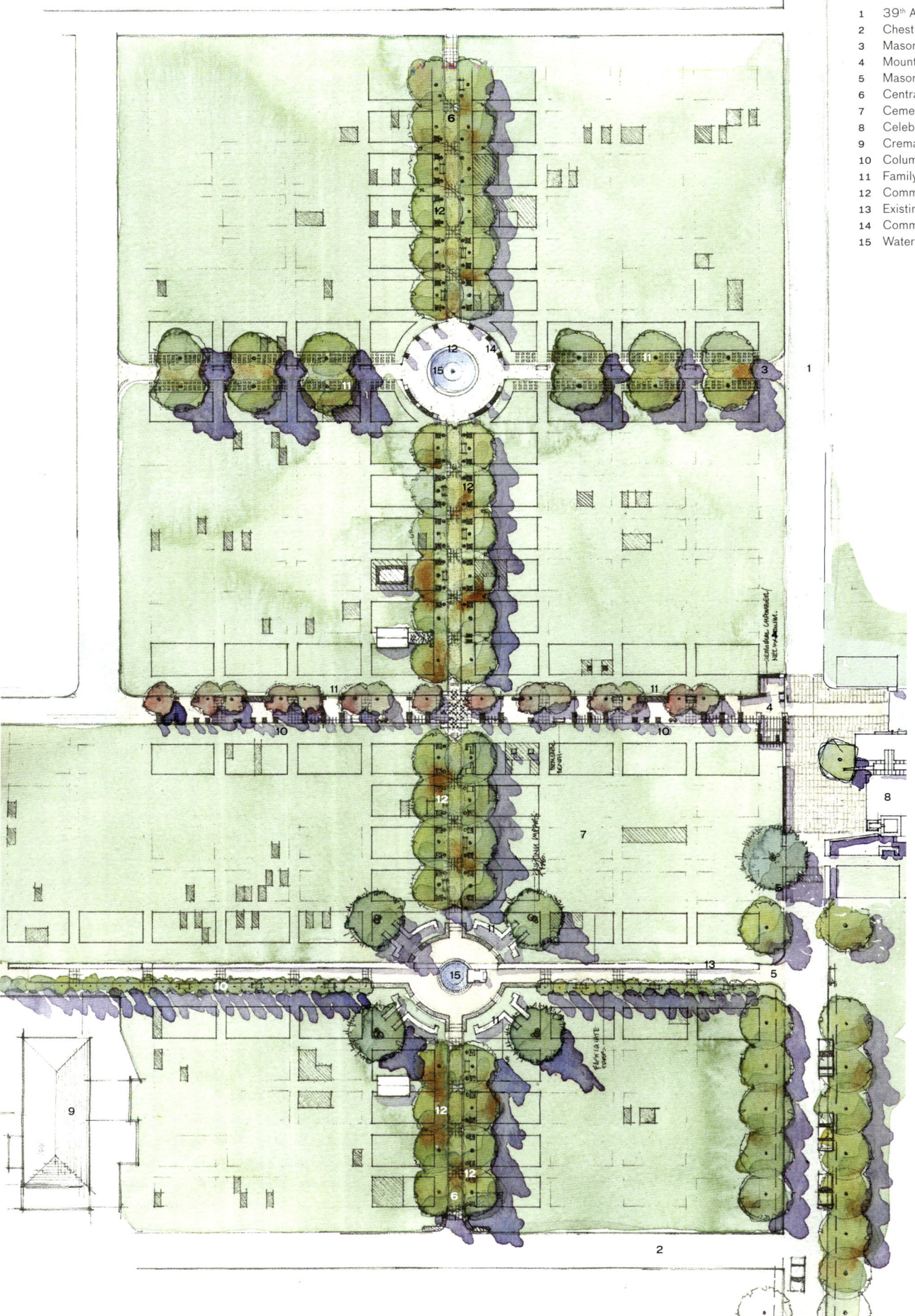

1   39th Avenue
2   Chestnut Street
3   Masonic West
4   Mountain View Way
5   Masonic East
6   Central Pathway
7   Cemetery Green
8   Celebration Hall and Administrative Centre
9   Crematorium
10 Columbaria Wall by Existing Cremation Borders
11 Family Columbaria
12 Community Columbaria
13 Existing Cremation Borders
14 Community Memorial Wall
15 Water Feature

1 Burrard Inlet
2 McGill Street
3 Hastings Street
4 Renfrew Street
5 New Brighton Park
6 The Sanctuary
7 Daylighted Stream
8 Relocated Horse Stables and Barns
9 Racetrack
10 Pacific Colosseum
11 Agridome
12 Italian Rain Gardens
13 Skatepark
14 Forum
15 Garden Auditorium
16 Proposed Pedestrian Underpass
17 Community Centre
18 Windermere Hill
19 Empire Sports Fields

LEFT Hastings Park Restoration Plan. RIGHT Aerial photo of Hastings Park circa 1990, prior to park redevelopment.

Hastings Park Restoration Plan
Vancouver, BC

Well-loved places invite discussion, and discussion is essential to the fostering of that love. In talking about one's home and environment, the knowledge, stories and imaginings that emerge in those discussions expand our interest in, caring for and respect for those places. A sense of citizenship also emerges. In the past great and small discussions were central to any built achievement. Most of today's participatory planning processes fail in this respect. Wrapped in bureaucratic intentions they curtail the passions and insights that are essential to the emergence and growth of great places. Hastings Park, on Vancouver's east side, is one PFS project that has been wrapped in discussions for many years. The conscious role of the firm was, and remains one, of honouring the best of those discussions.

Hastings Park is a 65 hectare site set aside by the provincial government in an 1889 legislative act, "for the use, and recreational enjoyment of the public." Over the years, the natural landscape was slowly replaced by race tracks, a city arena and exhibition buildings and grounds for Vancouver's major yearly gathering, the Pacific National Exhibition (PNE). By the 1970s the site, when not in use during the few weeks of the exhibition, had become a barren, paved, neglected landscape in the middle of East Vancouver where few green spaces remained. Local citizens wanted their park back and were, for a few brief years, given that opportunity. In 1994, the Hastings Park Restoration Committee was formed to guide the park's future. Working for over a year with various local and city-wide organizations, the committee proposed a detailed and passionate vision statement and program for the park. A year later the PFS team, led by Chris Phillips, was hired to elaborate upon that vision. The PNE in turn was asked to find an alternative location for the exhibition within the Greater Vancouver region.

The citizens' vision radiated out from the core idea of a sanctuary, a natural oasis-retreat in the middle of the site that would serve as the physical and symbolic heart of the park's restoration. The sanctuary would initiate the park's healing process. Renfrew Creek once flowed through the park, passing through New Brighton Park on its journey to the Burrard Inlet. Long ago the creek was covered with 9 or more metres of fill. PFS proposed a series of major ponds that

LEFT The Sanctuary, a reintroduced wetland and stormwater system, during construction. Buildings and parking lots were removed to introduce the wetlands. RIGHT The Sanctuary two years after construction.

would treat urban stormwater and symbolically mark the beginning of the stream's long-term daylighting. This move energized many of the subsequent master planning moves.

The proposed daylighting of the stream leading north from these ponds to the sea, however, was blocked by two significant barriers: the Hastings Park Racecourse's horse stables and barns and McGill Street, a major transportation corridor. PFS noted that many of the stables needed to be rebuilt and, by building them further to the east, the stream could continue its journey to the sea between the stables and the track. This bold move would also give the racecourse several options for improving the actual racing track and its overall image. By moving through the site at this location, the site grade was such that the stream could be bridged over McGill Street thereby assuring its continued journey into New Brighton Park and on to Burrard Inlet. The aspirations of the Sanctuary as a place for initiating the act of healing were being given real form.

To the south of the park, similar problems existed. Daylighting the streams leading into the Sanctuary would need to bridge under Hastings Street, a major east-west urban artery and barrier to adjacent neighbourhoods attempting to access the park and community centre. It was recognized that such bridging would allow for a pedestrian greenway that would strengthen the idea of a north-south spine through the middle of the site, vastly improving the cognitive structure of the park within the city.

To date, ponds have been built that now appear as though they have been there for years. The close attention paid to pond ecology, the proper use of native plant material and the generally rough way the landscape is allowed to emerge, speak of a natural healing process working at a rapid rate. At the same time the refined detailing of pedestrian bridges and walkways express the symbolic importance of the Sanctuary.

Four other broad sets of intentions and ideas expressed by the restoration committee and others are worth noting. The committee wanted the park's past history to be imaginatively retained. They also wanted the seasons of the Pacific Northwest, and particularly the rain, to be celebrated. They desired a coming together of all age groups. No one was to be left out. In this respect they sought also to assure that the many diverse groups living in the area would feel represented or recognized in the park development. These highly specific desires were given effective form by PFS.

Empire Stadium once occupied the southeast corner of the site. It was here that Roger Bannister and John Landy first broke the four minute mile at the 1954 Commonwealth Games. The location, general form and athletic functions of the stadium have been reclaimed from an exhibition parking lot. Aspiring young athletes can once again run the track in the same spot as Bannister and Landy while the embankments surrounding the track and fields express imagined bleachers of cheering fans. The past is embodied in images of future possibilities.

Along the west side of the site the best of a grouping of old Art Deco exhibition buildings have been retained for various community events. Where buildings have been torn down, they have been replaced by new activities such as a skate park, playgrounds and court games that maintain the spatial intensity of the area and bring various age groups together to play. These activities have been gently cloaked in details that embody delightful hints of former site activities and former Art Deco elements. For example, a large grass mound crowned with a sculpture of a cow (recalling the agricultural nature of earlier exhibitions) sits on axis with the older exhibition buildings and serves as a focal point to a children's playground. In addition, old roads through the exhibition site have been converted into grand pedestrian allées. The memory of the place's past structure surfaces through the structure of the new place.

The Italian Rain Gardens have also been located in the middle of this activity zone to provide an important entrance feature along the park's western boundary. The Italian community, a long established and active part of East Vancouver's population, wished to commemorate their role in the city through the creation of a garden that would recognize the rebirth of Hastings Park. PFS created a garden that is an exuberant translation of this community's heritage. The garden's structure harkens to the Italianate while being cloaked in details part 'Venice Carnival', part 'Carlo Scarpa' and part local history. The gardens, in their lushness and celebration of water, are also very local in their embellishment. While they were not without

THIS PAGE TOP, OPPOSITE PAGE TOP AND BOTTOM Boardwalk system through Sanctuary wetlands. THIS PAGE BOTTOM Sanctuary habitat three years after completion.

controversy (the donors were originally hoping for something more traditionally Italianate) their almost instantaneous success assuaged any concerns. The gardens have emerged to become part of a particular here and now, an essential act in the making of a specific place in a global world.

PFS continues their role in the discussions and has again been retained by the City of Vancouver as the lead consultant for the Hastings Park/PNE Master Plan, a comprehensive plan that will guide the future long-term development of Hastings Park and integrate an active, urban park with the PNE and the Hastings Racecourse.

Douglas Paterson   Place, Body, Memory   119

THIS PAGE The Dining Room in the Italian Rain Gardens.
OPPOSITE PAGE TOP Water, a potent stimulant to children's imagination.
BOTTOM The Braille Wall with poem entitled *Rain* by Maori poet Hone Tuwhare. Like many of the elements in the garden, the wall captures and playfully redirects rainwater during storm events.

Douglas Paterson   Place, Body, Memory   121

1 Ottawa River	12 West Terrace
2 Rideau Canal	13 Library Terrace
3 Wellington Street	14 Wellington Edge
4 Bank Street	15 Perimeter Plateau
5 Centre Block	16 North Escarpment
6 Library of Parliament	17 West Escarpment
7 Peace Tower	18 East Escarpment
8 West Block	19 Lovers' Walk
9 East Block	20 Parliamentary Woods
10 Parliamentary Forecourt	21 Bank Street Ravine
11 Upper Terrace	22 Bank Street Lookout

LEFT The site development and landscape plan for Parliament Hill gained Canadian Government Federal Land Use Approval in 2000.
RIGHT Presentation models of approved Landscape Plan for Parliament Hill. Parliament Hill is a Classified Site originally planned by Thomas Seaton Scott and Calvert Vaux.

Parliament Hill Landscape Plan
Ottawa, ON

Parliament Hill is Canada's grand house of democracy—the place that represents the best of who we are and what we aspire to as a nation. The forms and functions it assumes for such an important role demand precise intentions, a carefully critiqued set of real and symbolic activities, and a carefully managed unfolding of the ordinary and the extraordinary. It is not a place where one group is to be given priority over others, where the private is allowed to invade the public, nor where the sentimental is allowed to dominate public manners and sensibilities. Planning for such a place is not an easy or immediately resolvable task. It demands an ongoing conversation—one that is often tricky, loaded with potential conflicts and always changing in focus. Yet it is also a conversation that should be equally loaded with excitement, passion and the expression of noble inspirations. The conversation about the place is as important as the place itself.

Parliament Hill is comprised of four main buildings: the Centre Block (the central House of Parliament and Senate with its Peace Tower) and the Library of Parliament are flanked by the East and West Blocks that house the various ministries of government. The buildings form a U-shaped space facing south to the city. From a high bluff, the buildings overlook the Ottawa River Valley and distant Gatineau landscape. The setting is distinctly Canadian—a reminder that this is a northern, forested country, with wide and rapid rivers and great distances to be overcome. The building style is Canadian Gothic and is recognized internationally as one of the great complexes of Gothic Revival architecture. The front terrace, walls and steps that unite the three buildings were conceived by Calvert Vaux of the firm Olmsted and Vaux.

From the beginning, the complex has been open, friendly and, while somewhat grand, certainly not pompous. When the young nation's roads were first constructed, one could drive from just about anywhere in the country right up to the front door under the porte-cochere, immediately below the Peace Tower, the nation's grand axis mundi. The overall site was dotted with a few statues of founding fathers and the queen. Along the river and around the complex, to the delight of many, there was a Lovers' Walk.

Yet the place, as is the case with such places in the Canadian mind, has always been and probably always will be held with

Douglas Paterson   Place, Body, Memory

LEFT TO RIGHT Generative site sketches: Defining a contemporary Canadian Gothic, Exploring a more ordered landscape and Maintaining a creative tension.

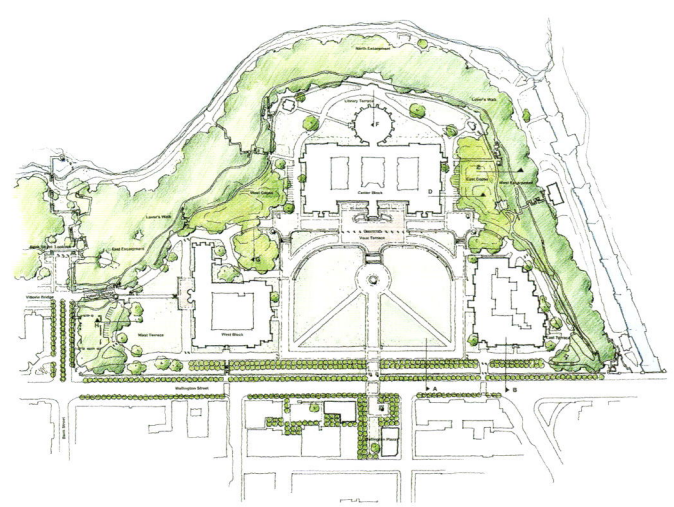

some suspicion. Some of this is a result of citizens' characteristic suspicions of power in any form, even if it is their duly-elected government. Some of it has to do with a central government being perceived as wasting taxpayers' money. And some of it has to do with distance, with the endless miles that separate most Canadians from Ottawa and their representatives in parliament. It is even fair to say that many of the representatives themselves who come to Ottawa to serve their constituents are suspicious of the place and its traditions and bureaucracies.

Over time, the easiness of the place, combined with these suspicions, took its toll. The site became one big parking lot. Tour buses made family photographs in front of the Peace Tower next to impossible. Senators liked to park as close as possible to Centre Block during cold winter months. And everyone expected their individual memorial to be 'parked' on the 'Hill' otherwise intended solely for heads of state. At the same time more and more visitors came to see the site and the Changing of the Guard, a ceremony once restricted to Rideau Hall, the official residence of the governor general. Or they thronged to Canada Day celebrations in such numbers that port-o-potties eventually lined the facades of the East and West Blocks while the advertisements of Canada Day sponsors 'slipped' into various venues. The pressures were more than the site could accommodate. At the same time, there was a reluctance to improve the precinct and the suspicions continued to dominate.

Over the years, ten master plans were made, each contributing new insights to the discussion but each eventually was ignored. The 1987 Parliamentary Precinct Plan by du Toit Allsopp Hillier (DTAH) was notable for the discipline it brought to the design management of the site and its recommendation that commemorations on the Hill be reserved for former prime ministers. In 1983 DTAH also planned a grand ceremonial route that would connect important civic sites on both sides of the Ottawa River, an important move for a nation's capital, but once again the suspicious and reluctant managed to curtail much of the design intention.

In 1998, PFS was hired to develop a detailed landscape plan to curtail the growing problems that existed on the Hill. A deteriorating site, fear of global terrorism, the need for more effective strategies to control visitors, and more complicated parking and servicing needs pushed the design agenda. The design brief they developed focused on four basic tenets: to identify, protect and enhance the aspects of the site that have made it great; to challenge, and where possible eliminate, the aspects of the site of low value that detract from the site's greatness; to integrate the increasingly complex set of programmatic demands on the site with the site's physical order and character; and finally, to add a strong contemporary layer onto the site that respected the site's heritage values but also demonstrated that Parliament Hill is a place that is capable of growing and evolving with its people.

The primary move was to emphasize an inside-outside, Gothic-Romantic structure. The inside forecourt was made more distinct by emphasizing its austerity and its clarity of space and order. By contrast, the surrounding perimeter plateau and the Wellington Street edge were made more complex, more intimate and sometimes even rougher and more in keeping with the romantic side of the Hill's location overlooking the Ottawa River.

The forecourt proposal is a controlled, masterful work of subtle reordering, grading and paving. The original geometry of the Vaux walls and terraces is reinstated. The upper terrace is stepped slightly to improve site circulation and to give the terrace a greater sense of presence as the foreground to the Peace Tower. The road around the entire forecourt is redefined and gathered into paved forecourts for both the East and West Blocks, giving these buildings a greater sense of prominence and providing pedestrians with clear priority over the automobile. Continuous paving from the central lawn to the building edges, the elimination of ineffective shrub beds and the exposing of the face of the Vaux wall add to the forecourt's sense of austerity. An energized sense of contemporary Canadian Gothic emerges, a place that is both of the past and the present.

The plan substantially reduces paving around the perimeter, increasing the area given over to lawns and significant tree planting. It reinstates Lovers' Walk while establishing a variety of views and experiences along the edge of the precinct that specifically reinforce Parliament Hill's historic and symbolic position on the promontory. This is further emphasized to the west of the site where, in the exten-

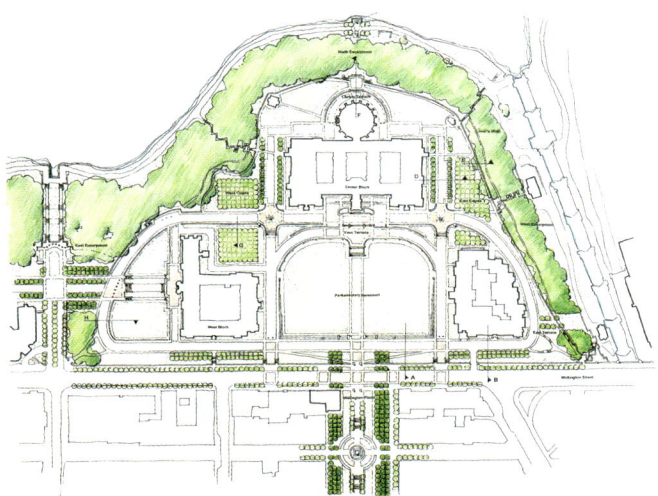

sion of Bank Street as a service street to the Hill, the Bank Street Ravine has been kept and enhanced to maintain and clarify the sense of promontory on all three sides of the site.

While the plan is notable for its controlled, disciplined and well-argued physical site interventions, it falls short on two other accounts: its lack of specific directives for daily and special programs that are part of the life of Parliament Hill, and for the manner in which site maintenance and operations are carried out. In such an important location these activities need definition because of their impact on how the place is 'read'. This is the democratic house of all Canadians. As such, the orchestration of events within the parliamentary forecourt is as important as the room itself. The place, its people and the nature of its activities and rituals go hand in hand to give Parliament Hill its full sense of place. Two brief examples warrant explication.

Canada Day celebrations 'radiate out' from the Hill to all parts of the country while 'gathering' various talents from around the country to perform on a stage erected on the lawn of the parliamentary forecourt. But the stage is generic, not unlike the stage one would find at an average rock concert, and during its construction the Hill is covered with large semitrailers hauling it in and dominating the scene. The ubiquitous nature of the stage and its erection casts a spell of mediocrity over the Hill and its performances and lacks any memorable physicality that might transform the event beyond the typical and common. Parliament Hill is a place that calls for its own unique stage that is inspiring in its form and wondrous in the manner in which it is assembled. This stage, perhaps a traveling stage that could be assembled in other parts of the country, would become a significant memory maker, elevating the value of both the celebration and the place for all citizens.

Winter is a major part of what defines who we are as Canadians. It is something that should delight. The clearing and management of snow and ice on Parliament Hill, like the stage, is perfunctory, an everyday necessity. Yet it could be an experience of magical theatre, a choreographed movement of snow, an evolving piece of winter art. Photographed and broadcast to all Canadians, the act would assert a pride of place rarely seen in these times.

Even without such attention to program and the daily activities of place, the PFS plan provides the strongest direction to date for an upgrading of Parliament Hill. Sadly, inaction remains; the places in our world that should inspire us to make a greater commitment to places everywhere are themselves in disrepair and disarray.

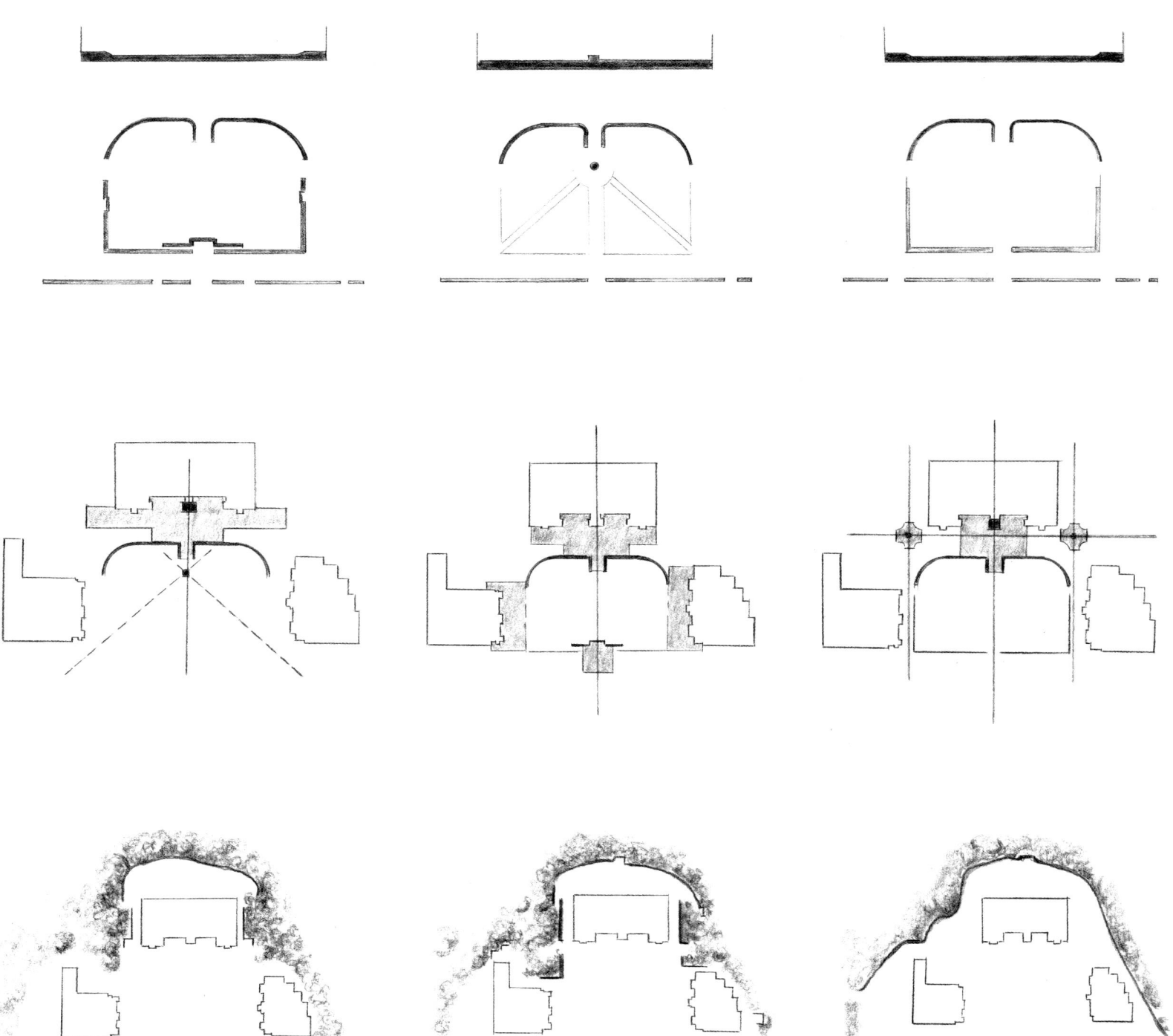

THIS PAGE TOP ROW Defining edges. MIDDLE ROW Exploring the equilibrium of the parliamentary forecourt. BOTTOM ROW Exploring the relationship of Parliament Hill to the river escarpment. OPPOSITE PAGE Aerial perspective rendering of approved Landscape Plan for Parliament Hill. The new plan increases the amount of soft landscape at the expense of paved surface with intensified tree coverage on the perimeter plateau and a rehabilitated escarpment. Stronger connections are made to the Ottawa River and the Rideau Canal to set Parliament Hill more clearly in its context.

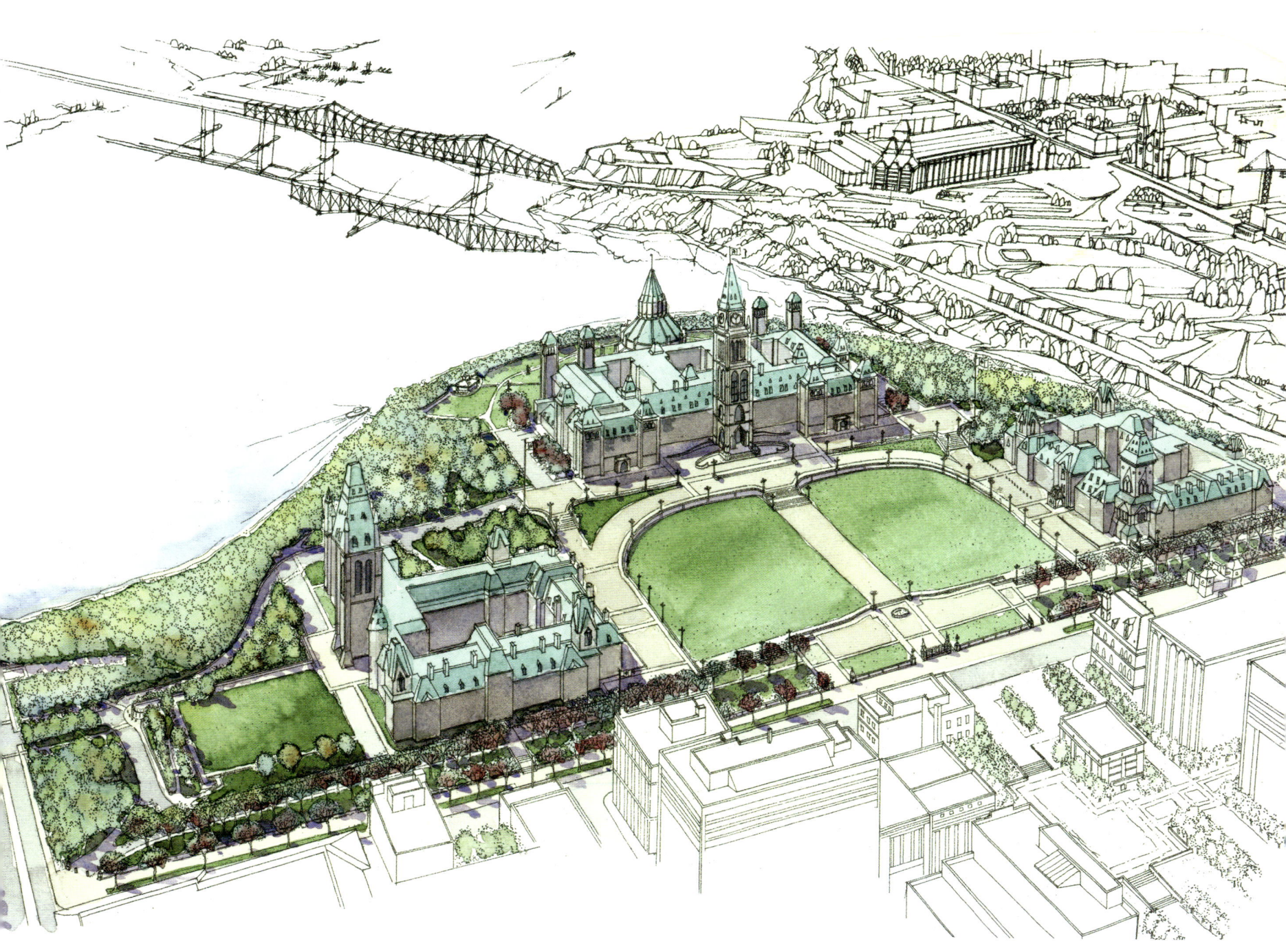

Douglas Paterson Place, Body, Memory

Conclusion

Canadian geographer Ted Relph defines the inauthentic as involving "a leveling down of the possibilities of being....The values are those of mediocrity and superficiality that have been borrowed or handed down from some external source."[11] The result is placelessness. Local failures and weaknesses, including a lack of public commitment to place, ubiquitous standards, single-purpose actions, a fear of experimentation and a loss of apparent social values seem to welcome the onslaught of the global and with it such placelessness. Yet the world still wants to resist the inauthentic. People, places and cultures are unique. And if the corollary to Relph's definition is true—that the authentic involves an elaboration and elevation of the possibilities for being—then the discovery and enhancement of the particular must play a central role in authentic placemaking.

The projects discussed here all seek to define the particular: the particular position of the place; its particular histories, activities, climates and people; and its contextual responsibilities. In their seeking of the particular, there is an opening up to new possibilities, new ways of experiencing one's everyday world and new ways of making. Each project is distinct and carries its own sense of order, character and careful response to context and place. There is no company branding, no slavish adherence to the latest fads and no reliance on catalogue shopping. Each project seeks to find its own place and hence its own authentic presence.

Ultimately the particular is the soul of imagination as well as the soul of place.

Notes

[1] Edward Casey, *The Fate of Place – A Philosophical History* (Berkeley: University of California Press, 1997), 18.
[2] Jane Amidon, *Radical Landscapes: Reinventing Outdoor Space* (New York: Thames & Hudson, 2001), 131.
[3] Paul Ricoeur, *History and Truth* (Evanston: Northwestern University Press, 1965), 277.
[4] Kenneth Frampton, "Towards a Critical Regionalism: Six Points for an Architecture of Resistance" in *The Anti-Aesthetic – Essays on Postmodern Culture*, edited by Hal Foster (Port Townsend: Bay Press, 1983).
[5] Lucy Lippard, *The Lure of the Local: Senses of Place in a Multicentred Society* (New York: The New Press, 1998), 286.
[6] Randolph Hester, *Design for Ecological Democracy* (Cambridge: MIT Press, 2006).
[7] Douglas Kelbaugh, "Towards an Architecture of Place" in *Arcade*, Dec./Jan. 1986 (Seattle).
[8] John Seely Brown as cited in C. Thomas Mitchell's *New Thinking in Design: Conversations on Theory and Practice* (New York: Van Nostrand Reinhold, 1996), 108.
[9] Christopher Alexander, *A New Theory of Urban Design* (New York: Oxford University Press, 1987), 77.
[10] Daniel Weil as quoted in C. Thomas Mitchell, *New Thinking in Design: Conversations on Theory and Practice* (New York: Van Nostrand Reinhold, 1996), 24.
[11] Ted Relph, *Place and Placelessness* (London: Pion, 1976), 80.

Interview

PFS's three partners—Chris Phillips, Marta Farevaag and Greg Smallenberg—were interviewed by Kelty McKinnon at Vancouver's Ouest Restaurant one late summer evening.

KM Phillips Farevaag Smallenberg has come to be respected as one of the foremost landscape architecture, planning and urban design offices in Canada. As PFS approaches its third decade how would each of you characterize your practice?

CP As a firm we're unable to articulate a definitive position on what we do. We move around a lot. Some people can express in three minutes who they are and what they do and how they approach things. We don't do that—we tend to reshape ourselves constantly.

MF There's a lot of intellectual content to what we do—I think that's why we've chosen this field. We've joked about this for years—if you want to make a lot of money you need to find something straightforward and repeat it over and over. But PFS does something completely different with every project. We're always figuring out new solutions. Even though there is knowledge and insight brought from previous projects, each assignment is a new line of inquiry. And we like that.

GS When you look at the range of work produced by our office you'd be hard pressed to think that it all came out of one firm. Reflecting on the hundreds of projects we sifted through to arrive at the ones we wanted to feature in this book, the level of diversity is quite surprising. I suppose that's one of the real strengths of PFS.

CP It's true, there's not one particular style that defines us. We aren't hired for a 'PFS look', but for an engaging process that builds on the uniqueness of place and community. We try to respect the individuality of place; its social, ecological, geological and cultural aspects. We tend toward an inclusive process—drawing out local qualities and influences as best we can. Marta is one of the great process gurus and works with different players to elicit ideas and values that create a vision for place. Greg immerses himself in an extraordinary variety of sites and cultures around the world. He has a knack for quickly understanding their unique qualities and potentials. He's become highly regarded and sought after for his innovative ideas and simultaneous respect for 'place'.

GS Our staff brings a range of unique approaches to the work we do—it would be hard to imagine a more talented and dedicated group of professionals. Without them, PFS couldn't

Canoe Landing Park. Toronto, ON.

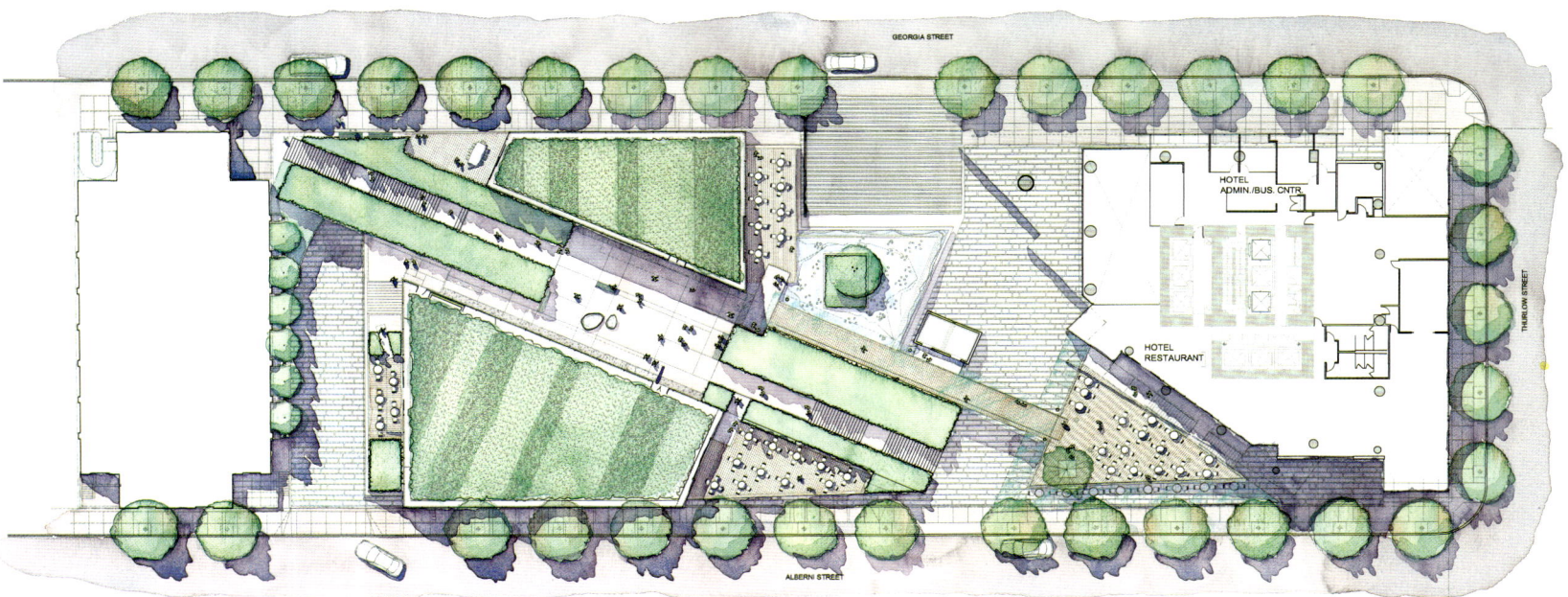

Shangri-La. Vancouver, BC.

have achieved what it has and we certainly wouldn't be going forward with the confidence we now have. I think they recognize what they've become a part of and this keeps all of us energized and motivated.

But Chris mentioned place-based process, and I agree. When I think about what distinguishes PFS, it's our emphasis on process that gets us to exceptional design solutions.

CP We have patience as well—we wade through the issues. We're pretty good listeners and that's important in understanding people, place, culture and community.

MF And we believe in the public process, to the extent that we do engage and listen and don't just give it lip service. As a result we really try to grapple with things people tell us. We don't just do the display and walk away—we try to use the process to advance the project.

CP Our focus on process really gives us clues as to how to proceed in an interesting and appropriate manner.

MF The best of our projects, where we had enough time and engagement, become a reflection of a much larger group than just us.

KM Can you talk more specifically about PFS's approach to both internal and public process?

MF Process should and does vary with every project. PFS's reputation is based on our openness and ability to adapt process strategically throughout a project to meet changing conditions. Over the years we've expanded our 'toolkit' of methods to involve the community, municipal interests, landowners and future user groups and to bring multidisciplinary teams and clients into design development. We like to use workshops to advance the dialogue, both internal to design teams and external involving stakeholders. Our public consultation processes focus on learning how people want to use the site and how they feel about it and its place in the larger community both historically and into the future. Our graphic communication tools have also evolved as we've learned to align our message to the clearest and most cost-effective visual tools suited to the particular stage of the process.

KM This kind of process demands a great deal of patience!

GS The patience needed for engaged listening and meaningful process is a sign of confidence. It allows us to sit back and defer judgment because we're confident that we'll be able to work with some of the thinking that's coming from other directions and craft it into something truly unique. If you don't have confidence in what it is that you can ultimately deliver, you're probably going to have some impatience with the process because you might want to avoid the threat of entertaining other ideas in the hopes of preserving some preconceived ones of your own.

CP I think we've learned to be patient because in the end it's beneficial. You can gain so many insights and ideas that enrich the project. Not to say that we don't at times experience conflict in the process, but I think we learn to include that as well...most of the time!

MF Process can be a two-edged thing. When we're hired to manage a project we can design the process, the public conversation. We can be fluid about the order we do things in, so if problems arise we can bring in more resources to grapple with them—all the things that you need to do in order to stay on top of where you're trying to get to. But it can be frustrating when we're not the prime consultant. Then we have to convince others to do the right thing. It can be like trying to push a string.

KM How does the interdisciplinary aspect of PFS, that Marta is a planner while Chris and Greg are landscape architects, differentiate the firm's practice?

GS There's a logical overlap between these two disciplines. This is also what defines the work of PFS—our ability to bring the dual perspectives of planning and landscape architecture to many of our larger assignments.

CP Years ago in Canada, planning and landscape architecture were actually together under one professional organization: The Canadian Society of Landscape Architects and Town Planners. There was an intimate connection between physical planning and policy that was about the larger idea of landscape or cityscape. Our professions have suffered from their separation. And landscape architecture has often become more about the application of other people's decisions—with landscape architects being more technicians than tacticians.

GS It would be a great day for Canada if the professions re-merged. That may never happen but at the very least we need to recognize how much we have in common and that, in most instances, we're playing for the same team. Separating landscape architecture and planning ideas and energy results in a lot of redundancy, unnecessary competition and incomplete work.

CP Offering both planning and landscape architecture at PFS allows us to be more strategic and to have more involvement earlier in the process. It allows us to steer rather than be driven by the process. Collaboration is fundamental to a lot of our work, so combining forces positions us to bridge the many disciplines that partake in the creative process. From community representatives to biologists, to artists, there is often an interesting range of expertise and interests that enter into a project.

GS Our office has earned the respect of governments, private sector clients and many of the best architects, engineers and artists in North America and internationally. And, although it's taken us a long time, for the past decade or so we've found ourselves in the role of prime consultant on projects more often than we are subconsultants to others. Having said that, we really enjoy collaborating on great teams, and when we do we usually find ourselves equals at the table. This means a lot. It's not only professionally satisfying but it always results in finer work.

Wall Centre. Vancouver, BC.

MF We've been fortunate during the economic boom that we've had enough work opportunities to be able to select who we work with. And we don't take projects where everything is already decided.

GS We really hope the success of our practice has had some influence on the way landscape architecture is perceived, particularly here in Canada. But I know for a lot of firms it is a tough slog.

KM Was it tough at the beginning for PFS as well?

GS Our practice has changed dramatically. We've worked hard to practice the way we want with people we respect on projects we enjoy. It wasn't always like that. In the beginning, despite best intentions, we often had to take on what would keep the doors open and I suppose this is typical for most young firms. Some clients were less than kind, many projects were quite ordinary and a lot of the people we worked for didn't carry a lot of respect for us or our professions. The early days were quite a dark time for me personally—I seriously considered leaving the profession. Moura Quayle was the one who convinced me to give it more time. I'm glad I did. Now we're careful to choose what's interesting and what's right. And if it's profitable, well, that's an added bonus.

MF I've seen a lot of change in the practice over the years and some is for the good and some isn't. There are a lot of professions out there that have begun 'poaching' the territory that should belong to planners and landscape architects. A lot of architects are now doing their own landscape design. In Vancouver's design lecture series a few years ago, every single architect spent most of their presentation discussing the landscape around their buildings—and many of them hadn't worked with landscape architects. Their landscapes were monotonous, unprogrammed open spaces. And polka dots were big! Perhaps if they had consulted with a landscape architect they would realize there is something more to landscape than a two-dimensional pattern.

Traditional landscape architecture is also being fragmented into separate specialized areas by so-called 'sustainability' experts, CPTED (Crime Prevention through Environmental Design) experts, and other such experts. And the notion that there's a discipline called 'urban design' that's separate from planning, architecture and landscape architecture that one can

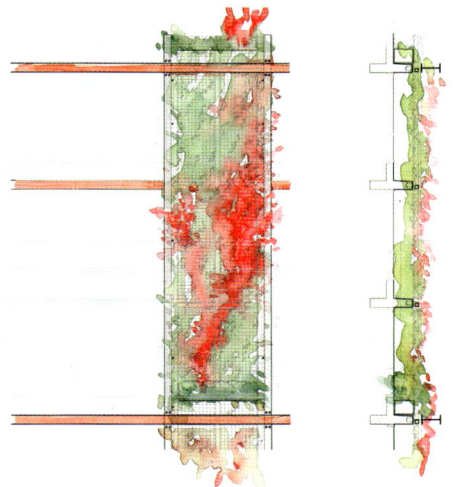

Woodward's Redevelopment. Vancouver, BC.

get a degree in—this is not helping. People think now that they can be urban designers without first qualifying in one of the three basic professions.

GS It sounds cliché, but as a profession we simply need to get our work in front of people. Too often landscape architects are dismissed for what might seem at first a crazy idea, only to have that idea come back to play a central role in framing a solution. It reminds me of Schopenhauer's thoughts on the 'trajectory of great ideas'. He defines three distinct stages: the first stage of a great idea is met by ridicule, the second stage with strong opposition and in the third stage the idea comes to be considered self-evident by everyone. So many times in the history of landscape architecture the profession has been faced with an initial rebuff of an idea that later turns out to be a smart, commonsense way to move forward. The most frustrating part is that quite often great ideas originate in landscape architecture only to be subsumed by others as their own.

KM What I appreciate about working with PFS is the broad research-based approach taken to each project. Many landscape firms take a limited approach to drawing a site's boundaries. They don't look at the greater relationships, how their site and context fit into larger urban and ecological networks or how it functions at a social or cultural level. Do you think PFS's planning perspective has something to do with this broader perspective?

CP Part of our definition of landscape is that every project is about a much bigger, interconnected context. As landscape architects we drive ideas—often the challenge is not the site but the context. Especially in the urban realm, design isn't about creating successful little bits and pieces; it's about working within an ecology of buildings, public realm, streets, natural process, community, history, etc. It's a systems approach. When we get random pieces of the landscape to work on, the challenge is to understand how these pieces fit into the larger community or landscape.

MF I think Vancouver's been a starting point for this idea. We've all gotten to know the city very well from many different points of view. Being involved on civic committees and having worked on so many projects, one can't help but see the larger patterns of how the city functions. You open up to more and more. And because we've gone into depth on specialized issues in different projects we innately bring that knowledge to the next projects that we do.

GS I do think that there is a fundamental difference between how landscape architects and planners might look at city-building versus how an architect might. So much architecture today doesn't seem to recognize broader urban systems, and the trend toward designing iconic one-offs that often don't fit into any contextual systems can be commonplace. Systems thinking is more intuitive to landscape architecture and we tend to draw in everything that concerns landscape: urban systems, environmental systems, events (temporal systems), etc. But having said all that, PFS is also well known for our interest in creating strong form in our projects, and delivering beautiful design in our built work. In the end, form is very important.

KM Let's talk about city-building. Over the years PFS has been quite influential in the City of Vancouver, affecting public art policy and the development of 'Vancouverism', and designing major public systems and public realm amenities within the city. Can you talk about this?

MF PFS worked on a number of projects that were key to the evolution of the 'Vancouverism' approach to dense development of residential and mixed-use projects downtown. 888 Beach Avenue was one of the first projects to ring a block with urban townhouses and to create a semi-private landscape for the enjoyment of residents on top of podium parking. Chris worked with architect James Cheng to develop the landscape concept for both streetscapes and courtyards.

Shortly afterward, Chris and I worked with City Planning and Engineering to prepare the Downtown South Streetscape Design Guidelines that essentially enshrined the townhouse

The Palisades. Vancouver, BC.

lined streetscape with narrow point towers as the form of redevelopment for this former light industrial area.

GS Our recent work has included the public realm for some of the more publicly recognizable, and at times controversial, projects in downtown Vancouver. For example, we worked with Henriquez Partners Architects on the Woodward's redevelopment in the Downtown Eastside as well as Shangri-La and a series of outstanding residential projects with James Cheng Architects. We recently also completed the Southeast False Creek Plaza with HBBH Architects in Vancouver's Olympic Village.

The Woodward's project is one of Vancouver's most ambitious mixed-use projects incorporating a strong mix of market and non-market housing, Simon Fraser University's new School for the Contemporary Arts, an anchor food and drugstore, retail, federal and civic offices, non-profit community space, a daycare, a public plaza and urban green space in the form of facade and roof top gardens.

With Shangri-La, as part of the negotiation for becoming one of the city's tallest buildings, there was an expectation that the project contribute to public life at the street level. Through innovative agreements with the Vancouver Art Gallery, a public outdoor gallery was conceived for temporary exhibits. A mid-block connection through and over retail below creates an integrated public realm between two of the city's major streets. And every roof space on this building is either an intensive or extensive green roof, including the sixtieth floor.

The Residences. Vancouver, BC.

We also worked continuously through a ten year phased build-out of Wall Centre, a project that saw three different architects, Freschi, Doyle and Busby, over the same period of time. It's located in the heart of the central business district with a major city hospital across the street. Half of the city block is designed as a major publicly accessible space surrounded by high-rises.

MF Early on Chris was active in implementing the City of Vancouver's public art process, and was the first chair of Vancouver's Public Art Committee. The City's public art process brought funding and support for artists to contribute to public space.

Our early design work was strongly influenced by the West Coast Modernism of the 1960s, especially the integration of indoors and outdoors. It also embraced Asian influences that were then reflective of the increasingly multicultural nature of our city. I would say that PFS has also contributed to Vancouver's West Coast Modern aesthetic in the public realm.

KM Has West Coast Modernism led to a recognizable PFS aesthetic?

GS If there is a recognizable aesthetic, I think it's most influenced by Chris. He has a very strong design sensibility, likes to work through each assignment very carefully, and in the end has developed a repertoire of beautiful, usable, meaningful landscapes. You can see it in PFS's early work such as The Residences or The Palisades in downtown Vancouver or more recently at Burnaby City Hall and North Vancouver Library. He also recently designed this amazing private garden for Waterfront Estate in West Vancouver that is truly 'west coast'.

CP I think there's a contemporary expression to many of PFS's projects that combines Modernist sensibilities with regional references to BC's dramatic natural landscape of sea, mountains, rain forest and desert. We're interested in abstraction and symbolism—not literal re-creations, but landscape as a metaphor.

For example, with the Richmond Olympic Oval we worked collaboratively with artist Janet Echelman to create a winding red boardwalk that runs through the reeds of a biofiltration garden that treats stormwater collected from the Oval's two hectare roof. The winding red boardwalk is homage to the large Asian community of Richmond. It's the winding lion dancer zigzagging through the streets at Chinese New Year. Working with artist Janet Echelman was great. She's a brilliant artist and was highly engaged in the design discussions, it was a very creative collaborative process. She developed an installation of a large illuminated net—a 'sky lantern' that responds to the wind and totally modifies the public space.

Back to the discussion of city-building, Marta and I were fortunate to start off working in Vancouver for an intense and visionary employer, Art Cowie. His working process was quite influential. We were right out of school and he'd just throw us into stuff. In over our heads!

As landscape architects we drive ideas. Often the challenge is not the site, but the context. Especially in the urban realm, design isn't about creating successful little bits and pieces—it's about working within an ecology of buildings, public realm, streets, natural process, community, history, etc. It's a systems approach. When we get random pieces of the landscape to work on, the challenge is to understand how these pieces fit into the larger community and landscape.

Waterfront Estate. West Vancouver, BC.

MF Art loved conceptualizing how the city should be, thinking up projects and writing about them. He did a lot of cold proposals which is something that doesn't happen much anymore. He would see something that needed doing and he'd write a proposal. There was no RFP—he'd go in and say, 'I've been thinking about your problem and this is how you should go about solving it and these people are going to do this for you.'

CP He was extraordinary. When BC Place was just starting to study their downtown land, he managed to convince BC Development Corporation to hire him to develop plans for the eighty hectare site. The thing about Art was that he loved to get these big jobs, and he liked to delegate. I was right out of school then and he assigned me to the project. I said 'What? Eighty hectares of brownfield in downtown Vancouver!' So I asked for some help. He had heard Doug Paterson speak in Winnipeg and the next thing I knew Doug arrived that summer to work with us. He was a real networker. Art, Doug and I spent almost a year working on these eighty hectares of dream land. And Doug was very impressive.

MF There is that wonderful ideas book with all of Doug's sketches.

GS Amazing document.

CP That book set some of the parameters that have driven Vancouver's development, and continue to drive them today. Working with Doug was fantastic. It turned my whole view of landscape architecture around. When I had to go for my licensure interview with the BC Society of Landscape Architects they asked me to present a project I'd been working on. So I arrived with these sheets showing eighty hectares of designed public realm in downtown Vancouver—streets, parks and plazas. Most of the people on the board were from horticulture school—they said, 'What are you *doing*!' They were completely baffled! They didn't know what to say and I realized these guys were on a different plane. It was a completely different world to them. It was the beginning of a big shift in Vancouver, and a whole new generation of landscape architects arrived at that time.

MF Art ran the only firm that did planning and landscape architecture in the city. He had both degrees. It put him in a position to do studies that other firms weren't able to do. He was a very ideas-driven person. He was very creative with his proposals. He would think,

Canoe Landing Park. Toronto, ON.

'Who do I know that knows useful things about this?' And he'd put a team together that was not at all requested by the RFP, bringing all kinds of different experts together—sociologists, archaeologists, etc.—just to get ideas going. This was before anyone else was doing this. PFS tries to maintain this tradition of including a diversity of expertise and creative thinkers on project teams.

CP We were fired by the Port of Vancouver on a study of their waterfront lands. They were looking at Main Street and how it was going to end at the port. When I looked at Main Street I thought it would be a great way to connect the waterfront with the east side. I did some quick analyses and sections and found a design solution. When I showed up at the meeting they presented a road design, a big cloverleaf! I said, 'You've just designed the off-ramp to a freeway! This is the worst thing you can do!' Of course the clients said, 'What did you say?! Are you with us or against us?' And I said, 'I can't support this, it's going to be a disaster. This is the one chance to unite the waterfront back to the city.' And they fired me. I went back to Art and told him we were fired. He said, 'Explain.' And then he said, 'You did the right thing.' That was Art, he supported us 100%.

MF The most impressive study I can remember working on with Art was a project he got when the government did the land swap with Marathon Realty and the provincial and the federal governments to assemble the site for Expo '86. Art did a study of what you could do with the parcels given in exchange, including where Wall Centre and the downtown library are now. It was my first experience with design charettes—he hired this wonderful group of people to sit around a table, share ideas, sketch concepts, explore and design.

KM It sounds like it was a visionary time in the City of Vancouver. How do you find working in Vancouver today—and how do you think this compares to other Canadian cities?

GS PFS has been a leader in urban design and landscape architecture in Vancouver for a long time now, but because it's such a small city, exceptional design and planning opportunities are infrequent and competitive. When great projects do come along we work hard to win them. Practicing in Vancouver has been a blessing and a challenge. It's a beautiful city with a considerable appetite for landscape architecture, but perhaps it's too beautiful for its own good—people seem rather complacent about design here.

CP Yes, in Vancouver, the presence of nature and wilderness is a driving force to who we are. We're surrounded by powerful views of mountains, sea, beaches, rocky shores and rain forest, thus our obsession with the outward view and with occupying the water's edge. There's an incredible amount of activity for miles along Vancouver's continuous public waterfront—people cycling, walking, playing, meeting. And our climate allows us to grow rich exotic landscapes. As landscape architects, creating innovative and edgy urban landscapes has always been a challenge in this context—everything is expected to be green, lush, beautiful and perhaps too naturalistic.

GS Vancouver is growing in terms of population and density and with that growth I think a greater commitment to public space needs to be made. You only need to look at the central parts of the city to see that it lacks a true civic heart. But I see Vancouver's preoccupation with its water's edge slowly transforming as the downtown becomes more populated. With more people in the core, an interest in creating better streets will grow and the need for great urban rooms will become more obvious.

Vancouverites seem relatively complacent about public space issues relative to, say, Toronto where a continuous public discussion on city-building has clearly fired people up and has caught the attention of the media there. Vancouver's media largely ignores urban space issues, which is tough because the only way firms like ours can push harder and deliver the best work is if the public understands what's at stake and speaks out on urban issues.

Burnaby City Hall. Burnaby, BC.

MF But on the other hand, Christopher Hume recently compared Toronto to Vancouver. One of his points was that Vancouver got making buildings as part of an urban block, but at the expense of getting great, starchitecture buildings. In Vancouver it's all about context, while Toronto has figured out how to make great foreground buildings, but not how to have a great supporting cast. It's about urban design. Vancouver has focused on the overall formation of the urban realm—through its urban design panel, through specific guidelines and through the kinds of people that have been leading its municipal departments.

KM Would you say that the City of Vancouver's focus on community process has affected the local practice of landscape architecture in any particular way?

MF I think the civic process has done a certain amount to legitimize landscape architecture. When I was on the urban design panel there was always a request that the landscape architect speak. If an architect showed up without their landscape architect, it was duly noted and commented on.

CP About ten or twelve years ago in Vancouver we had landscape architects chairing the Public Art Commission, the Planning Commission and the Vancouver Urban Design Panel—all three.

KM That's pretty significant.

CP Doug Paterson was on the Planning Commission, I chaired the Public Art Commission and Eriks Eglite chaired the Urban Design Panel. All three organizations, Planning, Public Art and Urban Design demand an ability to engage with the city on a broader level, and our profession is able to do this. It's all about city-building and placemaking.

GS In Toronto now there's an alliance between really good architects and landscape architects and an honest sense of mutual respect and responsibility. In some places I've worked there's mutual respect but not a mutual responsibility. In many cases the architecture community still trumps the landscape architecture community. But I think the really mature architects and landscape architects don't let that get in the way. In fact there seems to be a much closer relationship between the two now more than ever, particularly in Toronto. In

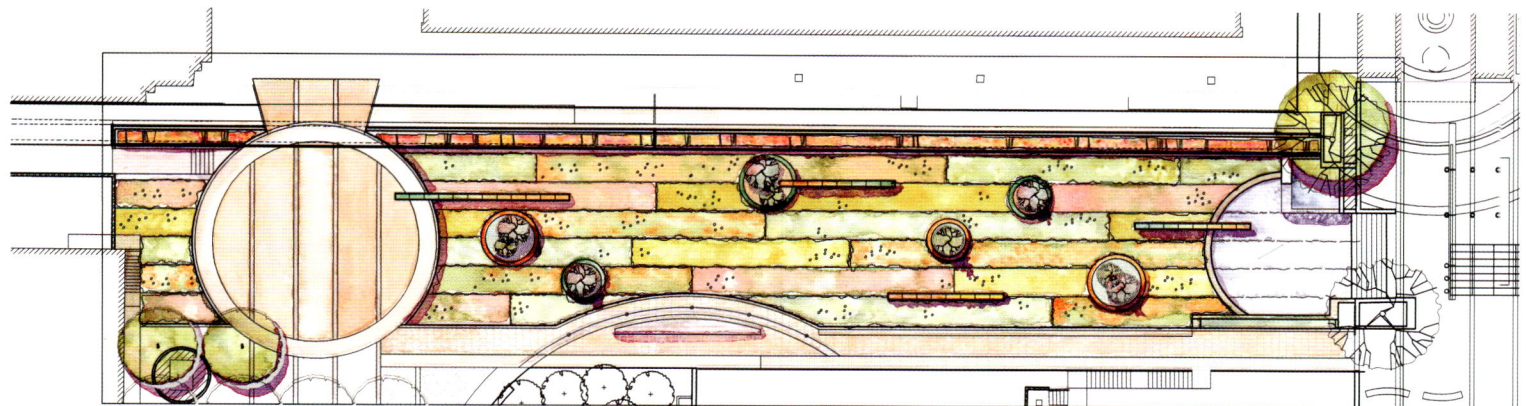

Garden of Transmutation, Davenport/Lash Miller Courtyard. University of Toronto, ON.

his discussions with Waterfront Toronto, Bruce Kuwabara coined the term 'Leading with Landscape'—and Toronto is currently doing just that. Communities are realizing that if they don't get landscape right, it doesn't matter what they do with the buildings because alone they will fail to create neighbourhood. So there have been some very thoughtful people in Toronto's architecture community like Siamak Hariri, Peter Clewes, George Baird, Don Schmitt and others who have helped to elevate this idea that in order to city-build, landscape architecture needs to frame the possibilities.

KM Can you talk about PFS's recent work in Toronto?

GS Toronto is a big focus for us now. We've been doing a lot of interesting work there collaborating with great architecture firms like Kuwabara Payne McKenna Blumberg Architects (KPMB) and Teeple Architects. We're also completing two major downtown parks, Canoe Landing and Sherbourne—both very exciting public realm designs that I think redefine a park's relationship with its surrounding community. We hope that these projects will help to bring attention to landscape architecture in Canadian and international circles. PFS is also central to two massive brown field urban developments initiated by Waterfront Toronto. In 2005 we established the public realm component of a plan led by Fred Koetter that became the DNA for the more refined plans of that area being developed by West 8 and du Toit Allsopp Hillier (DTAH). We're currently leading a design effort with The Planning Partnership (TPP) and Sweeny Sterling Finlayson & Co. Architects (&Co) to work through the details for the public realm of the West Don Lands, another Waterfront Toronto initiative that will ultimately see the development of a leading-edge, mixed-use neighbourhood structured by great streets and public spaces. Michael Van Valkenburgh Associates (MVVA) is designing a major park that will become the green heart of that community and the primary pedestrian connection to the Don River and new waterfront communities being created to the south along Lake Ontario, including the Lower Don Lands which we consulted on for MVVA.

We've been working in Ontario for almost twelve years—first in Ottawa where we were awarded a string of major government commissions, and then a few years later in Toronto where we started at the University of Toronto with what was then called the Garden of Transmutation at the Lash Miller/Davenport Chemistry Building. Unfortunately much of that design wasn't realized as the university was tugging considerably at our capital budget to contribute to repairs associated with deferred deficiencies in the below grade structure over which the garden was developed. I can say it looks good at night and seems to work well for the students. Maybe some of the lost design pieces will resurface in a future incarnation. You never know.

We have had a very long and mutually satisfying relationship with KPMB in Toronto. They're a terrific firm and we've worked together on many projects, first here in Vancouver on Richmond City Hall, then in Toronto on a variety of things including Vaughan City Hall,

Manitoba Hydro Headquarters Building. Winnipeg, MB.

5th and Madison. Seattle, WA.

Bridgepoint Health and the Balsille School of International Affairs in Waterloo. We also worked with KPMB on the Manitoba Hydro Building that won them the 'Best Tall Building in the Americas Award' for 2009. And we have a number of other things on the go in Toronto including the Shangri-La with James Cheng.

KM All of this work comes out of a generally strong civic understanding of how great design impacts cities on a global scale—and how the public realm is the progenitor of great place.

GS Last year I was invited to speak at Toronto's ROM (Royal Ontario Museum) along with James Corner, Michael Van Valkenburgh and Maarten Buijs from West 8. There was a public audience of 500 people, a lot of them designers themselves, and they were listening to ideas from our respective landscape architecture firms that are rethinking big parts of Toronto.

Toronto has a design community that is much more apparent than in Vancouver. And they *work* to make themselves apparent. Their design community seems so much more involved in the public life of the city.

MF Christopher Hume said that years ago his column was way in the back of the paper, and now he's on page one. When something design-related happens in Toronto they put it on the front page because people want to read about it. Their public is interested in it.

GS Years ago I was bemoaning the fact that there didn't seem to be any publicly oriented media focusing on public space from a landscape architectural perspective. In Vancouver, it's still lacking. They have a great dialogue in Toronto, in San Francisco and in New York. The New York Times has great writing about public space. In Vancouver journalists don't write about public space very much—and people don't seem to talk about it very much.

MF The conversation is a big part of the process of making great public space.

KM Yes, public space is definitely a practice—it's not something you can pin down. For me it's like writing. The more difficult the ideas that you try to articulate, the more fluent you will

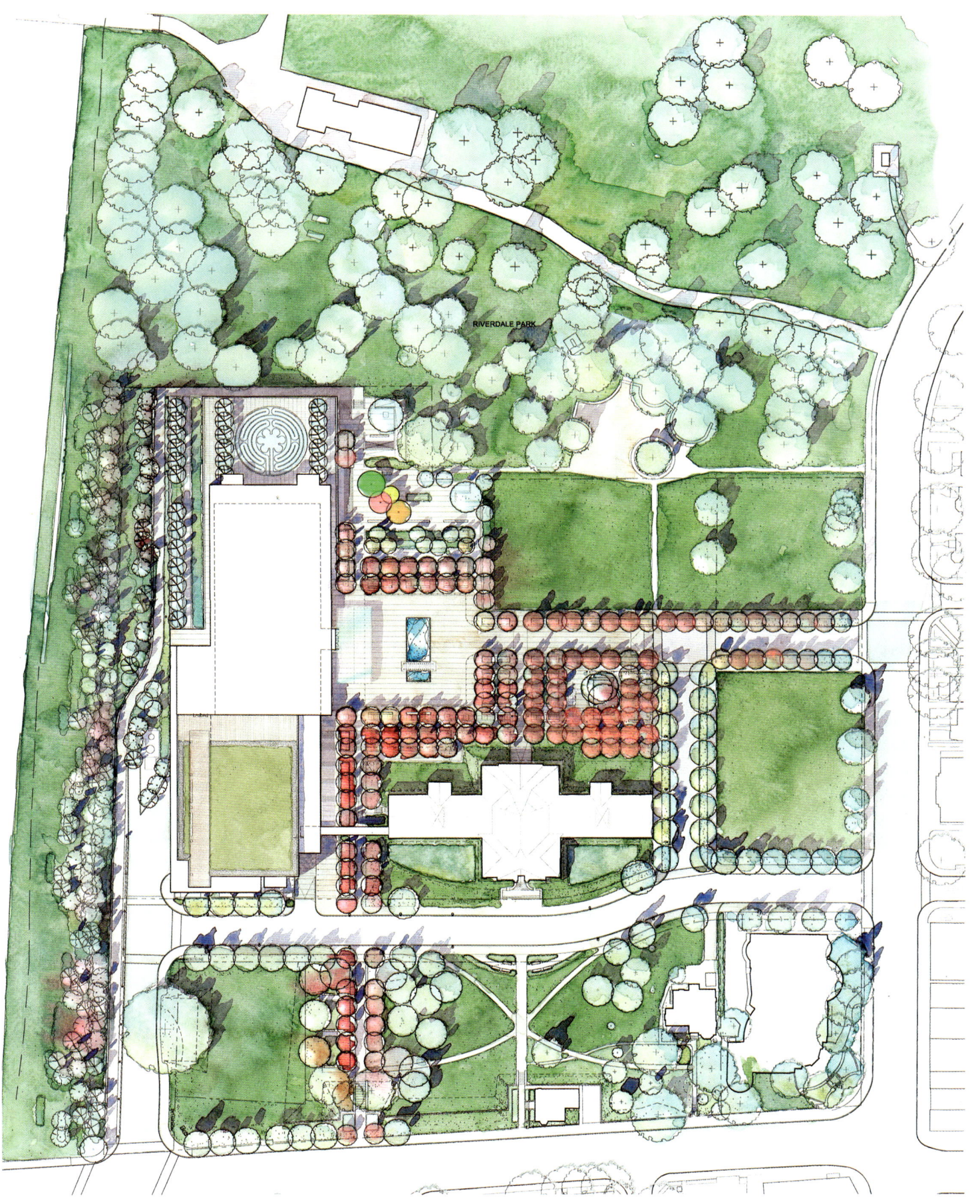

Bridgepoint Health Complex, Toronto, ON.

Interview 145

In Vancouver, the presence of nature and wilderness is a driving force to who we are. We're surrounded by powerful views of mountains, sea, beaches, rocky shores and rain forest, thus our obsession with the outward view and with occupying the water's edge. And our climate allows us to grow rich exotic landscapes. As landscape architects, creating innovative and edgy urban landscapes has always been a challenge in this context— everything is expected to be green, lush, beautiful and perhaps too naturalistic.

be through the practice of writing or the practice of having a dialogue. Public interaction—physical and communicative—is what public space is all about. Great physical design is just a part of it—it can help initiate these things but it can't *be* public on its own. The interaction and the discussion—this is what we need in Vancouver.

CP Well there are critics and there are creators. Sometimes critics make the mistake of trying to design. They might be great at observing how people use and understand space, they might have great imagery of public space—but it often falls apart when they try to design. Designing public space is a very difficult thing to do.

MF The beauty of design is that it can align so many complexities. And when a design begins to solve different issues at the same time, people recognize it and start to see the value of it. I've seen this happen over and over again with our work—we get it right with someplace and people say, 'How could it be otherwise?' Yet they don't necessarily know what went into the process.

CP Many people don't realize that public spaces are designed—they just assume they've always been there. Landscape is this nebulous kind of thing. People don't fully understand or appreciate it and that's always been the problem for our profession. Buildings are clear, bridges are clear, but landscape is so many things at once.

MF Granville Island is a perfect example. People think it's always been there just as it is now.

CP But so much of Granville Island is a result of major decision-making, programming and physical design—design is key. It's not just about organizing space—it's much more than that.

MF Public space is also layered. Every site can't be a major public destination. There need to be supportive spaces to great public places that bring people there and move them through. There needs to be deliberate and sustained programming.

CP It's a real challenge to grasp how public space works. There are 'ten essentials' that I often use to communicate to clients and the public how great public spaces work. These include things like a strong sense of enclosure; engaging, lively edges; a powerful inclusion of both civic and intimate scales; and great program.

It's a very hard thing to get right—it's intangible. It's not like a building with a defined program, and materials and structures that are given form—it's more abstract than that. Part of our challenge is how to communicate its importance, especially when working with the public.

KM Can you comment on the state of landscape architecture in Canada?

GS Landscape architecture in Canada is still struggling a lot. I'm not sure why because when you look at the work of Canadian landscape architects there are many examples of extraordinary work from coast to coast. So with all of these great minds and new ways of thinking and exciting opportunities, why isn't the profession in Canada flourishing? It's a real puzzle.

I think there are a lot of insecurities in the profession. The challenge for many is to get out from under architects and engineers. I prefer to look at these groups as allies—to learn to work with them or, better yet, show them how good it is to work with us.

MF For years I was involved in organizing Vancouver's design lecture series, and we always have at least one international landscape architect speak. I have had so many architects come and tell me that their favourite lectures throughout the series have been the landscape architects. They've said to me, 'This opened my mind in a way that really made me think.' And yet what Greg says is true—that engagement isn't happening with Canadian landscape architects.

GS One of the most curious backhanded compliments I've ever received was, 'You guys think like architects.' I think our design process integrates really well with the way architects often work. There are architects we work with that we respect, they respect us, there is an integration of thought process that everybody seems to be comfortable with. But it took a long time to find that. It used to be 70%, but now only 30% of our work is actually with architects.

MF That's why we put 'urban design' into our firm description—it's multidisciplinary. It combines architecture, landscape architecture, planning, ecology and economics.

KM Let's get personal. What or who inspired you to get into the profession?

CP I was fortunate to grow up in an environment where a sense of beauty, art and aesthetics was important. My parents appreciated beautiful places, both natural and cultural, and shared them with us. Today I relish visiting those same special places and I continue to be inspired with every visit. For example, when I was a child, my family would visit this wonderful New England amphitheatre by the sea that I recently discovered was designed by Fletcher Steele, one of the great American landscape architects.

Professionally I've had the good fortune to work with many thoughtful designers, community representatives, developers and thinkers, and each of them has influenced me in different ways. A key mentor has been landscape architect and academic Doug Paterson. Doug has shared his understanding of landscape in its fullest sense and has given me great insight into city-building, placemaking and experiential landscapes. He really taught me to appreciate the broader scale of landscape—that a site is part of a much larger context. And as a professional, one has a responsibility to understand the scale of what landscape architecture can affect.

MF What caused you to want to become a landscape architect?

GS It's because he hated engineering.

CP I was in engineering for three years. In my third year, the dean called me into his office. The dean! When I got there he closed the door and said, 'We've got a problem. It's been pointed out to me that you've taken three fine arts courses in the last two years—how the hell did you manage to do that? Engineers don't take fine arts.' That was the state of engineering back then! Art had no value whatsoever. I quit that year. That interaction with the dean reminded me that my original intention was to go into architecture. That summer I met a landscape architect from the Université de Montréal who gave me McHarg's *Design with Nature*. I'd never heard of landscape architecture, and that book initiated my foray into the discipline. As soon as I finished it, I applied to study landscape architecture and ended up at the University of Guelph. After graduating I headed to the west coast to check it out. And I've been here ever since—I fell in love with Vancouver and the profession.

GS I've been very lucky to find a discipline that I continue to be absolutely passionate about. Passion for creating great public space that is not only beautiful but meaningful has been the primary influence on my view of landscape architecture and of the world in general. It's the modern or the contemporary that really interests me, which is funny because we've worked on so many historic projects. But there is always a contemporary layer that we add to each project, otherwise we'd all get bored and go home.

A number of practitioners have inspired me over the years but my main historic influences are Fletcher Steele and Tommy Church. Fletcher Steele created Modernist landscapes almost on the heels of the Beaux Arts movement. When you think about it, that seems an impossible move! All of a sudden there was this guy out there with embedded steel and forced perspective and clean lines. His mid-career work after his Art Deco phase is the strongest. He

Glenlyon Business Park. Burnaby, BC.

consistently overstretched his peers and developed exciting possibilities for landscape. I love Naumkeag. And Tommy Church had a way of integrating competing geometries of built form and site into beautiful Modernist compositions that were so fluid and elegant.

Two contemporary landscape architects that I respect a great deal are Alain Provost and Michael Van Valkenburgh. Alain Provost understands form, scale and composition so well—I'm thinking particularly of the Thames Barrier Park, Parc Andre Citröen and the Jardin Diderot at La Defense. And Michael Van Valkenburgh has this remarkable ability to read places. He has a studied approach to all of his work which results in poetic space and memorable places. His experimentation with urban landscapes is provocative and pushes the profession forward.

Two outstanding thinkers were teaching at UBC (University of British Columbia) when I was there—Doug Paterson and Moura Quayle. I learned a lot from them. I've also been fortunate to have met and worked with some of the brightest and most interesting people I could imagine.

MF So Greg, when did you have your 'I-should-be-a-landscape-architect' moment?

GS I was living on Vancouver Island at the time. One weekend my wife Susan and I came upon a UBC open house promoting a number of programs including landscape architecture.

Interview   149

Safeco Roof Garden. Seattle, WA.

Susan knew I was always interested in design and landscape and immediately said, 'You should look at this.' I applied within a couple of months and was accepted into the program the following year. I think my interest in landscape came to me at a very early age. I spent a lot of time with my grandmother in her garden and I really connected with it—gardening forms some of my strongest childhood memories actually.

CP I have strong childhood connections that way myself. To gardening, to the outdoors—to urban and wild landscapes.

GS William Lyon Mackenzie King once said 'You can tell the character of a man by the quality of his garden.' And Doug Paterson used to say that many of his students were embarrassed by the term 'gardener' or 'garden design' or anything with 'garden' in it. He always tried to make the point that the garden is one of the noblest things that we can create, so why should someone be embarrassed by that? I have some very fond memories of watching things grow, getting dirt under my fingernails and being amazed by the whole experience. I spend a great deal of time in my own garden today. Of course the profession and our careers have turned out to be something much different than this, but gardening has definitely played a role in my interest in landscape.

KM Gardening connects us to landscape processes of so many kinds.

CP As a kid I worked for this amazing house of elderly ladies—five sisters, all spinsters, and some of the first women to graduate from McGill University. They had an immense house and garden—an unbelievable garden. I gardened for them a few times a week—during the winter I shoveled their garden and paths to their bird feeders and compost system (at a time when having a composting system was very unusual). They had a lot of unusual plants and were keen birdwatchers—they often took me birding.

   I also remember manipulating this stream that ran through my parents' garden, making different gardens along its length—digging it up and planting irises. It's these childhood connections—these formative things in my life that were probably very powerful. I would constantly fabricate these environments—I had an ever-changing city in my bedroom made of boxes and boxes of building blocks that I would turn into streets, buildings and bridges. And in the summer I lived for the sandbox. My brother and I would build towns, roads and mountains.

KM It's fascinating how these early experiences of manipulating space and working with the land really affect our later relationships to the world.

MF I think that's one of the most amazing things—how different interests and experiences intersect and come together to influence people's later careers.

CP The connections can be quite subliminal.

MF It's part of practicing what you do, even before you recognize the pattern.

CP There's the creative process of constantly moving, changing and making.

KM The confidence to build—to manipulate space.

MF And the interest to keep changing it.

KM Marta, what's your story? How did you come into planning—who or what influenced you?

MF My undergraduate degree was in psychology. I didn't know about careers in planning and landscape architecture then. I moved to Vancouver to join my boyfriend, now husband. After several jobs, my father-in-law, a planner, hired me to research and help write an environmental impact study. I was taken by the subject and began reading a lot about it. *Design with Nature* by Ian McHarg, and other books, started me thinking about landscape. I took some night school classes in landscape design at BCIT (British Columbia Institute of Technology).

When the report with my father-in-law was finished, I set out to get a job in a planning or landscape firm, with no qualifications but definite interest. I was hired at IBI Group in a low level position to do presentation graphics and put reports and proposals together. The two people who hired me, planner Doug Spaeth and architect Ron Yuen, became mentors and encouraged me to go back to school for a professional degree. I wanted to stay in Vancouver and UBC was just starting its landscape architecture program. So I enrolled in planning and took the four landscape courses offered by Dr. John Neill with the intention of bridging the two professions in my career. A few years later, I applied to work at Art Cowie's firm, Eikos, because it was the only firm in Vancouver at the time that did landscape architecture and planning. Chris and I were hired within a couple of weeks of each other.

CP I'd been traveling for months, living out of my car in a tent. I'd written a letter to Art for a job. I was totally broke, I'd run out of money. I couldn't even buy gas for my car. So I knocked on his door and said, 'I'm here, I sent a letter to you, you probably don't remember me.' He said, 'Where the hell have you been? I've been waiting for you for two months!' I didn't realize it. Don Wuori put a good word in for me so I started the next morning.

GS My early landscape experience was with Don Vaughan. He was kind enough to take me under his wing at his office that he ran with Jane Durante. Like Art, Don was involved in some of the better work in the city, so I was exposed to that. First to draft Don's ideas, and eventually I was allowed to do some more interesting stuff. One of the more important things I learned from him was taught to me inadvertently and then explained to me later. He had this remarkable ability of presenting ideas in ways that had almost everyone on board by the time he was finished. He used honesty and good humour, and if he saw the presentation unravelling, he somehow managed to redirect the conversation, get through the rough parts and then bring it back on course. Don was master at gaining consensus.

MF Consensus-building is very complicated. It's interesting as we look at young people in the firm and think, would they be suitable partners? There are many different things one needs to be able to do.

KM I know that you, Chris and Marta, met at work. How did you meet Greg?

Wyndansea. Ucluelet, BC.

CP I first met Greg in Quebec City.

GS That's right, I got frostbite.

CP There was a Canadian Society of Landscape Architects conference in Quebec City. Doug Paterson was planning to go and share a room with Greg, but at the last minute Doug got sick. So he said to me, 'Take my hotel room—it's paid for but you have to share with this guy Greg. You guys will have fun—but I'll warn you, he talks a lot.' He told me how he first met Greg—driving to Vancouver Island, and he said they drove for four hours and Greg never stopped talking, he had so many questions. Doug was exhausted by the end of it. Greg had a million questions, his brain was running at a hundred miles an hour and Doug could hardly keep up with him. And I thought, well that's interesting—someone who can keep up with Doug! So I went and roomed with this guy I'd never met before. Greg was hilarious, and really interesting. We had a lot of fun.

GS We had a good time!

CP I really wanted to share Quebec. I was very passionate about it, having grown up in Montreal. And Greg was like me; he liked to absorb the city, and really get into things. So we had a really interesting time—I had to show him everything.

GS It was forty below zero.

CP We walked for miles. Ah, we had fun. So we kept in touch after that.

GS A couple years later Chris had his firm going here in Vancouver. Marta was an associate there with Chris. Chris had taken Eikos over when the economy fell out and I was working in Calgary. Doug Paterson thought we should do something together. So Chris and I chatted, we sent a couple letters back and forth, and then we had lunch. Soon after, I decided to move from Calgary to Vancouver to join Chris. Marta joined the partnership at the same time. That was in 1991.

GS Nineteen years! Wow! The three of us have a strong, equitable and agreeable partnership. We really like and trust one another and have worked all these years together without any major disagreements. That amazes me at times because we're all very strong willed. Chris and I work independently of each other because, for the most part, our design interests and skill sets are similar. As a planner, Marta bridges our work and our partnership quite effectively. She's a stabilizing force in the firm, leading our planning assignments in addition to working closely with Chris or myself on our more complex projects.

KM PFS had two branch offices—one in Ottawa and one in Shanghai. Within the office there's great ambition to do work intensely committed to both local and global landscapes. How did this come about?

GS Without too much strategic thinking about it I began to look outside of Vancouver in the mid-1990s, sensing that Vancouver was a pretty small pond and in order to have enough opportunity for all of us to pursue the projects that interested us, we needed to fan out. I started by pursuing work in Ontario which has turned out to account for a considerable percentage of our work. We established a small office in Ottawa while working on Confederation Square and Parliament Hill. When things cooled a bit in Ottawa and before they began to heat up in Toronto, I set my sights on Asia. We were there long before the gold rush of foreign consulting began. At that time there were a number of North American and European firms doing good work, but eventually mediocre firms, probably with little work in their own home markets, began peddling really bad ideas to Chinese clients, essentially selling some version of 'the western style'—whatever that means.

We set up an office in Shanghai with Ramsay Worden, an allied architecture firm here in Vancouver, and ran that for a few years before finding that we simply couldn't service it properly. While we were there we worked on some very interesting projects and continue to do so today but with more of a 'parachute-in' approach, collaborating with local Chinese design offices. I think it's gotten a bit easier now, but working in China is a very complex undertaking for a small office like ours. The rewards are great but the demands are greater. We will continue to work there on a selective basis because we enjoy it and because we've established a good reputation and have made so many contacts and friends there.

We just try to be as responsive as possible to the communities we work in. So whether it's Manila, Shanghai, Ottawa or Scottsdale, we're committed to the idea that local history, social patterns, ecology and demographics add up to placemaking. As designers, we see ourselves as placemakers—honest to the places we're working in. It's interesting that we're sometimes criticized in China for not being 'western' enough in our approach to projects there. We're constantly challenging clients with what we want to do that makes the best sense for the people we're designing for.

KM What do the next twenty years look like for PFS, and for landscape architecture and planning in general?

CP Green is the future. Landscape architects are critical to meeting the challenge of creating cities that are sustainable in the broadest sense—high-density, compact and desirable places to live, work and play; places where we can walk or cycle instead of drive; places that plan for their green networks first and foremost; where stormwater systems, the growing of food, and the provision of wildlife habitat are creatively and effectively integrated. Landscape architects are poised to contribute innovative strategies in the creation of these kinds of healthy, livable, ecologically diverse cities that are socially and culturally rich. Hopefully everything PFS engages in contributes to this vision in a meaningful way.

GS In large part landscape architects have been trying to make this planet a lot greener, a lot healthier and a lot happier for decades. Look at McHarg's work. He nailed down a lot of the problems facing us in the 1960s, but he didn't get the kind of traction he deserved. So here we are a half century later, and it's taken some sort of a green rating system (LEED®) to have politicians, developers and designers stand up and take notice. For us, we'll just keep doing what we've always done and in a small way that's good news for the environment. A million acts of green, right?

We've been involved in some very diverse projects where environment and sustainability are the primary shapers of the design. Glenlyon, here in the Lower Mainland for example, fuses protected natural lands and new ecologically functioning naturalized landscapes with some very contemporary architecture to create one of the most sought after business park environments in Western Canada.

Our work in the Pacific Northwest is expected to deliver a green solution wherever possible. Recent projects in Seattle include the Washington Mutual Roof Garden, Safeco Roof Garden and the re-imagined 5th and Madison mixed-use project adjacent to Koolhaas's Seattle Public Library. They're all about creating green in the heart of the city where little existed previously. We also recently developed the concept plan for Wyndansea, a proposed LEED® gold resort in Ucluelet on the Pacific Rim of Vancouver Island.

MF Planners and landscape architects grapple with complex issues and are experienced in evolving nuanced and layered solutions to physical, ecological and spatial change. Politicians and the public are becoming increasingly aware of the need for energy conservation, stormwater management, water conservation, green roofs and other aspects of sustainability, and they are now seen as priorities. These issues should be factored into planning and design processes along with the more traditional objectives of creating livable communities, enhancing walkability and revealing a strong sense of place. In communicating with people who seek sustainability in civic projects, it's challenging to avoid trendy and less than optimum solutions while also trying to communicate the complexity of decision making. Trying to communicate the qualities and benefits of proposals in ways that can be understood and appreciated by non-professionals—politicians, municipal staff and the general public—this is the ever-present challenge.

GS I really think we're at a crossroads for landscape architecture in general. If we want the profession to flourish we need to assert ourselves and our ideas for building healthier, greener, more beautiful cities and communities. The coming decades could belong to landscape architecture as people become weary of the way cities are rolling out or, in some cases, imploding. Urban design discussions these days seem to revolve around streets, parks, civic spaces and the environment. How we close in on all of this will decide the medium and long-term future of PFS and the profession.

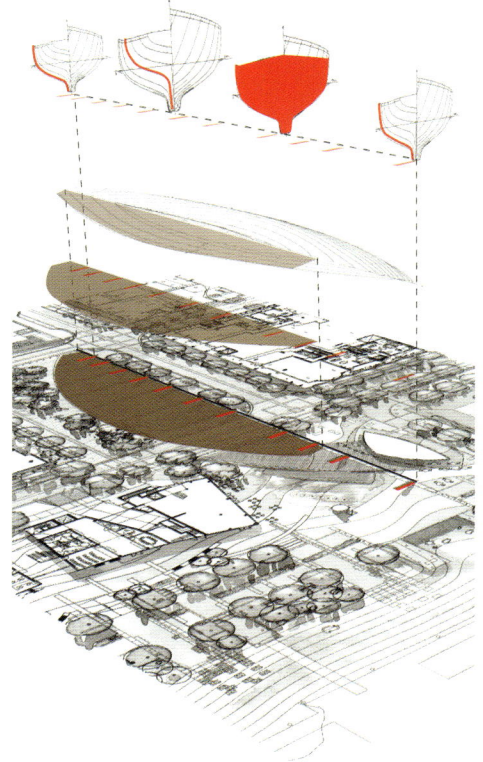

LEFT AND RIGHT Southeast False Creek Plaza. Vancouver, BC.

If architects were the primary form-givers in the 20th century, landscape architects will be the primary placemakers in the 21st century. We are beginning to understand, once again, that buildings are simply components of their urban, rural or wilderness settings; that landscape is the primordial base of a sense of place and identity. This is a return to a pre-Modernist understanding of landscape, the acceptance of the dynamic quality of landscapes as part of their enduring and sustainable quality—a significant shift from the Modernist attitude that buildings are the markers of place and identity.

Cultural Landscapes
Architecture and landscape in the 21ˢᵗ century

by Julian Smith

The 20th century will be looked back upon as a time when people were obsessed by objects. The physical sciences in the 19th century had made great strides by focusing on objects: observing them, cataloguing them, sorting them into hierarchies. And society gradually followed suit, several generations later, as scientific theory gradually emerged in the form of cultural assumptions. Twentieth century western culture will be remembered for collecting and displaying objects, and developing what one could call an objective approach to understanding the world.

The shorthand term for this 20th century attitude was Modernism: a conscious effort to break free from the emotional baggage of inherited wisdom and traditional tribalism, and to search instead for a more rational and universal understanding of the human condition. The First World War was the great instigator of Modernism, and the Second World War only solidified its hold. Two classic Modernist institutions are the museum and the university. The former is a literal translation of the idea of collecting, sorting and interpreting objects. The university is a more abstract translation of ordering information and putting it into objective form. The idea of 'publish or perish' as the compelling mantra for the professor in academe reflects this underlying assumption. To publish is to create an object, a collection of truths in tangible form that can then be put into the university library, the true museum of the information age.

Design professions in the 20th century followed this pattern. The planners and architects of the early 20th century made buildings the primordial objects of the new world order. Buildings became sculptures set into the landscape, reflecting the rationale that had been used to develop the sculpture gardens of museums. Buildings became the focus of urban design, dominating the coding of planning maps and the development of design assumptions for zoning bylaws. Architectural journals photographed buildings as objects, and theorists and critics evaluated buildings as entities unto themselves.

As an example, the profession of urban planning blossomed in the early 20th century and came into its own in the western world by mid-century. It used blue, red and yellow as the primary colours for planning maps, both existing and proposed. These colours were not arbitrary; they were the colours used by designers and builders for centuries to represent respectively stone, brick and wood. In planning maps, blue (stone) represented institutional use, red (brick) represented commercial and yellow (wood) represented residential. The objects that made up the city became the coding used to control its analysis and its development.

In this context, the architect was the key design professional shaping the urban and rural landscape. The building as object became the identifier of change, of progress, of the 'Modern' city. And in a seeming justification of Philip Johnson's and Henry-Russell Hitchcock's use of the use of the term 'International Style' in their famous Museum of Modern Art display of architectural Modernism in the 1930s, this role of architects' buildings as object-signifiers spread from Europe and North America to every country on the globe. It is interesting to note how often museums, university buildings and other institutional buildings where knowledge is objectified and codified have been the focus of Modernist architecture in the 20th century.

The rise of the photograph as a means of communicating information and knowledge coincided with the rise of Modernism. There was not a more powerful tool for objectifying the landscape and for separating the observer and the observed. In the 20th century the photograph became the most important tool for teaching architecture; for transmitting the knowledge of architectural historians, theorists and critics to new generations of students; and for shaping the understanding of the world around us in both the professional and popular media.

Times are changing. The 21ˢᵗ century is already seeing the signs of a paradigm shift in understanding the environment we inhabit, and theorizing about the design process within that environment. The obsession with objects is giving way to an obsession with ritual, the focus on observation is giving way to a focus on experience, and the concern with buildings is giving way to a concern with landscape. The new paradigm stems from an interest in, even an obsession with, ecology. Ecology is not about objects—it is about the relationships between objects. It is dynamic rather than static.

This is not a stylistic change; this is a more fundamental change in how the environment is understood. It is not about classifying objects, but about describing their interrelationship. It is about

PAGE 156 The Plaza Bridge and grand stair linking Confederation Square to the Rideau Canal below. Ottawa, ON. THIS PAGE A portal to Confederation Square and the reconstructed regional pathway below the city streets.

more recent advances in scientific theory, including relativity and uncertainty, and the impact of the observer on that which is observed being integrated into cultural patterns and assumptions. It is also increasingly a view of our actions within the context of sustainability, which fits much more easily into the dynamic context of ecology than into the static context of objective observation and classification.

This shift can be understood in the expanding use of the term 'cultural landscape'. This term refers to something that is not observable; it is a landscape as understood from within a cultural perspective. It is a landscape mapped by ritual. It is a cultural idea embedded in a place. It has to be experienced to be understood.

UNESCO established the World Heritage Convention in the 1970s to enable the greatest design achievements in the world to be recognized and protected. The object approach was fundamental to the establishment of this organization. Cultural and natural sites were considered according to independent and objective criteria, and each had to be delineated by hard boundaries to be considered for inclusion. Although natural sites were analyzed in terms of ecological systems, these had to be relatively self-contained, and human activity was considered extraneous. Gradually the idea of cultural landscapes was introduced, for both cultural and natural sites, to deal with complex sites where human and natural ecologies were inseparable, and where 20th century classifications and distinctions did not seem to work.

First Nations communities in Canada have had a significant role in defining a new paradigm for this overlap between cultural and natural realities. The Eurocentric insistence on separating nature and culture had never been accepted. Nor was the dominance of object over ritual. For most First Nations, the museum has always been a troubling institution because it took objects, including sacred objects, out of the context of ritual that gave them their meaning. The Eurocentric community is gradually learning to appreciate this cultural insight and intellectual framework as a new worldview.

Even the idea of cultural landscape, when first developed by UNESCO, was classified and sorted into three types: designed, evolved and associative. Designed landscapes were those from any period of human history that most easily fit the Modernist paradigm as isolated, static representatives of great individual design intent. Evolved landscapes were those that represented a collection over time of individually designed objects, and that contained the possibility of change. And associative landscapes were the most dynamic of all, assumed at the outset to be applicable primarily to aboriginal cultures where natural and cultural realities were intertwined.

As we enter the 21st century, we are beginning to understand that 'associative cultural landscape' may be the term that most closely captures the essence of any cultural landscape. It signifies a landscape understandable only through cultural association, which is neither solely cultural nor natural, which is not self conscious the way designed landscapes are, nor purely collections of objects the way evolved cultural landscapes are.

Julian Smith Cultural Landscapes 159

If architects were the primary form-givers in the 20th century, landscape architects will be the primary placemakers in the 21st century. We are beginning to understand, once again, that buildings are simply components of their urban, rural or wilderness settings; that landscape is the primordial base of a sense of place and identity. This is a return to a pre-Modernist understanding of landscape, the acceptance of the dynamic quality of landscapes as part of their enduring and sustainable quality—a significant shift from the Modernist attitude that buildings are the markers of place and identity.

In planning terms, this means a rethinking of the entire basis of zoning as a planning tool, and more generally of utopian visions as the framework for official plans and zoning bylaws. When healthy urban or rural landscapes are understood and evaluated from an ecological and dynamic basis rather than a static and objective basis, then planning tools become mechanisms for managing change rather than specifying utopian ideals. In a truly ecological approach to design within the environment, there is no predictable end result. Rather, each change is simply a step towards improving the ecology of the whole. Continuity and change are both essential.

A number of projects undertaken in recent years involving our architectural firm Julian Smith & Associates Architects and landscape architects and planners Phillips Farevaag Smallenberg (PFS) have forced us to grapple with the paradigm shift that surrounds us. They provide some useful commentary on emerging trends in design.

Our firm has a strong background in architectural conservation focusing on questions of continuity applied to individual buildings, complexes, heritage districts and rural landscapes. PFS has a strong background in contemporary design that focuses on change and adding powerful new layers to existing sites and districts. Our collaboration has brought the opportunity to explore this relationship between continuity and change, the central question of any preoccupation with sustainability and an ecological perspective on environmental issues.

Both heritage and contemporary design are emerging simultaneously from their 20th century preoccupations. Both were focused on objects, and each became isolated in its own world. In the field of heritage, as much as in that of contemporary design, the key references in both theory and practice were individual buildings and sites. Everything was classified, observed, evaluated and protected. The idea was to create a static record of past achievement, and the field of heritage is well known for its resistance to contemporary design interventions. In fact, much popular support for heritage conservation has come from people opposed in principle to the tenets and practices of Modernism.

At the same time, contemporary design firms were equally obsessed with the self conscious expression of individual design instincts. Rupture rather than continuity was often used to emphasize value and identity, and to draw clear boundaries around creative achievement.

The projects where our firms collaborated tended to be on cultural sites of national and international significance. They were not museums, they were working environments. There was therefore a simultaneous need to achieve static continuity and dynamic change. It was this challenge that created the framework for debate, for design, and for implementation, collaborating with partners from across the heritage/contemporary divide. This divide was a major characteristic of many communities in the late 20th century, and continues to be a concern in many places today.

The following comments describe casual incidents from four shared projects to illustrate these larger issues: Confederation Square and Rideau Hall Landscape Design and Management Plan in Ottawa; Villa Grazioli, the Canadian Embassy in Rome; and Central Experimental Farm Management Plan, also in Ottawa.

Villa Grazioli

Central Experimental Farm

Confederation Square

Rideau Hall

The 'Grand Escalier' connecting two previously segregated topographic layers.

Confederation Square
Ottawa, ON

Our first encounter with PFS was in a collaboration to restructure an area known as Confederation Square. This was an urban design project at the heart of Ottawa's central urban node, the historical bridge connection between Uppertown and Lowertown that is still the nexus of the central city.

Because our firm specializes in work involving the conservation of significant cultural properties, historians and conservators are essential members of our team. We were met with some suspicion by the design team from PFS, Greg Smallenberg and Chris Mramor, because those involved in heritage conservation have a well deserved reputation for being suspicious of contemporary interventions of any kind. We have found many contemporary designers to be deliberately or naively insensitive to cultural identity and heritage character. They seem resistant to accepting the richness of previous cultural layers, and the advantages that a historical reading can bring to thinking about a project.

Sure enough, initial PFS sketches for the redesign of the Plaza Bridge complex seemed at odds with our proposal to consider the evolution of the site as a starting point for its contemporary reformulation. But at a subsequent meeting Greg and Chris drew a sweeping curve between the two halves of the bridge and suggested creating a large opening down to the canal below. The intent was to break up the large plaza with an intervention that would not only recall the 19th century reality of the site, with its paired bridges at different angles, but also solve a long-standing urban problem of connecting the upper and lower layers of the city at the Rideau Canal crossing.

It is this kind of design insight that creates a fresh contemporary layer while uncovering historical truths that I call a cultural landscape approach to design. If cultural landscapes are about cultural identity, they require dynamic forms of continuity because cultural identity is constantly changing. Surprisingly, it is often the most important historical and cultural sites that need the strongest and most creative contemporary design sensitivity. But strength and creativity are dangerous unless coupled with an ability to read the cultural and historical realities of a place. Such readings cannot be done purely through 20th century modes of observation. They must be done with the involvement of cultural historians and anthropologists and others who emphasize a process of experiencing a place rather than just observing it.

The Confederation Square project, and the Plaza Bridge intervention in particular, involved many design decisions that created new urban design elements within a rich existing historic fabric. The experience of working together made it clear that our firms could collectively address part of the void that had developed between the heritage community, with its paranoia about contemporary design, and the contemporary design community, with its paranoia about designated places.

The international charters that address the conservation of important historic sites use the French term *mise en valeur*, which unfortunately has no English counterpart. *Mise en valeur* suggests a process that is dynamic, not static, and addresses not only protection but enhancement. Protection is well understood by those in the heritage conservation field, but enhancement much less so. Yet appropriate enhancement is key to the making of significant cultural places that are continuing sources of cultural pride and identity.

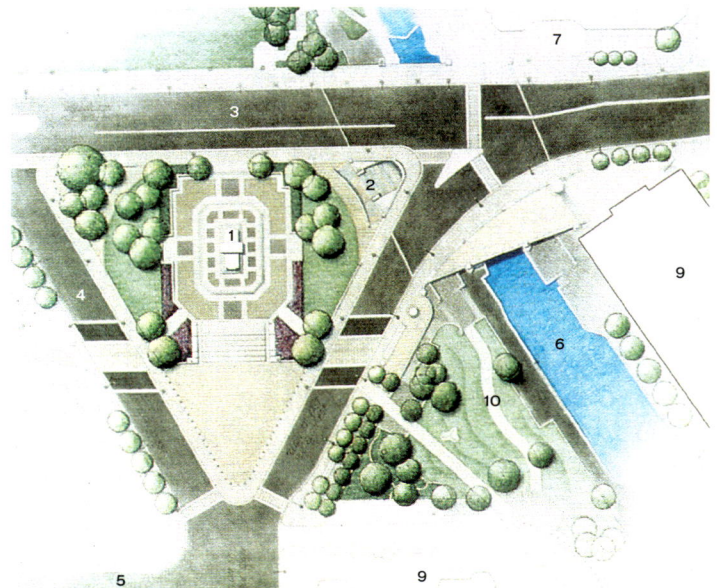

1 National War Memorial
2 Steps to Rideau Canal
3 Wellington Street
4 Elgin Street
5 Sparks Street
6 Rideau Canal
7 Chateau Laurier
8 Conference Centre
9 National Arts Centre
10 Regional Pathway

OPPOSITE PAGE TOP Looking up through the opening created in the Plaza Bridge reconstruction. This design move provided a much needed visual and physical connection between the Rideau Canal and Confederation Square above while referencing the historic configuration of two earlier bridges, the Dufferin Bridge and the Sappers' and Miners' Bridge. BOTTOM Rendered site plan of Confederation Square. THIS PAGE TOP A view toward Confederation Square from the east bank of the Rideau Canal. BOTTOM The lighting of Confederation Square was a critical component of the work. PFS collaborated with Martin Conboy Lighting Design Inc. (MCLD) to achieve dramatic results. PAGES 166–167 The Square is a grand celebration space for Canadians every Canada Day, July 1st.

Julian Smith   Cultural Landscapes

Rideau Hall Landscape Design and Management Plan
Ottawa, ON

The Rideau Hall project continued our joint involvement in places with high cultural significance but uncertain design futures. Rideau Hall began as a private residence and, in the mid-19th century, was designated the official residence of the governor general of Canada. The project involved the preparation of a landscape master plan for the 29 hectare site.

As with Confederation Square, there was a discernible tension between heritage and contemporary design advocates from the start. This site was fresh from controversy over a recent memorial rose garden, and there was an inevitable sense of 'either/or'.

Julian Smith & Associates Architects and PFS needed a cultural landscape approach to overcome these suspicions. The key factor at this site was the difference between initial observation and subsequent experience. It is in how a place is experienced that continuity and change can intersect in fruitful ways.

The focus on observation had led the National Capital Commission to propose a large new visitor centre at the entrance to the site, with large windowed public areas providing dramatic views of the Rideau Hall grounds and entrance drive winding up to the house in the distance. The house was seen as an object in the landscape, and the visitor centre was meant to frame this view. The problem was that the visitor centre would solidify the idea of the residence as an object to be observed, rather than allowing it to be an experiential environment. As the historians pointed out in our discussions with them, the primary intent of the original landscape design was to draw one in to the centre of the site and to organize the landscape from that point outwards. It would not be possible to understand the subtleties of the design from the outside. One had to enter the site and experience it from the inside.

The pivotal moment in the design process occurred when Greg Smallenberg asked if we could enter all of the rooms inside the house to view the landscape from the interior. It was explained, with some embarrassment that, in fact, all of the windows had had sheer curtains fixed in place for years, and that one was not really able to see the landscape from inside. It was then that we realized that the reason the landscape was in danger was that no one was experiencing the landscape the way it was intended to be experienced. Tens of thousands of visitors every year were reinforcing what the governors general themselves were feeling—that the residence was an object set entirely apart from the setting within which it had been built.

Once the curtains were removed to allow our inspection, the quality of both the house and the landscape were irrevocably altered. The curtains never went back. A new governor general was just settling in, and in her tenure the relationship between the house and the grounds became the basis for all major planning decisions. The visitor centre was built at the centre of the landscape, within the residential compound, looking out rather than looking in. The landscape also became a productive part of the estate, with replanted vegetable gardens and orchards. And the original design intentions were easily translated into a new sustainable design approach: a design that considered natural and cultural resource conservation simultaneously. The new interventions were contemporary, but the spirit was in keeping with the site's long history.

The magnificent grounds of Rideau Hall, home to the governor general of Canada.

THIS PAGE TOP Looking toward the cricket field of Rideau Hall.
BOTTOM The well-established Rideau Hall arboretum. OPPOSITE PAGE View from the ceremonial entry drive to the residential forecourt.

Contemporary design details combine with the Italian Gothic Revival restoration of the Canadian Embassy in Rome.

Villa Grazioli – Canadian Embassy
Rome, Italy

The Canadian government purchased the historic Villa Grazioli estate in Rome, as a place to consolidate all of its embassy functions within the city. These functions had previously been scattered in several buildings in downtown Rome. Our offices were asked to prepare a master plan, and subsequent more detailed and interrelated architectural and landscape designs.

Again we were challenged with developing a site with a rich history to reflect both continuity and change. The desire for continuity was obvious: the gardens are a registered historic monument in Italy. But the desire for change was also powerful, because the site was to take on dual nationalities intersecting traditional Italian attitudes and contemporary Canadian values. Since Canada is a country that respects a variety of cultural values, this was not an easy design task. The process of carefully restoring the impressive 19th century villa had already begun, and to complicate things further the City of Rome does not allow contemporary design within the historic city limits.

The gardens became the locus of play between interpreting past, present and future, and the intersection of Italian and Canadian identities. Once the master plan was in place, the first phase of the new landscape treatment was detailed. This phase has now been implemented, and already there is an appreciation by those who visit the site of how good contemporary design can successfully intersect with strong cultural traditions. Again, the starting point moved beyond observable, visual issues to questions of experience and ritual. The embassy forecourt expresses Italian sensibilities, particularly their brilliant use of planting and paving materials to blur the distinction between pedestrian and vehicular space, to create a public space that reflects specifically Canadian ideas of how to merge the public and the private. Unlike most embassies, which create walled gardens in the European tradition, the Canadian Embassy opens to the street in a series of gestures that works even in the atmosphere of heightened security. After preparing a series of sketches, Greg Smallenberg worked closely with Italian nurserymen on the design and implementation. The result was an innovative idea: the use of an Italian vocabulary to express Canadian ideas, rather than the expected approach of using a Canadian vocabulary to express Italian ideas.

The same approach was then used to develop the design concepts for the new embassy building. It took as its cue the 19th century Italian Gothic Revival style of the existing villa. This was the same style used by Thomas Fuller in his winning 1859 design for the new Parliament Buildings in Ottawa. There the style was used to create one of the few world capitals where the buildings are set within the landscape. That same attitude, an Italian vocabulary adapted to Canadian ideas, was used to design a contemporary building comfortably placed within the historic garden. When the officials in Rome, including the Superintendent of Historic Gardens, the Superintendent of Archaeology, the Superintendent of Monuments, the Director of Architecture, and the Deputy Mayor met together to approve the design, they clearly appreciated the team's approach that touched on architecture within the context not just of landscape, but of landscape culturally interpreted and experienced.

THIS PAGE LEFT The grounds and stone-lined gravel entry drive at night.
TOP RIGHT View to the main entry forecourt from the offices above.
MIDDLE RIGHT Paving and planting details inside the main gate.
BOTTOM RIGHT View of the main entry drive and grounds from the upper floor of the embassy. OPPOSITE PAGE The paving materials and patterns of the main entry forecourt interpret those found in neighbouring streets and private gardens.

LEFT The site plan establishes the boundaries and general uses of the Central Experimental Farm, a 400 hectare agricultural preserve and research facility surrounded by the city of Ottawa. The Management Plan preserves the activities that are intrinsic to the cultural landscape, allowing Agriculture and Agri-Food Canada to expand and develop its research activities while bringing this National Historic Site back in line with its original landscape design intentions. RIGHT Rendered westward view across the fields. The Central Experimental Farm is one of Ottawa's most significant heritage landscapes and a well used open space on the regional parkway system.

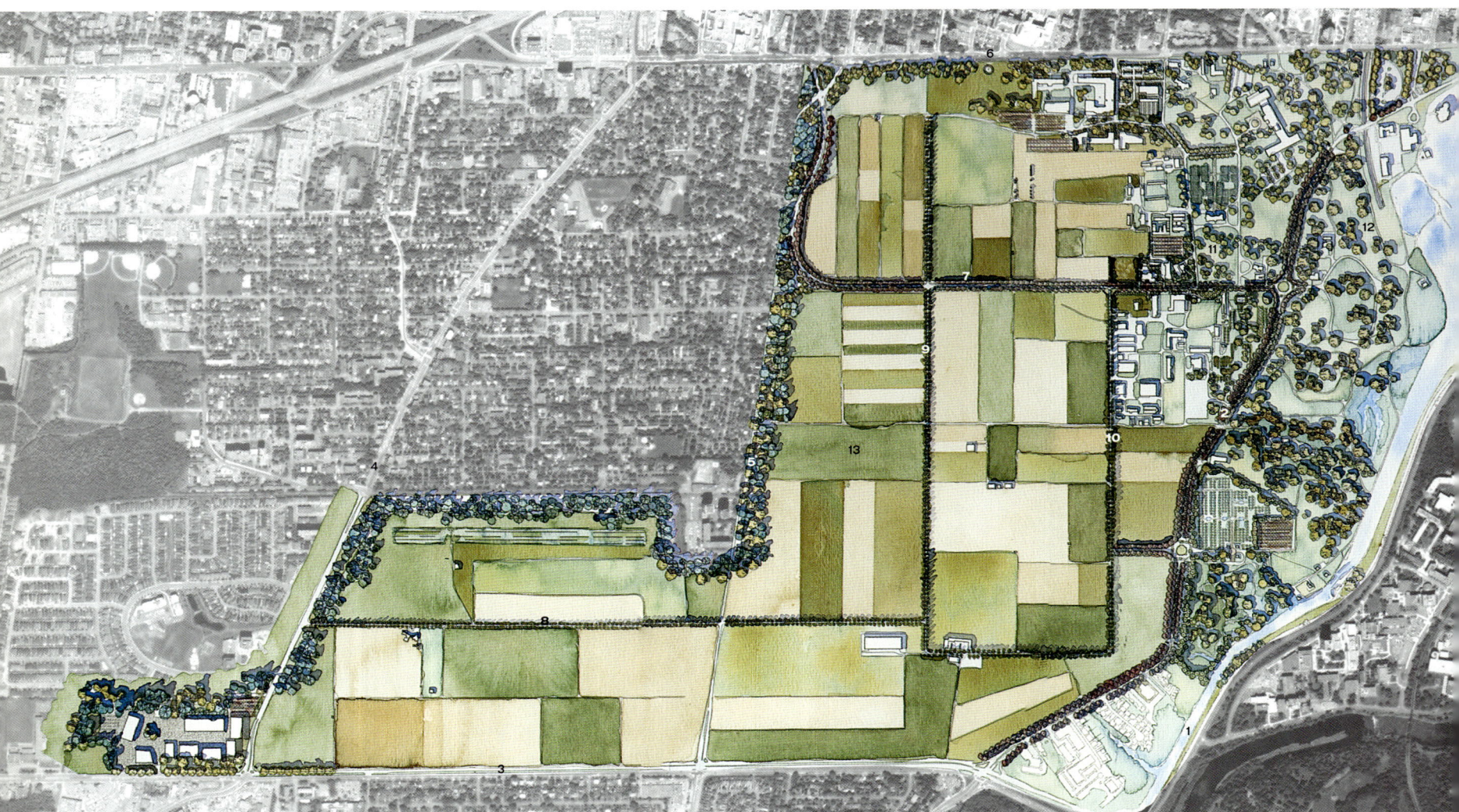

1 Rideau Canal
2 Prince of Wales Drive
3 Baseline Road
4 Merivale Road
5 Fisher Avenue
6 Carling Avenue
7 NCC Scenic Drive
8 MCooey Lane
9 Ash Lane
10 Morningside Lane
11 Central Green
12 Dominion Arboretum
13 Experimental Fields

Central Experimental Farm Management Plan
Ottawa, ON

No other joint project involving Julian Smith & Associates Architects and PFS is as expressive of the power of a cultural landscape approach to design as the Central Experimental Farm Management Plan. At the outset of the project, which was to develop a long-term management plan, the consultant team was told that Agriculture Canada had essentially decided to abandon the entire site. It had recently been designated a National Historic Site and Agriculture Canada was concerned about how to manage a healthy research agenda within a landscape labeled 'picturesque' by the Historic Sites and Monuments Board.

At the end of the project Agriculture Canada not only decided to remain at the location, they announced that they would invest $110 million in the site to upgrade their research facilities and to signal their long-term commitment to the property.

Once again the challenge was to overcome the inherent hostility between heritage advocates, who wanted to use the National Historic Site designation to limit visual interventions, and the contemporary design advocates, who saw many potential building sites within a powerful landscape setting but were unappreciative of the site's history. Both of these attitudes could best be understood in the context of 20th century Modernism, and both were equally problematic.

Central Experimental Farm is a major 567 hectare parcel in the centre of Ottawa. At the outset, a detailed process of cognitive mapping was carried out. The intent was to understand how the landscape was experienced, not just how it was observed. There were many communities of interest: research scientists, headquarters staff, museum personnel, local visitors, dog walkers and the transient public. What became evident was that multiple cultural landscapes existed, each with its own rituals and boundaries, and that the old Central Green was not on anyone's cognitive map. No one was using the site in the way it was originally designed and intended, and the result was that no one appreciated its richness and the logic of its component parts.

At the same time project historian Julie Harris, a historian of science, renamed the landscape a 'research' landscape rather than a 'picturesque' landscape, not because of its current reality but because of its original design intentions and its subsequent historical associations. Only by understanding 19th century science and research practices could one understand the internal and external parameters of the site design. That design had been sustained by the rituals of inhabitation—by the patterns of undertaking and communicating agricultural research for more than a century.

Contemporary problems with the site were as much about changing rituals as changing objects. Many historic objects were still intact, and the heritage community had focused on these objects in isolation. Their individual historic value was clear, yet each one was threatened if Agriculture Canada abandoned the site.

Once the situation was recast in terms of the rituals of inhabitation, and once it was clearly set within the idea of 'research', the discussions with Agriculture Canada became focused and productive. The idea of a research landscape was completely understandable, in both its historic and contemporary contexts. And the dynamic nature of that landscape in physical terms was easily placed within the context of continuity of attitude and practice, in both tangible and intangible dimensions.

THIS PAGE TOP Elevated view of the structuring elements found in the picturesque areas of the farm – narrow curvilinear roadways, groves of large trees and generous areas of lawn and garden. MIDDLE Northwest view across the expansive farmland of the Central Experimental Farm. BOTTOM Cow pasture at the Central Experimental Farm. OPPOSITE PAGE TOP Rendering of the existing framework of the concentrated northeast quadrant with a re-energized and intensified research zone and revitalized Prince of Wales Drive. BOTTOM Rendering of the proposed visitor centre and collections facility on the base of a restructured Agriculture Canada headquarters building.

The values of the landscape were then developed in relation to this revised historical perspective. One of the major challenges was to examine whether the Central Green could be reanimated to make sense of the original logic. This raised the issue of the public face of research and the interaction between research scientists and the broader constituency of farmers, consumers and activists. Another part of the discussion was the function of a museum in shaping contemporary research. In the end the new plan called for returning to the original design intentions but using contemporary as well as historic interventions as part of this approach.

When Agriculture Canada's headquarters were moved to this site in the 1960s, they took a Modernist approach to landscape. Using a Modernist building in a picturesque setting, they were oblivious to the rupture it created to the subtle connections between the research landscape and the people who inhabited it. The headquarter function had never been a sustainable fit. The management plan called for its removal to a neighbouring property, and the research scientists recognized that they would be able to reclaim the site. It was then an easy transition to have them interact with the public around the Central Green, and to further engage the museum in a contemporary role linked to the idea of making research publicly engaging. It was this renewed continuity between past, present and future that animated the management plan and that in turn animated the department and its research staff.

1 Carling Avenue
2 Prince of Wales Drive
3 Central Green
4 Agricultural Museum Complex
5 Research Precinct
6 Visitor Centre
7 Dominion Observatory
8 Greenhouses
9 Perennial Gardens
10 Dominion Arboretum
11 Hedge Research
12 Experimental Fields

Julian Smith Cultural Landscapes 179

Conclusion

The relationship between Julian Smith & Associates Architects and PFS has been central to my own exploration of shifts in design practice: in cultural expectations and understandings of how we integrate theory and practice, new and old, object and ritual, architecture and landscape. Our firms start at very different places, and believe strongly in what we do. That is why the dialogues are so intense and so productive, because there is much to be learned and much to gain.

It is surprising how easy it is to slip into the solitudes of specialized areas of theory and practice. Even sustainability is facing that danger, becoming one more area where specialist practices hope to find a comfortable niche. But design is not a comfortable undertaking, at least not if we respect the uncomfortable experiment that John Ralston Saul so eloquently described in *Reflections of a Siamese Twin* as fundamental to Canadian identity. Discomfort brings its own rewards when the issues are worth fighting over, and when there is the possibility of a resolution in which the whole is greater than the sum of its parts.

Managing risk also takes particular skill. One of the great pleasures of our association over the years has been the presence, on a number of these projects, of a project manager of rare strength and ability. This is Marc Monette, a person dedicated to the ideals of managing change in creative and satisfying ways. It was he who brought us together, because he believes that passion is as important as reason, and that the most important sites need the most intense debates. This is not a typical approach for project managers in either the public or private sectors, and yet it is fundamental to good theory and good practice. And to return to this essay's original idea, it is no coincidence that Marc is a landscape architect by training. I am convinced that the emerging world view that will colour many of our practices in the years to come will be articulated and put into play by such people. These are people for whom landscape in its broadest sense, as the locus of human ecology, is both enormously powerful and surprisingly fragile. It is their wisdom which will be essential in exploring our joint future.

In Chinese, the English word 'urbane' translates into 'well-mannered' (you li mao de) *or 'cultured'* (wen ya de), *thus ridding it of its association with city life. Even the Chinese word for 'civilization'* (wen ming), *which has figured so prominently in the Party-State's promotion of an image of Beijing, does not connote city life as does the English, which shares with 'city' the same Latin root of 'civis'* (citizen).

Global Acculturation
Urbanism in contemporary China

by Dr. Eduard Koegel

Since 1978, economic and political reforms in China have generated a new condition for Chinese urbanization, with major effects on global development. From 1978 to 2004, the average housing space per person in urban areas changed from 8.1 to 27.2 square metres. In 2004, the urban population reached 41%, compared to 28% in 1995. And between 1998 and 2004, China lost 72 million hectares of cultivated land to infrastructure and urban development. Growing hunger for energy and raw materials necessitates sustainable solutions. This is not just a Chinese problem. Western standards of living also consume huge quantities of natural resources. Foreign urban experts can contribute to sustainable models of development both abroad and at home.

To help understand current urban design practices in China, it is essential to understand the history of Chinese urbanism as well as the history and effects of foreign influence. The first difference between Chinese and Western approaches to urban design is rooted in vocabulary: the English word 'urbane' translates into 'well-mannered' *(you li mao de)* or 'cultured' *(wen ya de)*, thus ridding it of its association with city life. Even the Chinese word for 'civilization' *(wen ming)*, which has figured so prominently in the Party-State's promotion of an image of Beijing, does not connote city life as does the English, which shares with 'city' the same Latin root 'civis' (citizen).[1]

Apart from this theoretical but important point, rapid urbanization in China produces extreme practical difficulties such as shortage of land and water; pollution of air, water and soil; and social pressures between city and country. Such rapid societal transformation from an agricultural to an urban lifestyle has never progressed so quickly and the massive scale of such problems challenges local institutions and professionals. All parties involved know that they must simultaneously address environmental issues, societal social balance, and global exchange and influence. They are therefore receptive to foreign expertise in the field of sustainable development. Foreign consultants are urgently sought to improve the quality of new developments, even when their concepts are at times radically altered purposely or through intercultural misinterpretation.

To better understand the initial position of Chinese clients, it is helpful to understand where the discourse on Chinese urbanism originates. Ideas are partially rooted in Chinese tradition and partially adopted from Western concepts that arrived via foreign consultants working in China and Chinese architects and planners educated in the West. This East-West exchange of ideas in modern architecture and urban design began about a century ago.

In the semi-colonial developments of the late 19th century, the first Western experts came to the concessions of big cities like Shanghai, Tianjin, Qingdao, Canton and Beijing. The first North American advisors and engineers arrived in China after the fall of the Qing dynasty in 1911.[2] The first Canadian is thought to have been Harry Hussey, who came as an architectural consultant to Beijing just before the 1911 Revolution.[3] Between 1916 and 1918 he worked on a commission for the Rockefeller Foundation to design the Peking Union Medical College which today belongs to Tsinghua University.

During the same period, American architect Henry K. Murphy became so fascinated by traditional Chinese architecture that he searched for a new style combining Eastern formal vocabulary with Western technique. He developed the idea of an 'adaptive architecture' that influenced the Chinese creation of the 'Chinese Renaissance Style' in the 1920s.[4] At the same time, young Chinese architects studying in the West returned home with Western conceptions of architecture and urban development. Many of them had studied in the United States and were deeply influenced by the formal ideas of the École des Beaux Arts. Technical developments and new infrastructural functions made it necessary to develop new building standards for power stations, railway stations, apartment houses, bank buildings and offices. In addition, urban behaviour and lifestyle changed rapidly in cities like Shanghai, Canton, Tianjin and Beijing in the 1920s.

Especially in Shanghai, commercial pressure in the International Settlement resulted in the vision of a high-rise metropolis based on the Art Deco model of Manhattan's 'skyscraper city'. These visions were not realized until after the Japanese started war in China in 1937. The cinema, particularly Hollywood, was also influential in transporting new ideas of Western urban cultural behaviour and fashion.[5]

During World War II the Republican Chinese government developed a new urban structure with the help of American advisors such

PAGE 182 Blue Mountain. Shanghai, China. THIS PAGE TOP Bustling streets of Qingdao, Shandong Province, China. BOTTOM Three eras of housing – the Lilong, Communist housing block and contemporary high-rise – collide in Shanghai.

as Ralph Eberlin and Norman J. Gordon. Eberlin was a civil engineer who worked with Clarence Stein[6] to implement the 'Neighbourhood Unit' concept in Sunnyside and Radburn. In the United States, Clarence Perry originated the Neighbourhood Unit concept in the 1920s, but Stein was the first architect to translate the theoretical idea into a new settlement pattern. He combined the ideas of Ebenezer Howard's 'Garden Cities of Tomorrow' in Great Britain with the new mobility of private cars in the United States to create an 'American Garden City'. In 1929, Stein developed the following elements for Radburn: 'The Superblock', to replace the characteristic narrow, rectangular block; specialized roads planned and built for single uses; complete separation of pedestrians and automobiles; reversed housing with living and sleeping rooms facing gardens and parks, and service rooms facing access roads; and the park as the backbone of the neighbourhood.

This new neighbourhood type was planned for 5,000 to 10,000 inhabitants. A combined school and community centre located within walking distance from each house formed the heart of each neighbourhood.[7]

The idea of the Neighbourhood Unit fit very well with the traditional Chinese spatial organization principles of Bao-Jia. According to Bao-Jia, ten families were organized as one unit (Jia) and ten units formed a larger circle (Bao). Historically the emperor used this system to control local administrative power and to simultaneously control the activities of all residents. Norman J. Gordon, advisor to the Chinese Ministry of the Interior on city planning and housing programs in the 1940s, later reported,

> We attempted to combine the neighbourhood planning standards of 20th century United States with the social institutions of the 5th century B.C. in China....No fewer than ten nor more than thirty families will compose a Jia....The Ministry of Education has declared its intention to provide an elementary school for every Bao.[8]

In this standard, several Jia were tied together as a Bao. They were planned with 2,000 persons per Bao and around 360 families in a unit. The difference between the Neighbourhood Unit and Bao-Jia concepts was based on conceptions of open space. In traditional

Ballroom dancing on city streets.

Bao-Jia spatial organization, the family or clan lived together in one compound of enclosed courtyards, sometimes including private gardens. The 'outside' was conceived of as uncertain; an 'empty space' without social relations. Apart from some projects designed around the idea of the Neighbourhood Unit in the war capital of 1940s Chongqing and for the planning of Greater Shanghai, between 1945 and 1949, its influence was mainly theoretical. But in departments of urban planning at postwar universities, the Neighbourhood Unit became the guiding concept for urban planning education.

After the establishment of the People's Republic in 1949, the new administration took parts of the Neighbourhood Unit system and adapted them in a socialist societal reorganization. The social and spatial roots of the work unit *(dan wei)* and street committee were influenced by Bao-Jia principles, Neighbourhood Unit developments in the West and advice from consultants from Moscow. The work unit took care of individuals' working, living and social needs and replaced traditionally close family ties.

The radical development of the 'Great Leap Forward' in 1958 and the Cultural Revolution of the 1960s resulted in a chaotic situation that led to a massive reorganization of society into self-sufficient communes. Work units became enclosed islands with all the necessary institutions for daily life behind walls. In the 1960s, Mao Zedong replaced long-term site specific planning with standardized models, promoted with the catchphrase, 'Learning from' the agricultural commune Dazhai or the new semi-urban communes in the oilfield of Daqing. The oilfield of Daqing[9] in the north of China was discovered in the early 1960s, and many workers from all over the country came to build a new kind of urban model according to the principles of Maoist self help. Prime Minister Zhou Enlai described this as "combining cities with the countryside and workers with peasants and creating conditions conducive to production and convenience for people's lives."[10] The idea of 'development through shining example' was developed in two models (rural and urban) for a new society. In the utopia of Chinese socialism, the city was meant to dissolve into the countryside, and the rural areas to become industrialized in a 'war against nature'.[11]

In the 1980s, under the leadership of Deng Xiaoping, the Open Door Policy of the Chinese Communist Party set the economic conditions for the transformation of urban development, and the 'Learning from' model was extended to foreign examples. Urbanization accelerated at lightning speed throughout the 1980s due to economic and political liberalization. In the 1990s Rem Koolhaas and the Harvard Design School investigated this urban condition in the Pearl River Delta. They described this phenomenon as "a synthetic idyll in memory of the city."[12] What they found was a new urban landscape with quickly changing, dichotomous patterns of urbanization.[13] Informally developed cheap space for the floating work force that moved from the country to the city was contrasted with themed housing resorts for the urban middle-class, developed by commercial investors.

Before economic reforms, the state and work unit had been responsible for providing housing. Not until the late 1980s did state law change and housing became a product of the market. For the first time since 1949, people could purchase their own apartment. Private investors in new housing focused on one particular societal group—those with money. While the state and the work unit had a social responsibility, private enterprise was only interested in a quick return of investment. They developed exclusive gated housing projects with spectacular names like 'Golden Flowers Estate' and 'Life Green Residence', spatially derived from the former enclosed work unit. These so called Micro-Residential Districts (MRDs) are the basic module for commercial housing in China today.[14]

Besides the physical alteration of the environment, social behaviour has also changed dramatically. What has emerged is a new demand for public space and public landscapes that respond to the dissolution of the homogeneous community, and the need for recreation and health. In the work unit, an individual's time was managed by the collective administration. For example, workers were required to attend evening classes where the Communist Party educated the masses with ideological phrases. The new market economy emphasizes individual responsibility, and the family as a social institution has once again become more important. Societal focus has shifted to individual recreation and the organization of one's leisure time, but also to issues of ecology.

In most cases, developers and local authorities decide on future development. In the new middle-class MRDs, the landscape often becomes the advertisement for the single flat. Green space has become such a valuable commodity in growing cities that environmental integrity and the climatic and biological needs of plants are the least of investors' concerns. The long-term ecological consequences of intensive maintenance regimes, and the copious use of potable water for fountains in regions with water shortages raise the question of whether new gardens and semipublic spaces are provided for the use of inhabitants or as a short-term strategy to sell housing units. A popular saying amongst potential Chinese clients alludes to the problem: 'As long as water is still running in the fountain, not all apartments are sold.'

Chinese cities will often only specify the basic function for a piece of land, with no requirements for streetscape design or connectivity between housing estates. Only by chance does the placement of buildings create meaningful public space for both visitors and residents. As described previously, the separation of enclaves, such as the work unit and the MRD, was not conducive to developing collective social space for diverse societal groups.

Uneven social development, characterized by millions of temporary residents in big cities (the so-called floating population) is a result of the 1958 Hukou Registration Regulation that still separates society into urban and rural populations. In 2005, the Central Committee of the Party established the goal of 'construction of a harmonious society' for their eleventh five-year plan. They recognized that the previously championed technocratic-scientific model of development was not effective, and established a new 'human-oriented' principle which would transform 'social contradictions' into 'social harmony' because "several contradictions among the people, which are not properly dealt with, might even develop into incidents with a mass character."[15] Indeed, the underprivileged class and those disadvantaged as a result of city-country registration are not satisfied with recent development. They want to participate equally in economic development, but believe that the administration is slow to resolve their problems and that it neglects existing laws for personal profit. The central government aims to address this growing intolerance of social and economic difference that could easily undermine efforts toward a safe and sustainable future.[16]

Sustainability must be considered technically, politically and ecologically, as well as socially. But having an intercultural dialogue about sustainability is difficult when there are differing concepts of memory, history, nature and human interaction. In China, any discussion about urban history begins with the axiom, 'Urban development in China started 3,000 years ago'. This is more than just a saying. It literally reflects the collective accumulation of idealized development in an enclosed space of time (history), whereas in the West development is portrayed as improvement along a linear timeline. The French sinologist and philosopher François Jullien notes that this abstract homogeneous idea of time, with a strict separation between beginning and end, was never considered in China. Instead the Chinese think of simultaneous yearly seasons, processes, moments, possibilities and the 'as-well-as'.[17] This flexible system differs radically from the common Western understanding and causes a great deal of misunderstanding.

In China it is not important whether an artifact is 1,000 years old or only 200, what matters is that it is part of history and that it adds value to the same cultural circle. It becomes part of common history, in many cases without reference to an original root. The Chinese cultural critic Bo Yang describes this phenomenon: "the Chinese can hardly accept that foreign ideas influenced their cultural development. Therefore they put everything into a 'pot of soy sauce', until Chinese flavour dominates."[18] Intercultural battles revolve around issues of copyright and the struggle to maintain control of a project through to implementation.

Beyond these traditional differences, there are also contemporary issues such as the new 'culture industry'. The Chinese government announced recently that all 'cultural resources' should be turned into 'cultural products'.[19] This intention, to perceive everything in terms of its economic value, makes it difficult to argue for long-term environmental sustainability, particularly for strategies with no immediate economic return.

In China there are three philosophical lines: Daoism looks to accommodate nature (harmony between heaven and humankind),

Dense housing along an urban canal system.

Buddhism has reverence for all living creatures, and Confucianism respects authority (nature is mastered by man). For Mao Zedong, the Confucian tradition best fit his project of industrialization and collectivization. Under his leadership, the major slogans in the 1960s and 1970s were 'Man must conquer nature' and 'Let us move mountains and rivers.'[20] In her book *Mao's War Against Nature*, Judith Shapiro describes Mao's attempts to conquer the natural environment: "mountains were moved, dams were built, rivers relocated and wasteland cultivated."[21] The ancient Chinese fable of the Foolish Old Man Who Moves the Mountain was changed to the Not-so-Foolish Old Man. In Mao's version, Foolish becomes courageous. After the Open Door Policy of the 1980s, this spirit of the 1960s and 1970s was reinterpreted in the commercial context of new urbanization:

> A whole region...was turned from hills into flat plains in less than two decades. The new generation (was) committed to conquering Nature, Heaven, or whatever (lay) in the way of economic prosperity...they...succeeded in creating a vast unnatural landscape, stripped of topography, mature trees, indigenous vegetation and any identity.[22]

In this context of absolute tabula rasa, sensible concepts of site integration become extremely important. Ecological strategies that contribute to sustainable development and a healthy environment are needed to balance urban consumption of natural resources.

For foreigners in China it is difficult to negotiate such things as multitudinous relationships, saving face, cultural misunderstandings, hierarchy and communication problems. A central Chinese concept for networking, communication and social interaction is *guan xi*. *Guan xi* is difficult to translate without losing part of its meaning, but it generally describes one's personal relationship to people at all levels of society. In urban planning and building, it is necessary to have a network that reaches the political decision makers in the Communist Party, the local and regional administration, other planners involved in the project, workers on site and multiple levels within the client's firm. It is important that all tiers are covered from the boss to the secretary. Only if one has good *guan xi*, is one able to successfully negotiate a project.[23]

Foreign planners must learn to work with simple and strong concepts, to integrate and learn from the oddest of cultural misunderstandings and to build *guan xi* at all levels of decision-making. A clear idea and personal presence are needed for meaningful solutions within fast paced Chinese development, otherwise all efforts will blur and vanish in the unforeseeable development. But the general openness to learning from the best solutions and to adapting them to local conditions in practical ways keeps things going in China.

As the transpacific economic and cultural network has exploded in the last 25 years, the parameters of Western value systems are challenged. With rapid economic development and growing political and cultural ambitions, Chinese influence is growing. By learning from the best solutions and acculturating foreign concepts, Chinese society is on the way to more sustainable future, with the help of foreign experts like Phillips Farevaag Smallenberg (PFS).

Shouqiu Shaohao
Historic Site

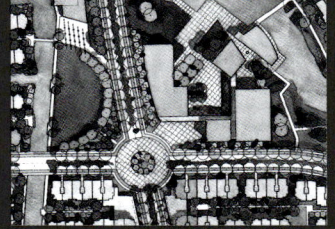

CMHC Shanghai Sustainable
Community Standard

Metropolitan Apartments

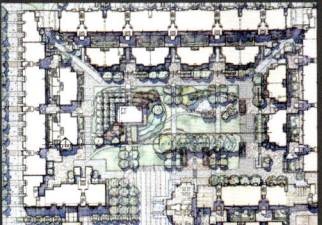

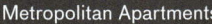

Blue Mountain

Hui Tian Ran CityPark

Golden Ox Mountain

Hui Tian Ran CityPark Master Plan
Zhuzhou, Hunan Province, China

The city of Zhuzhou is an industrial centre located in the Province of Hunan. Historically, its railway infrastructure and the Xiang Jiang River made it an important centre for communication. China's recent economic boom has promoted national programs for investment in Western and interior China, resulting in Zhuzhou's intensive development. Today its population has reached more than 3.5 million. Outside of the central city next to the Xiang Jiang River, PFS created a master plan for a new 720 hectare community of interrelated neighbourhoods, parks and schools oriented around a vibrant town centre.

This area of Hunan is known as the birthplace of agriculture in China, and its verdant green valleys, terraced fields, ponds and streams are a result of hundreds of years of farming activity. The master plan was created to preserve the beauty and heritage of this landscape, but to also highlight agriculture as relevant, viable and necessary in a 21st century community development. High-density clusters are sensitively sited to preserve farmland and to support additional low-density areas. Clustered high density (4–6 FAR) and the concentration of 35,000 people on less than 30% of the site make this integration with open countryside possible. The incorporation of urban agriculture connects to historic land-uses, leading to a gentler transformation of cultural patterns on the site.

Preserving the land for urban agriculture could become the hallmark of excellence for CityPark. In the course of economic prosperity, Chinese health has suffered. Today about 30% of Chinese are overweight, and about 6% suffer from diabetes. Fast food and low physical activity are the main reasons for this development. The younger generation has lost their connection to healthy living conditions. A close connection between food production and consumption could help to make a difference.

Development is primarily focused on slopes and out of the flood plains, preserving valley bottoms for recreation, agriculture and water resources. Development is to occur with as little disturbance as possible in order to protect the ecological role of forested slopes for natural habitat, erosion control and high quality water filtration. Shade trees are an important component of an energy use reduction strategy. The master plan aims to cover 35% of the site with tree canopy. Due to Zhuzhou's latitude and prevailing temperature patterns, the usual recommendation for a south facing aspect is forfeited to allow for dense shade on all building surfaces, particularly the east and west surfaces and roof.

Centuries old historic paths through the hills and low lying agricultural lands are the primary locations for new roads, pedestrian paths and services connecting the different clusters. Streets and paths are interconnected to encourage walking and bicycling to recreation, transit and commercial centres, and to ensure that suburban arterials do not become congested with traffic.

The intended mix of urban, natural, residential, agricultural and recreational spaces brings value to the city of Zhuzhou. PFS's CityPark plan is based on the three pillars of sustainability: social, economic and environmental. But in the end, clients and final users will show what they support and understand of the positive intentions. The development is planned for a happy few who have enough money for such a lifestyle and there is a tendency for pragmatic usage of the automobile over walking. The car in China is still a status symbol, as is the house. Control of the architecture and its integration into the landscape will be necessary during implementation to not spoil the natural beauty of the site.

The balancing of dense clusters with urban agriculture could help to establish sensitivity toward the landscape and the culture that it shaped. But with the Chinese tendency for ad hoc decisions in favour of short-term economic benefits, the gem can quickly turn into trash. The first step for a sustainable future will be to convince developers, the local administration and the final inhabitants. With China's recent history of social, political and economic development the challenge is daunting, but so are the problems that await a solution. PFS has taken the first step through planning. The Chinese people must work towards the ideas to protect their resources for future generations.

Rendered master plan of Hui Tian Ran CityPark.

1 Xiang Jiang River
2 Town Centre
3 Library
4 Civic Recreation Centre
5 Town Centre Park
6 Elementary School
7 Secondary School
8 Cultural Village / Farming Co-op
9 Lineal River Park
10 Preserved Agricultural Lands

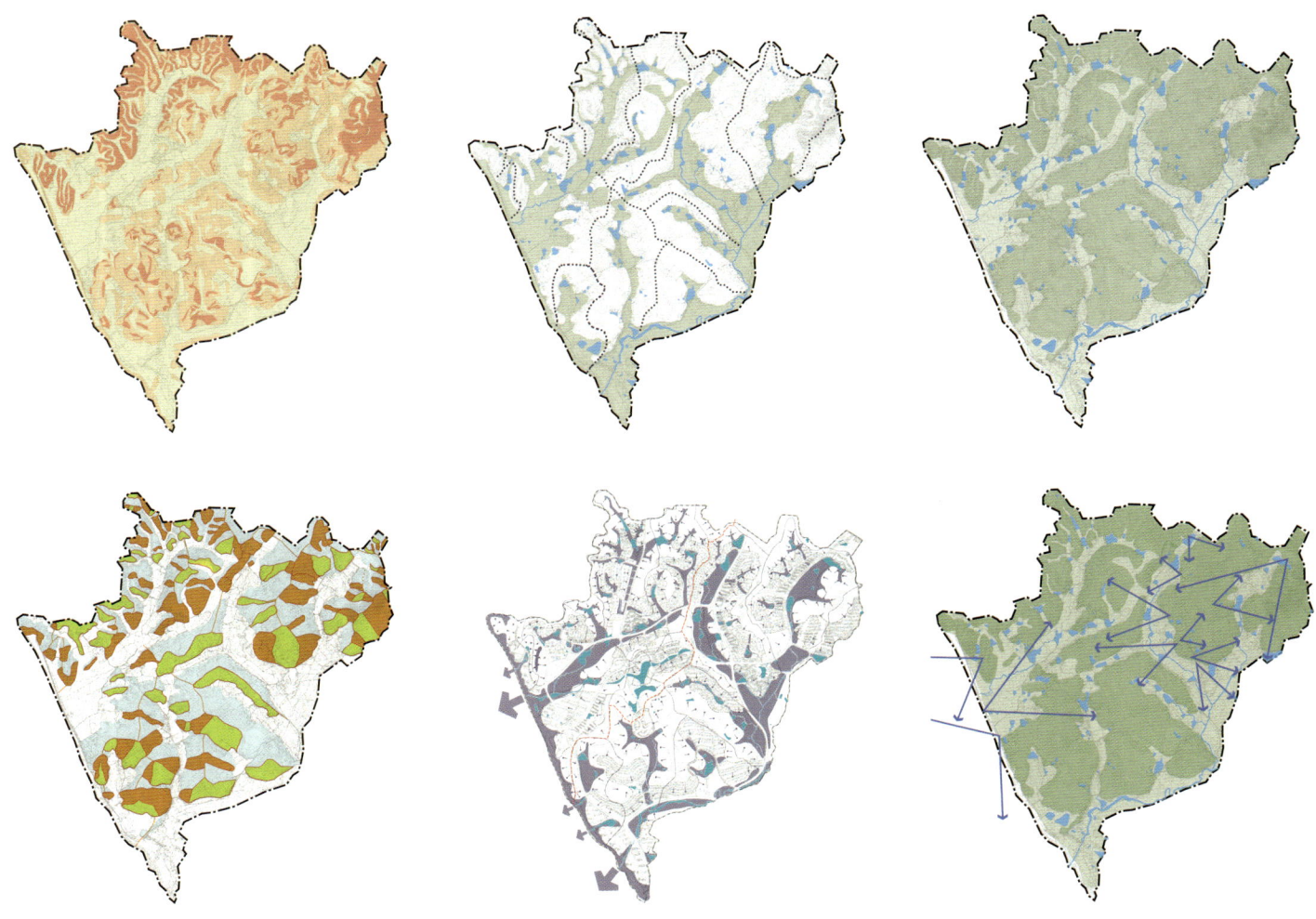

THIS PAGE TOP Diagrams: Slopes, Hydrology, Landscape Typology, Sun / Shade, Drainage, Key Views BOTTOM LEFT AND RIGHT Expanses of existing farmland on site.
OPPOSITE PAGE TOP Rendered model of the proposed Town Centre.
BOTTOM Rendered model of the Cultural Village and working agriculture centre.

Dr. Eduard Koegel   Global Acculturation   193

LEFT Proposed high-density development along the Xiang Jiang River.
RIGHT Rendered plan of Town Centre surrounded by mid-density residential development, recreational amenities and preserved farmland. The Town Centre is focused on a water feature providing stormwater management functions integrated with an extensive existing system of streams and ponds. The patterns, scale and dimensioning of the agriculture centre and Cultural Village east of the Town Centre are derived from those found in neighbouring villages.

1 Xiang Jiang River
2 Town Centre
3 Library
4 Civic Recreation Centre
5 Town Centre Park
6 Elementary School
7 Secondary School
8 Lineal River Park

1   Miaogong River
2   Perimeter Canal
3   Sanctuary Stormwater Canal
4   Jinhai Road
5   Main Entrance
6   Neighbourhood Parkway
7   Central Park
8   Event Centre
9   East / West Greenway
10 Pedestrian Lanes
11 Autocourt Linkages
12 Community Centre
13 Commercial / Entertainment
14 Mid-density Apartments
15 Town Homes

LEFT The Blue Mountain community is built around a lineal park.
RIGHT Blue Mountain site plan. The community is comprised of dense row houses and mid-rise development structured by a central park, a looping internal circulation system and a stormwater system of channels, streams and an existing canal.

Blue Mountain
Shanghai, China

The residential development of Blue Mountain is located in Shanghai-Pudong, about 30 kilometres from the centre of the city. The entire neighbourhood is 144 hectares, filling out one mesh in the huge grid of infrastructure that has been superimposed on the existing landscape. Blue Mountain is a cloistered community, sheltered from oversized roads by stone walls and thick buffer plantings. After passing through one of two entrance gates, an ideal living environment unfurls for the residents.

Within the suburban gated model of the MRD, Blue Mountain attempts to incorporate some key ecologically sustainable moves. The neighbourhood is structured by two landscape systems: open spaces and waterways.

The open space framework is comprised of a series of interconnected semipublic courtyards surrounded by multifamily housing, and a hierarchy of narrow streets that are detailed as pedestrian pathways. Each courtyard is surrounded by twenty to thirty homes, and is shared by pedestrians and vehicles. The courtyards provide necessary distance between buildings, maximizing solar exposure for all units, allowing for a sense of privacy, and creating a neighbourhood open space for adults and children to socialize within a safe environment. Framed by walls and hedges, the courtyards function as outdoor garden rooms. Roads within the development are narrow and detailed as pedestrian pathways. Parking is designed as part of the courtyard, minimizing hard surface and maximizing pedestrian space. The courtyard and pathway network is structured around a central lineal park composed of a long sequence of unfolding spaces offering a wide variety of programmatic and recreational opportunities. Dense planting of trees within the park, courtyards and along roads softens the density of buildings while greening the entire neighbourhood.

The second landscape system to structure the neighbourhood is a series of introduced and existing waterways. The low land in Pudong is drained by a traditional network of rivers, streams and canals. Blue Mountain integrates a river and several of these existing canals to form an effective stormwater management infrastructure that also serves as green corridors knitting the community together.

By using existing green infrastructure and by softening the living environment with intensive planting design, the Blue Mountain community becomes an island, but it is still connected to the harsh environmental conditions outside its walls. Existing water pollution in canals, streams and rivers needs to be mentioned in order to argue for a more comprehensive approach to sustainable development.

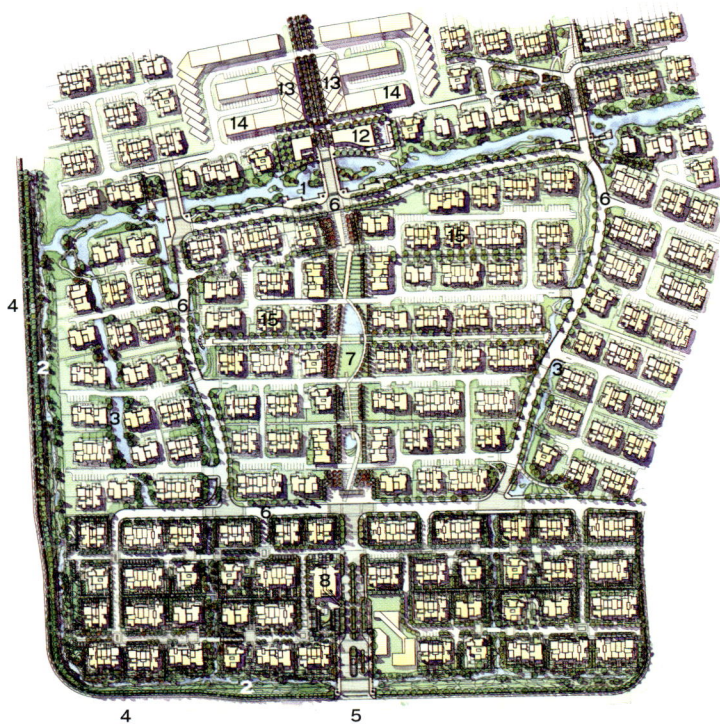

OPPOSITE PAGE TOP A stone and glass pergola marks the threshold to the central park. BOTTOM View of a revitalized canal flowing through the site.
THIS PAGE TOP The craftsmanship of landscape construction was exceptional. BOTTOM A willow-lined boardwalk in the central park.

THIS PAGE TOP Landscape terrace adjacent to a neighbourhood cafe. BOTTOM Gingko sentinels with traditional staking. OPPOSITE PAGE TOP A highly structured landscape of clipped shrubs and stately trees is characteristic of Blue Mountain's primary open spaces. BOTTOM LEFT A meticulously maintained landscape with entry banners celebrates the completion of the development. BOTTOM RIGHT Lush landscape, permeable paving and integrated parking promote the concept of shared streets.

Dr. Eduard Koegel Global Acculturation 201

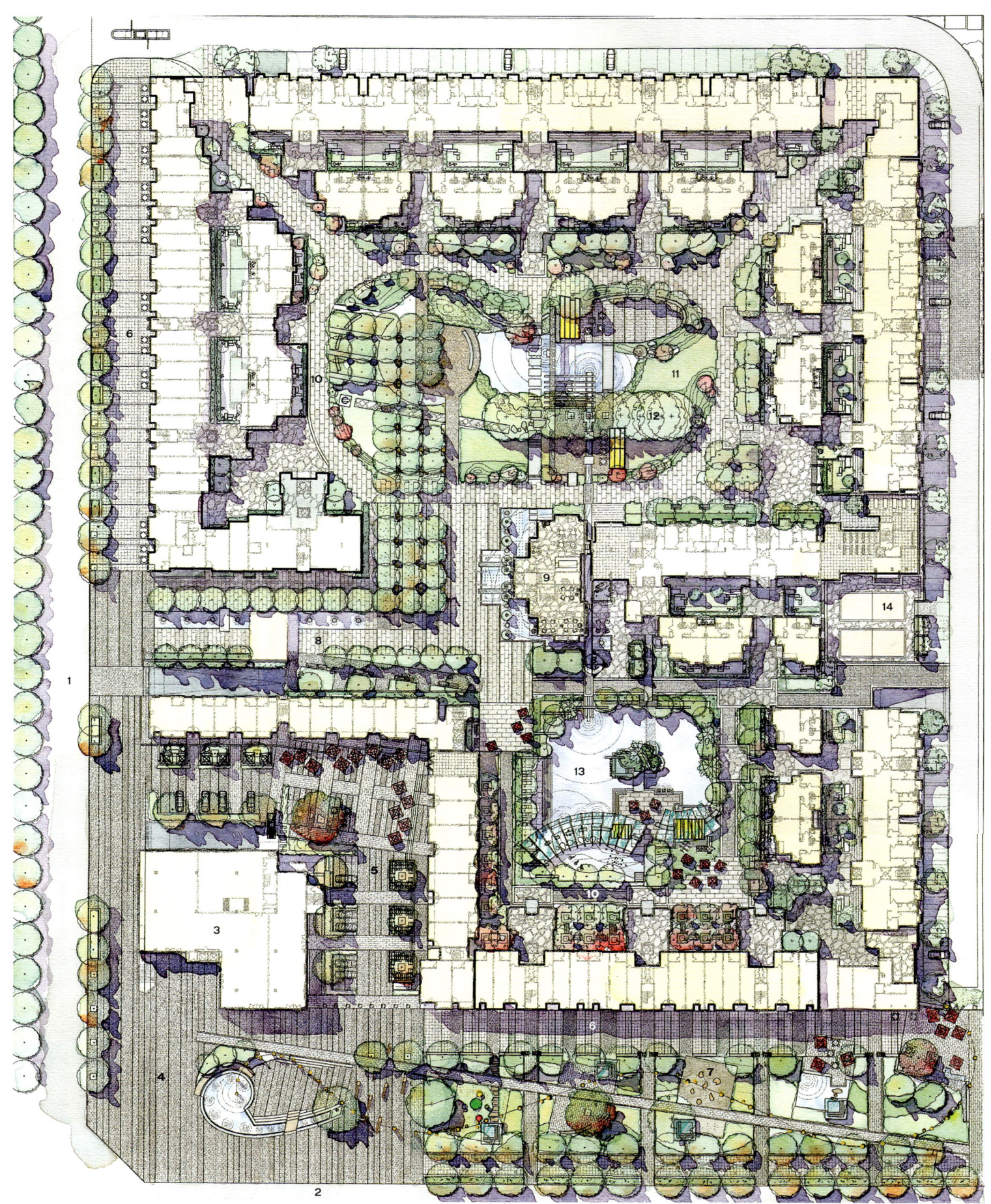

Rendered site plan.

1. Qianfeng Road
2. First Ring Road
3. Commercial Building
4. Qianfeng Plaza
5. Retail Court
6. Retail Streetscape
7. Public Gardens
8. Entry Mews
9. Arrival Court and Breezeway
10. Pedestrian Promenade
11. Garden Court
12. Mature Eucalyptus Trees
13. Pool Court
14. Exercise Court

Metropolitan Apartments
Chengdu, Sichaun Province, China

An example of the new need for quality public space can be seen in PFS's Metropolitan Apartments project in Chengdu. The landscape design for this high-end commercial apartment block integrates a semiprivate garden court with adjacent private patios, while also addressing the surrounding streetscape. Along the First Ring Road, a buffer of urban gardens and canopy trees gives pedestrians a protected setback from the busy street. Retail shops at ground level are open to the public, emphasizing the urban by merging the housing block to the larger workings of the city. A commercial building, located in the rectangular plaza at the corner of Qianfeng Road and the First Ring Road, is also lined with small shops around its perimeter. The mix of small-scale uses and the controlled interaction between private and public contributes to the urbanity of the developing community. Shade trees and seating for shoppers, residents and passing pedestrians structure both Qianfeng Plaza and the retail street. Value is added to the surrounding neighbourhood by the access to street merchants and high quality public space integrated into the overall development.

Metropolitan Apartments demonstrates that the disconnection of new housing estates from the urban fabric of the surrounding city, so common in contemporary Chinese development, can be avoided. At the same time, the careful design of open space with clear distinctions between private and semiprivate neighbourhood spaces and the larger public realm establishes the spatial condition for interaction between different social groups. Considering the uneven development of contemporary Chinese society, this is an extremely salient move.

CMHC Shanghai Sustainable Community Standard
Shanghai, China

Commissioned by Canada Mortgage and Housing Corporation International (CMHC), PFS was a key consultant for the Shanghai Sustainable Community Standard, created for the Shanghai Land Group Company (SLG) to guide the development of new communities in the Shanghai region. The Sustainable Community Standard was developed under the leadership of Ramsay Worden Architects, in close cooperation with SLG. The team customized the database for the Shanghai Sustainable Community Standard in response to local conditions and Canadian precedents. With this tool SLG is able to guide the development of both comprehensive community master planning and individual urban developments. This new standard fills the gaps between the many existing standards at local and national levels in China for sustainability at the scale of individual buildings, the city and the region. It also provides links to locally existing green building programs to guide the design and construction of individual projects.

Consulting on the management of knowledge is extremely important in overcoming the hurdles created by the usual lack of cooperation between different government bodies and local authorities. Connecting local, regional and national standards for urban development is quite difficult because, in many cases, each professional field has unique standards and does not communicate with other governmental bodies. In the hierarchy of the traditional administration, the related fields of water management, urban planning, landscape planning, infrastructure development and regional planning operate strictly on their own. It is a paramount goal to connect existing standards and to encourage collaboration amongst all parties involved. This genre of foreign aid to Chinese urban development is critical as it not only provides a tool for Chinese partnerships; it also brings transparency to the hierarchy of reliance in the jungle of guidelines. Through collaboration, new scientific knowledge is amalgamated with existing Chinese regulation to form a matrix for improved sustainability.

1 Main Entry
2 Existing Pine Forest
3 Existing Mandarin Groves
4 Expanded Water Reservoir System
5 Corporate Headquarters
6 Recreation Complex
7 Retreat
8 Hotel
9 Mid-density Employee Housing
10 Townhouse Complex
11 Detached Residential
12 Driving Range

LEFT PFS Asia's international competition winning site plan submission.
RIGHT A cross section through the site reveals the integral relationship of development objectives to the dramatic topography of the forested hillsides.

Golden Ox Mountain
Changsha, Hunan Province, China

Set within valleys and hillsides of pine forest, bamboo groves, terraced grids of mandarin orange trees and the sculpted remnants of agricultural land, PFS Asia's[24] concept for a new community near Changsha (the capital of Hunan Province) is based on the integration of natural resources with new development. The urban program attempts to mutually benefit the environment and future residents. Existing topography, vegetation, land use and local climatic conditions were analyzed to reach a solution that minimally disturbed the natural environment. The concept respects existing patterns, integrating infrastructure into the natural topography of the site. Stormwater processes are made visible through the treatment of overland flow in surficial streams and ponds. Development is clustered to minimize the disturbance of natural resources and to preserve them for collective enjoyment. The sensibility of this project approach becomes clear when contrasted with the radical urbanization of recent years. Extra expense, due to human impacts on the environment and the subsequent damage of natural resources, has had lasting effects on the administration, who now in some cases seek sustainable forms of development.

THIS PAGE The pyramidal tomb of Shao Hao. OPPOSITE PAGE TOP LEFT Ancient cypress bosque. TOP RIGHT Surrounding farmland. BOTTOM Aerial perspective of proposed processional landscape framework leading to the mausoleum. The surrounding villages form edges along the axis, integrating everyday village life into the visitors' experience of the region. Villagers are able to offer local food and arts to tourists, generating a new source of income.

Shouqiu Shaohao Historic Site
Qufu, Shandong Province, China

Qufu is the hometown of Confucius, the great ancient Chinese ideologist, educator, statesman and philosopher. In 2004, an unprecedented four million tourists, most of them Chinese, came to visit the city. The developing tourism and cultural industries for foreign and Chinese tourists necessitated a new scale and type of urban space generally not needed in China up to this point.

In addition to Confucius' home, Qufu is the location of a diverse array of cultural sites and relics. One such site is a mausoleum, a pyramidal tomb built in 1111, to honour Shao Hao (also named Jin Tian, a mythical emperor in 2600 BC), one of the legendary five emperors who succeeded the first Chinese emperor Huang Di (the Yellow Emperor). In the area of the mausoleum is Shou Qiu, the possible birthplace of the Yellow Emperor; the historic Song Dynasty (960–1279) City Moat; Jingling Temple and archaeological site; and a Neolithic archaeological site of 6,000 year old Dawen culture. This rich and diverse field of cultural relics needed a robust public space design to connect them and to accommodate the masses of expected visitors, a functional wayfinding system and a clear and evocative communication strategy. In addition, functional features such as recreational space, a visitor centre, shopping and eating venues, parking and restrooms needed to be sensitively integrated.

PFS worked with Commonwealth Historic Resource Management and a multidisciplinary team under a Canadian International Development Agency grant to develop a conceptual plan that strings each of the tourist destinations together along a central axis, structuring space at a grand scale and accommodating large crowds of people in generous public spaces for each cultural site. Public spaces for active sport, picnicking and informal recreation are designed for both local residents and tourists, and provide a broad range of flexible space for future development opportunities. A green buffer zone around the historic site and the planting of mature trees complement the already existing ancient cypress trees along the Song Dynasty City Moat. The buffer will cool and filter overland stormwater flow, improving water quality and raising the water level in the moat. Historic water levels will be restored to provide an amenity that is an aesthetically and ecologically appropriate setting for teahouses and other public activities.

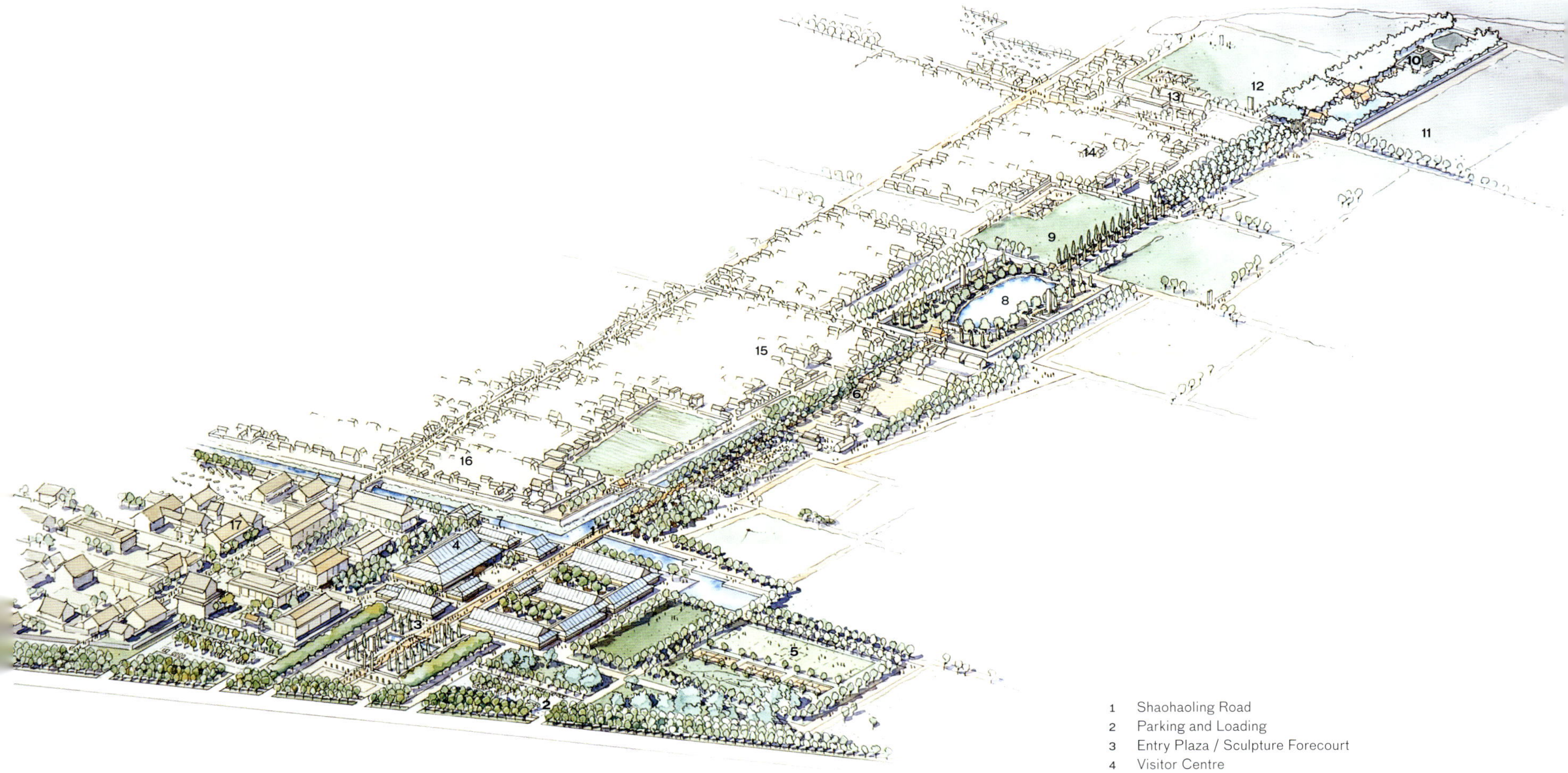

1 Shaohaoling Road
2 Parking and Loading
3 Entry Plaza / Sculpture Forecourt
4 Visitor Centre
5 New Public Park
6 Pottery Factory
7 Song Dynasty City Moat
8 Shouqiu Garden
9 Jingling Temple and Archaeological Site
10 Shaohao Mausoleum
11 Han Burial Site
12 Neolithic Archaeological Site
13 Archaeological Research Centre
14 Jiuxian Village I
15 Jiuxian Village II
16 Jiuxian Village III
17 Jiuxian Village IV

Dr. Eduard Koegel   Global Acculturation

TOP Roofed threshold from one ancient room to the next.
BOTTOM The mausoleum viewed through the bosque of ancient cypress trees.

Notes

1. Susan Brownell, "Making Dream Bodies in Beijing: Athletes, Fashion Models, and the Urban Mystique in China," in Nancy N. Chen, Constance D. Clarke, Suzanne Z. Gottschang and Lyn Jeffery, eds. *China Urban: Ethnographies of Contemporary Culture* (Durham: Duke University Press, 2001), 125.
2. Jeffrey W. Cody, "American Planning in Republican China, 1911–1937," in *Planning Perspectives*, 11 (1996), 339–377.
3. Hussey wrote an autobiography, but says little about his work in China. See Harry Hussey, *My Pleasures and Palaces: An Informal Memoir of Forty Years in Modern China* (Garden City, NY: Doubleday, 1968).
4. See Henry Killam Murphy, "An Architectural Renaissance in China," *Asia* (June 1928), 468–475. Cody analyzed the work of Murphy in China. See Jeffrey W. Cody, *Building in China: Henry K. Murphy's "Adaptive Architecture" 1914–1935* (Seattle: University of Washington Press, 2001).
5. Leo Ou-Fan Lee, *Shanghai Modern: The Flowering of a New Urban Culture in China 1930–1945* (Cambridge: Harvard University Press, 1999).
6. Clarence Stein also knew the influential Chinese architect and planner Liang Sicheng very well. The two first met in 1935 in Peking and again after the war in the United States. See Wilma Fairbank, *Liang and Lin – Partners in Exploring China's Architectural Past* (Philadelphia: University of Pennsylvania Press, 1994), 92.
7. Clarence Stein, *Toward New Towns for America* (Cambridge: MIT Press, 1957), 59. In his dissertation, the author discusses the development of the 'Neighbourhood Unit' in China. See Dr. Eduard Koegel, *Zwei Poelzigschueler in der Emigration: Rudolf Hamburger und Richard Paulick zwischen Shanghai und Ost-Berlin (1930–1955)*. E-publication: http://e-pub.uni-weimar.de/volltexte/2007/991/
8. Norman J. Gordon, "China and the 'Neighbourhood Unit'," *The American City* (October 1946), 122.
9. Dr. Eduard Koegel, "How to Urbanize a Special Economic Zone? The 2005 Biennale of Urbanism and Architecture in Shenzhen," *Yishu – Journal of Contemporary Chinese Art* 5 (Spring/March 2006), 6–12.
10. Ching Fa, "Days the Taching People Will Not Forget," *China Reconstructs XXVI* (April 1977), 16.
11. Foreign Languages Publishing House, ed., *Learning from Dazhai – China's Masses Move Mountains* (Beijing 1976).
12. Chuihua Judy Chung, Jeffrey Inaba, Rem Koolhaas and Sze Tsung Leong, eds., *Great Leap Forward* (Cologne: Taschen, 2001), 27.
13. Detlev Ipsen, Yongning Li, and Holger Weichler, eds., *The Genesis of Urban Landscape: The Pearl River Delta in South China* (Kassel: University of Kassel, Faculty of Architecture, Urban Planning and Landscape Planning, 2005).
14. Barbara Muench, "Verborgene Kontinuität des Chinesischen Urbanismus," *Archplus* 168 (Feb. 2004), 44–49.
15. The euphemism 'incidents with a mass character' stands for 'social unrest and protest'. Zhang Zhiping, "The 11th Five-Year-Plan: Putting the Human Being at the Centre," *Beijing Review* 45, 2005.
16. Dr. Eduard Koegel, "Urbanization Between Control and Campaign" in *totalstadt – Beijing case – High Speed Urbanisation in China*, Gregor Jansen, ed. (Cologne: Walther Koenig, 2006), 364–366.
17. François Jullien, *Du 'temps' – Elements d'une philosphie du vivre* (Paris: Grasset, 2001).
18. Bo Yang, *The Ugly Chinaman and the Crisis of Chinese Culture* (North Sydney, NSW: Allen & Unwin, 1992).
19. Mark Siemons, "Rote Kulturindustrie," *Lettre International* 79 (Winter 2007), 40–45.
20. Foreign Languages Publishing House, ed., *Learning from Dazhai – China's Masses Move Mountains* (Beijing 1976).
21. Judith Shapiro, *Mao's War Against Nature: Politics and the Environment in Revolutionary China* (Cambridge: Cambridge University Press, 2001).
22. Yung Ho Chang, "Preface" in *Yung Ho Chang: Atelier Feichang Jianzhu – A Chinese Practice*, eds. Gutierrez and Portefaix (Hong Kong: Map Book Publishers, 2003).
23. Lu Xin, *China, China... : Western Architects and City Planners in China* (Ostfildern Ruit: Hatje Cantz Publishers, 2008).
24. PFS Asia was a joint venture with Ramsay Worden Architects.

It is the language of landscape that circles back through the First World War and Gettysburg to the days when the Romantic Movement first confronted the primordial wilderness of the New World and saw in the landscape an expression of divine omnipotence.

Elysian Fields
Nature in the service of commemoration

by Jacqueline Hucker

The concept of nature has played an important role in shaping Canadian history and in moulding our cultural and national identities. In the service of commemoration, the variable light and colour of nature's changing seasons can create an elegiac tone, deepening the solemnity of the experience. As an element in military commemoration, nature's sublime power has the ability to touch spiritual and national chords and express our collective sense of obligation to our military dead.

Nature as a poetic idea became a new form of self expression with the rise of Romanticism in Western Europe in the mid-18th century.[1] Partly as a reaction to the Enlightenment and its scientific rationalization of nature, Romanticism elevated intuition, imagination and feeling above reason, and stressed strong emotion as a source of aesthetic experience. In an earlier period, artists, poets and writers had appreciated nature for its picturesque potential and the moral lessons it taught. Romanticism, in contrast, caused them to explore how they felt in the presence of nature. The Romantic process of discovering oneself through nature was quite distinct from the earlier projection of ideas upon nature.

Romanticism arrived in North America in the late 18th and early 19th centuries. In Canada, its emergence coincided with the era of early European settlement. A protagonist in one of the earliest novels written in English Canada expressed the Romantic impact on settlers' imagination of the vast primordial wilderness:

> Sublimity is the characteristic of this western world; the loftiness of the mountains, the grandeur of the lakes and rivers, the majesty of the rocks shaded with a picturesque variety of beautiful trees and shrubs, and crowned with the noblest of the offspring of the forest, which forms the banks of the latter, are as much beyond the power of fancy as that of description.[2]

Romanticism embraced the beautiful, the picturesque and the sublime; the exhilarating sense of awe of the unknown and the unknowable in the presence of nature. As the previous passage makes clear, from the time of their arrival, Europeans in Canada thrilled to the metaphysical power of the wilderness.

At first the preserve of the writer, poet and artist, by the mid-19th century Romanticism had extended beyond the page and canvas to exert its experiential influence on the way buildings related to their natural surroundings. The most notable early Canadian example is Parliament Hill in Ottawa. The site had been a small military outpost of British engineers, positioned to protect the Rideau Canal from invading Americans. In 1856, at a time when the civilian settlement around the garrison amounted to little more than a shantytown in the wilderness, a trio of High Victorian Gothic buildings began to take shape on the edge of a rocky promontory. In contrast to the utilitarian structures they replaced, their bold shapes and picturesque silhouettes exploited to the fullest the sublime nature of their surroundings. As the novelist Anthony Trollope observed when he visited Ottawa in 1862, "I know of no modern Gothic purer of its kind, or less sullied with fictitious ornamentation, and I know no site for such a set of buildings so happy as regards both beauty and grandeur."[3]

The development of Parliament Hill transformed Ottawa. When the town became the capital of the newly created country of Canada in 1867, the image of the Canadian Parliament in a wilderness setting became a visual metaphor for the new country's cultural identity.[4] City dwellers and visitors alike were drawn to the site and, not content to view the perspective from the safety of the plateau, they would venture along an old trail that edged the steep escarpment to experience the sensation of being enveloped by nature. They named the path 'Lovers' Walk'.

By this time, the ideas of 'nature' and God had become intertwined and the sublimity of nature was understood as a testament to God's immanence.[5] In North America, this belief found its most fertile ground in the eastern United States. There, Romanticism was absorbed into a flourishing intellectual and artistic scene centred on Ralph Waldo Emerson. He was the leader of a circle of pre-Civil War writers, artists and reformers who extolled nature's beauty and power, claiming that sublimity in nature emphasized that which was beyond human understanding. Emerson employed natural and cyclical imagery to express his credo that there is no end in nature, that every end is a beginning, and humanity is bonded to nature and the universe by an interconnected circle. Man, he exhorted, could transcend his senses and attain an understanding of beauty, good-

PAGE 210 Vimy Memorial's Mother Canada. Vimy, France.
THIS PAGE Leaf silhouettes are etched randomly in the granite paving below the Canadian Veterans' Memorial wall. Toronto, ON.

ness and truth via meditation and communing with nature through physical work and art.[6]

'Transcendentalism' was the name given to these new beliefs, which can be seen as a rejection of the puritan ideals of the more orthodox religions that held sway over the cultural life of the colonies. Religious leaders had always insisted on a separation of God and nature. They preached that life on earth was insignificant, little more than a preparation for death and the beginning of the true life of the spirit. Nothing illustrated this theological belief better than the New England burying grounds. To emphasize the insignificance of the earthly body, these churchyards were deliberately cut off from the living and left in a neglected, decaying condition.[7] The Transcendentalists viewed the burying grounds as a communal disgrace; a denial of man's spiritual life on earth and a negation of the memory of his past. The movement played an important role in creating a very different approach to burial: the rural cemetery, initiated at Mount Auburn on the outskirts of Cambridge, Massachusetts in 1831.

The word 'cemetery' is derived from Greek, and Mount Auburn was inspired by the ancient Athenian burying ground on the edge of the city near the groves of the Akademy.[8] Representing a return to nature and a reaction against the theological gloom of the churchyard, Mount Auburn was laid out as an expansive park with lawns, mature trees, winding paths and artistic monuments, not unlike the plans for English private parks developed by such landscape architects as William Kent, Capability Brown and Humphry Repton.[9] In such a setting, advocates of the rural cemetery believed, the living could commune with the dead and find solace through the presence of nature.

The impact of Mount Auburn was profound, and by the end of the decade, rural cemeteries had appeared in Western Europe and North America. In 1844, the architect and artist John Howard, having borrowed a guidebook to Mount Auburn, laid out the first Canadian rural cemetery on the scenic property belonging to the Church of St. James in Toronto. Mount Royal and Notre Dame des Neiges cemeteries were opened in Montreal the following decade, as was Cataraqui Cemetery near Kingston, Ontario. These early

Jacqueline Hucker   Elysian Fields

rural cemeteries also functioned as the first public parks, places of fashionable resort where people could escape the bustle of the city to spend a peaceful hour or two strolling through beautiful, natural surroundings.

During the American Civil War, the rural cemetery became the model for another cultural innovation, the military cemetery. In the past, rank and file military dead had been unceremoniously buried in unmarked mass graves. Once modern communications brought the brutal reality of modern warfare to the attention of civilians, this practice could no longer be sustained. Established in 1863 on the Civil War battleground, the Soldiers National Cemetery at Gettysburg represents one of the first cemeteries where the ordinary soldier is honoured in death. It was designed by William Saunders, a Scottish horticulturalist and landscape architect. Having designed a number of early rural cemeteries, Saunders was well acquainted with their picturesque style. At Gettysburg, he sought to evoke a more solemn mood. Each soldier would be buried in his own grave and each grave would be marked by a simple, identical headstone. The graves were arranged in a hemisphere around a central space reserved for the Soldier's National Monument, the cornerstone of which would be laid the following summer. In a report he prepared in 1865 Saunders elaborated on the character he sought through his design. Evoking Edmond Burke's theory of the sublime, he explained his purpose, using Transcendentalist imagery:

> The prevailing expression of the Cemetery should be that of *simple grandeur*. Simplicity is that element of beauty in a scene that leads gradually from one object to another, in easy harmony....Grandeur, in this application, is closely allied to solemnity. Solemnity is an attribute of the sublime. The sublime in scenery may be defined as continuity of extent, the repetition of objects in themselves simple and commonplace....To produce an expression of grandeur, we must avoid intricacy and great variety of parts....Ample spaces of lawns are provided; these will form vistas as seen from the drive, showing the monument and other prominent points. As the trees spread and extend, the quiet beauty produced by these open spaces of lawn will yearly become more striking.[10]

At the end of the dedication ceremony, the officiating clergyman employed similar Transcendentalist imagery in his closing prayer, intoning that, "As the trees are not dead, though their foliage is gone, so our heroes are not dead, though their forms are fallen."[11]

The Soldiers National Cemetery at Gettysburg subsequently served as a strong source of inspiration for the First World War soldier cemeteries. As at Gettysburg, the First World War battle landscape became a metaphor for death.[12] For those who sought to find meaning in the carnage, it took on a sacred identity. Poets, writers and artists imagined the war in terms of this myth, and their work frequently expressed elegiac sensibilities of loss and obligation which demanded that "somehow the past be kept present."[13]

Canadian Police and Peace Officers' Memorial

Tomb of the Unknown Soldier

Canadian Veterans' Memorial

Vimy Memorial Restoration

LEFT Allward's original intention for subtle grading to seamlessly bind the monument to the earth was fulfilled in the restoration. RIGHT A weighty horizontal stone marker crafted from three massive blocks of Belgian bluestone was used to subtly indicate the main entry to the Vimy Monument area. PAGES 218–219 A soft south light captures one mood of Allward's masterpiece. The dramatic scale and form of the Vimy Monument called for a very simple approach to its adjacent landscape. Originally sited within the devastated, pockmarked WWI battlefield, the immediate surrounding land was carefully chiseled into a crisp ribbon leading to the monument while the remaining ground endures as untouched battlefield terrain.

Vimy Memorial Restoration
Vimy, France

Canada's First World War memorial stands on Vimy Ridge, a height of land in northern France whose capture in April 1917 was arguably this country's greatest military accomplishment of the war. It has also come to be viewed as an event that awakened a nascent sense of Canadian nationalism. In Canadian eyes, the loss of lives during the battle transformed the ridge into a sacred site, sanctified by the blood of its fallen soldiers, many of whom had disappeared forever into the denuded and pockmarked landscape. When the architect and sculptor of the Vimy Monument, Walter Allward, was asked in 1921 for an explanation of its meaning, his response that he had been inspired by a dream of a war landscape haunted by the ghosts of fallen Canadians reveals the pervasiveness of the myth.[14]

Prime Minister Mackenzie King showed a similar sensibility to the war-torn landscape, noting in his diary:

> I made a strong plea for conserving a tract of one or two square miles of Vimy Ridge as consecrated hallowed ground around Allward's memorial to be erected. The real memorial being the ridge itself, one of earth's altars, on which Canadians sacrificed for the cause of humanity....This is Canada's altar on European soil.[15]

Following the prime minister's suggestion, in 1922 France ceded 100 hectares on Vimy Ridge to Canada to be laid out as a memorial park. More than 3,000 Canadians had died taking the ridge. By the time Canada took possession of the site, most of their bodies had been removed from the battlefield and laid to rest in one of two cemeteries located within the boundaries. As at Gettysburg, the belief that the land was sacred ensured for it a commemorative role equal to that of the monument.

If Vimy Ridge possessed metaphysical qualities for Canada, physically it was a barren stretch of land. The area had been mercilessly pounded by artillery for three weeks prior to the April 1917 assault and was in terrible condition. Pitted underfoot with deep dugouts, mine craters, trenches and shell holes, the ridge presented an image of nature annihilated by war. It took more than two years to clear the site of war debris such as barbed wire entanglements, burst cannons and shells before the memorial park could be contemplated.

The design principles that guided the layout of Vimy Memorial Park echo those enunciated by William Saunders for the Civil War cemetery. The monument was prominently sited at the highest point of the ridge and was designed to appear as though it was rising directly from the battlefield. Its outline was silhouetted above the horizon line, the Transcendentalist image of where 'heaven and earth meet'. When the monument was completed in 1936, the land around it was seeded with grass but otherwise deliberately left in its scarred, undulating state. Tens of thousands of young Austrian pines were planted across the remainder of the site. Their dark, repetitive forms reinforced the elegiac mood of the site. As the trees grew, they were pruned to allow light to filter through the understory to bring life back to the ground below. Two wide allées were planted through this forest to provide long, expansive vistas of the monument against the sky. Not surprisingly, more myths have been established about the site, including the erroneous but poignant belief that a tree had been planted for every Canadian soldier who lost their life in France.

It has been said that the only response to tragic events like the First World War lies in the resilience with which the situation is confronted, and "the depth and artistry with which it is framed."[16] At Vimy Ridge, Canadians vowed to preserve in perpetuity both the memory of military victory and the price it extracted in human life

and suffering. An unflinching acknowledgement of the true cost of the war is rooted in the cultural landscape. Such a wish for permanence was not new, but the extent to which those involved were prepared to go to ensure permanence is, in the words of the cultural historian Thomas Laqueur, "fraught with the thoroughly modern, historicist fear of forgetting."[17]

The approach to commemoration arising out of the First World War has served as a model for remembering all who die in the line of public duty. However, in spite of the ongoing respect shown to the memory of Canada's fallen servicemen, the metaphysical character that was once unhesitatingly attributed to the Vimy landscape in the years between the wars had largely evaporated by the 1960s. The site's contemplative character had been gradually undermined by careless interventions and incremental changes to meet real or perceived visitor requirements. Moreover, from the 1970s onwards, the battle landscape was increasingly interpreted only in terms of military history, and ceremonies of remembrance were confined to the area around the monument. The battle landscape was simultaneously made off limits in the name of public safety, and visitors could no longer tread the sacred ground.

A major restoration of the memorial from 2005 to 2007 offered a much needed opportunity to rehabilitate part of the park and restore a sense of the sacred to the site. Julian Smith, principal of Julian Smith & Associates Architects in Ottawa, teamed with Daniel Lefèvre, principal of Cabinet Lefèvre of Paris, to oversee the restoration of the Vimy Memorial. Greg Smallenberg of Phillips Farevaag Smallenberg (PFS) oversaw the restoration of the landscape around the monument. Inspired by the principles of the original landscape plan, extraneous features that had appeared across the site were removed and the ground around the monument was regraded in order to fulfill Walter Allward's vision of a seamless connection between the monument and the battlefield. With these improvements, the clarity of the site's original design has re-emerged.

Change can, of course, embody its own poetic qualities. Sensitive change signals the continuing value of a commemorative site for its community. The memorial park had never had a suitable entranceway, one that clearly established a threshold separating the sacred site from the adjoining land. Accordingly, as part of the restoration project, a new entrance was built to communicate to visitors their passage into a special place. A stand of white birch now shelters the entrance from the approaching public roadway. Through their natural life cycle, the trees will embody the spiritual message of regeneration that underlies the symbolic meaning of the whole park. A new management plan for the site has recently been prepared. Among its recommendations are that the forest should be protected and extended in accordance with the original design of the memorial park and that some of its pathways should again be opened to the public. If adopted, the recommendations would be relatively easy to introduce, but their impact would be profound. Walking through the silent forest, a visitor becomes enveloped by the Elysian power of place where, even though the past is now thoroughly past, the landscape still bears witness to war.

One of the podium walls carved with the names of the more than 11,000 Canadian soldiers who fought in WWI but whose remains were never recovered. A simple approach to the ground plane and the careful detailing of new uplighting at the base of the wall ensure that nothing detracts from the solemnity of this work. PAGES 222–223 Mother Canada and a fellow Canadian quietly survey the coal-rich Douai Plains and the expansive French landscape that so many fought and died for.

Jacqueline Hucker   Elysian Fields

OPPOSITE PAGE Haunting stands of Austrian pine are found throughout the memorial site. The 80-year-old monoculture is threatened as this species is not long lived. Efforts to establish a comprehensive reforestation strategy will hopefully ensure that the spirit of these woods remains in perpetuity.
THIS PAGE TOP The monument viewed from a distance through one of two cleared axes that were established in the original 20th century plan.
BOTTOM Sheep graze throughout the battlefield terrain. After more than 80 years and repeated attempts to locate and remove them, the land is still riddled with unexploded ordnances. The sheep are a safer means of maintaining this powerful landscape. PAGES 226–227 An early autumn morning at Vimy Ridge.

Tomb of the Unknown Soldier
National War Memorial, Confederation Square
Ottawa, ON

The landscape of the Vimy Memorial is Canadian rather than European in spirit. It plays upon unfettered scale, wide horizon lines and an infinite sky, not unlike the landscape surveyed by Canada's Parliament Buildings. The city of Ottawa grew out of a landscape of water, distant hills and sky. Three waterways, the Ottawa River, the Rideau River and the Rideau Canal[18] lapped around its edges, playing a large role in industry, commerce and transportation.[19] As the city matured and new forms of transport emerged, Ottawa's relationship to the water became less overt. By the late 1930s, Ottawa was attempting to change its structure and character based upon grand, Beaux Arts city planning principles. It was in this context that the National War Memorial was erected in a newly created city square near the Parliament Buildings. It has since become the focus of a national memorial service held on November 11th each year.

Confederation Square, the site of the memorial, was fashioned out of two 19th century bridges spanning the Rideau Canal at the point where it emptied into the Ottawa River.

The new square transformed the centre of Ottawa, but in the process severed old connections between the upper town and the waterways. Ringed with motor traffic, the square was never a total success. Over the years, as traffic steadily increased, the National War Memorial suffered the fate of many of its urban counterparts, becoming less accessible, less visible and arguably less relevant for the population.[20]

In 2000, Confederation Square became the focus of another act of military commemoration charged with Canadian nationalism when the federal government repatriated the body of an unknown Canadian soldier of the First World War. The Unknown Soldier had become a powerful symbol of commemoration since the burial on November 11th 1920 of the first such individual, among kings and poets in Westminster Abbey. Eighty years later, the body of a Canadian soldier was exhumed from a cemetery near Vimy Ridge and laid to rest in a specially designed tomb set into Confederation Square in front of the National War Memorial. Here the tomb is watched over by a ceremonial military guard. The presence of a Canadian Unknown Soldier in the national capital has served to lessen the temporal and spatial distance between Canada and its overseas

LEFT The tomb is carved from three large pieces of Caledonia dark granite intended to complement but not mimic the granite of the war memorial itself. RIGHT The terrace was subtly modified to provide steps that integrate with sloped, barrier free access to the upper plinth. Both the restoration of Confederation Square and the addition of the Tomb of the Unknown Soldier were the focus of a carefully orchestrated lighting concept developed by Martin Conboy Lighting Design Inc. (MCLD). To communicate the design intentions and the impact that the tomb would have on the National War Memorial, full size site mock-ups of the options were prepared along with many night-lighting tests.

Jacqueline Hucker   Elysian Fields   229

THIS PAGE November 11th Remembrance Day ceremony at the National War Memorial. OPPOSITE PAGE TOP The lid of the sarcophagus was carved by Maurice Joanisse, a Dominion carver with the Government of Canada. British Columbian artist Mary Ann Lui was responsible for the highly crafted bronzework on the sarcophagus—a composition of the symbols of the altar at Vimy: the helmet, sword, laurel branch and maple leaves. BOTTOM SERIES The repatriation of the remains of Canada's Unknown Soldier on May 28, 2000.

battle sites. At the same time, it has also made the National War Memorial more relevant.

To accommodate the Tomb of the Unknown Soldier, the National War Memorial was increased in size and refurbished with new stonework and a new landscape plan, whose features echo those found in military cemeteries. The original siting of the National War Memorial had been carefully planned to ensure that it would remain silhouetted against the broad sky above the Ottawa River. The expansion of the square provided a matching sense of open space, reflecting the importance of the war memorial to the nation.

To lessen the impact of circulating traffic on pedestrians, a flight of steps was built descending from the square under the ring road to the Rideau Canal below. From there a pedestrian way runs along the canal beneath the road system, to emerge into the landscape of the Ottawa River valley. The result of this innovative feature has been very positive: the square has been reintegrated into the fabric of the city, while the pedestrian way has created a new and interesting route across a historical area. At the same time, the city has been reconnected to its waterways, thereby bringing nature back into the city. The Confederation Square project has succeeded in reaffirming Ottawa's experiential relationship to its landscape while reinvigorating its military history and commemorative ceremonies.

Jacqueline Hucker Elysian Fields

LEFT The memorial is composed of panels of etched glass and sandblasted stainless steel interconnected with a stainless steel frame and set on a cut stone base. RIGHT A design development detail showing the careful incorporation of the memorial with the historical perimeter fence that surrounds the escarpment of Parliament Hill. PAGES 234–235 Etched glass units, narrow in width and set with generous interstitial spaces, are modulated by the rhythm set by the historical fence stanchions behind. This design approach helped to address the issue of permeability to the dramatic views of the Ottawa River and Supreme Court of Canada beyond.

Canadian Police and Peace Officers' Memorial
Parliament Hill, Ottawa, ON

The understanding of nature as a poetic idea is illustrated in a second contemporary memorial in Ottawa, the Canadian Police and Peace Officers' Memorial. Located on Parliament Hill, the memorial to police officers was first unveiled in 1994. It consisted of a granite stone engraved with the name of 227 officers who had been slain since the establishment of the force in 1879. A few months later a second stone, commemorating peace officers who had died in the line of duty, was unveiled. The memorial list was subsequently expanded again to include the names of slain officers from other Canadian law enforcement agencies. If the ever-increasing list of people deserving commemoration by a memorial stone on the Hill was not to overrun an already crowded site, a new commemorative approach was needed.

The solution realized for the Canadian Police and Peace Officers' Memorial was simple and Romantic in spirit. The names were etched into thick glass panels, which were then installed with military-like precision along an iron fence that runs around the edge of the steep cliff. Their location affords a most sublime view up the Ottawa River to a far horizon line. The simple Gothic posts silhouetted against the skyline are an elegant framing device for the glass panels, which become visible when light is caught along the edges of the etched names. Together they encapsulate the Romantic ideas of experience and aspiration. Enveloped in the expansive landscape of the river and illuminated by an ever-changing natural light, this simple memorial creates a dialogue between law and freedom, humanity and divinity, death and spiritual rebirth.

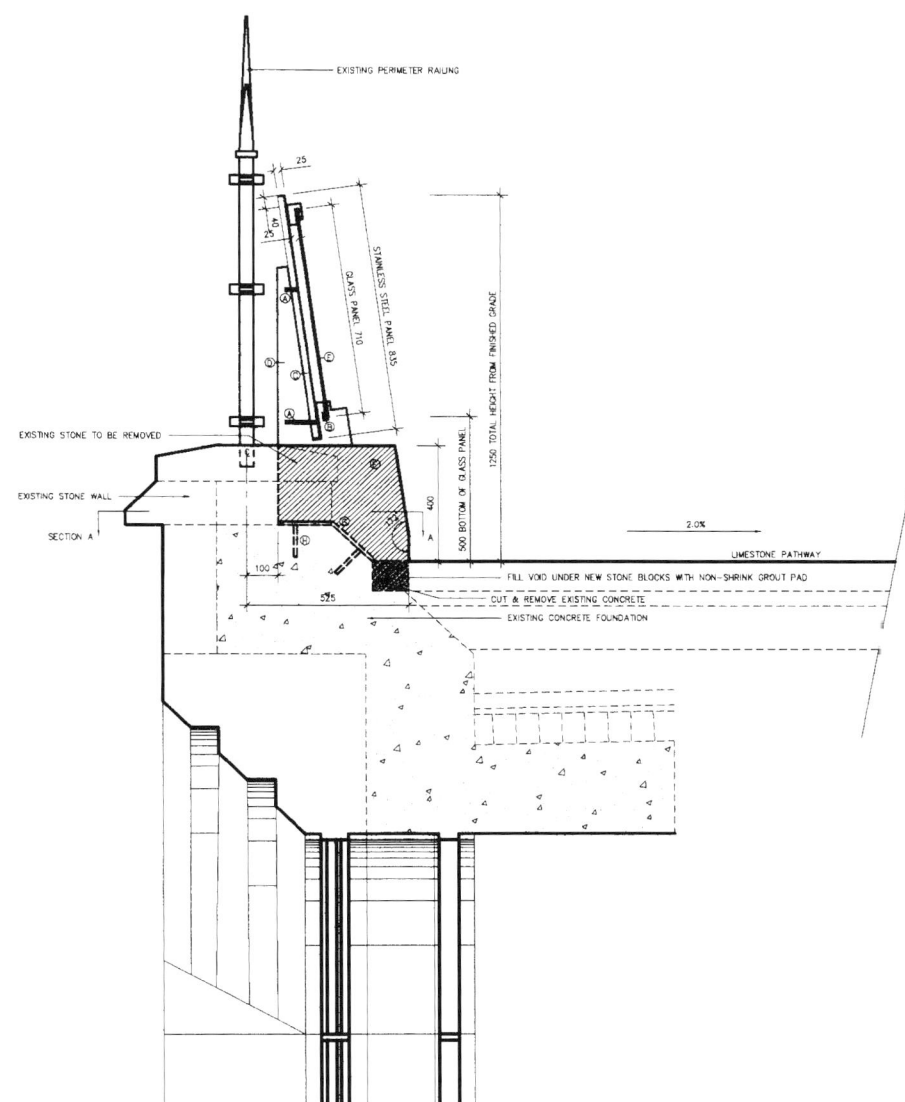

Canadian Veterans' Memorial
Queen's Park, Toronto, ON

As demonstrated by the Canadian Police and Peace Officers' Memorial, organizations understandably wish to see their monuments in conspicuous places in the community. Often this will involve locations where space is at a premium, and where insertion of a new structure must be undertaken with care to ensure the character of the cultural landscape is not undermined. Such was the challenge associated with the Canadian Veterans' Memorial in Toronto. Veterans pressed for the erection of a prominent memorial on the grounds of the Ontario Legislature and were subsequently granted a site at the southwest corner of the grounds in close proximity to the Legislative Building. The prominent location spoke not only to the community's appreciation of the veterans' contribution to Ontario history, but also to the veterans' political power. PFS was given the task of balancing the wishes of the veterans for a distinguished structure with the need to protect the character of the historic cultural landscape. With this consideration in mind, the designers created a monument in the form of a long low lying wall made up of highly polished black granite panels. A laser-etched photographic collage along these panels, by Canadian military war artist Alan McKay Harding, traces Ontario's military engagements and peacekeeping activities since the 1860s.

The Canadian Veterans' Memorial is one of a number of new monuments that reveal the influence of the Vietnam Veterans Memorial in Washington, DC. Sharing its predecessor's desire not to detract from important sight lines, it lies low in the landscape. But unlike the Vietnam Veterans Memorial, which is set into an open landscape and was designed to respond to the needs of a generation in mourning, the Ontario monument is partially hidden from view by a grove of mature trees. The trees create a private space where a second seating wall invites passersby to pause and contemplate our long military history and its implications for the future.

Rising behind the Canadian Veterans' Memorial, aligned with its midpoint, is a newly planted young red maple. Selected for its blazing red autumn colour, the tree is identified as the Memorial Maple Tree, a symbol of sacrifice and regeneration. As one of Canada's primary national symbols, the history of the 'red maple leaf' dates to the mid-19th century when the 100th Regiment, the precursor to the Royal Canadian Regiment, adopted it as an official symbol.[21]

In the autumn, the symbolic language of the red maple deepens one's experience of the memorial. It is the language of landscape that circles back through the First World War and Gettysburg to the days when the Romantic movement first confronted the primordial wilderness of the New World and saw in the landscape an expression of divine omnipotence.

Designing military monuments whose rhetorical message will remain relevant from one generation to the next presents obvious challenges. Those like the Canadian Veterans' Memorial, where landscape plays an equal role with stone and bronze, can create an evocative mood that is not easily duplicated or sustained in these other materials. Landscape features can change and deteriorate, and when they are not maintained, a monument's metaphysical quality may weaken. But, under the best conditions, the symbolic power of landscape can touch our souls and elide the gulf between past and present.

TOP Early napkin sketch of the winning scheme. BOTTOM The memorial carefully integrated with the historic grounds of Queen's Park.

Jacqueline Hucker   Elysian Fields

1 Black Granite Landscape Wall
2 Alan McKay Harding Collage
3 Black Granite Seating Wall
4 Bronze End Walls
5 Bronze Dedication Podium
6 Memorial Maple Tree
7 Existing Trees

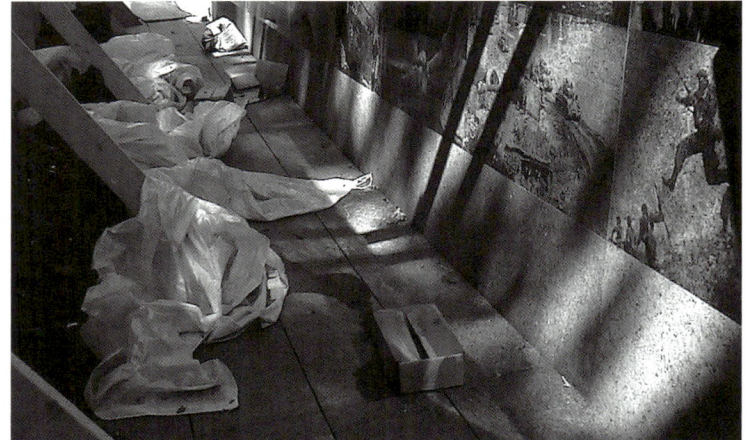

OPPOSITE PAGE TOP Rendered site plan. BOTTOM LEFT AND RIGHT The installation of granite panels and Allan McKay Harding's imagery was kept under hoarding until the memorial's grand opening. THIS PAGE The placement of the 3-metre high wall creates two topographic planes that allow the memorial to express a grand scale while receding into the landscape to preserve views within Queen's Park. The wall tilts forward in the eastern section and backward in the western section as a metaphor of the strategies employed in war and in peace.

Jacqueline Hucker Elysian Fields

Looking west to the memorial in fall. Future hedge planting along the wall's east and west planes will expand its visual length by another 20 metres.

Notes

1. The phrase 'nature as a poetic idea' has been borrowed from Anne Whiston Spirn, *The Language of Landscape* (New Haven and London: Yale University Press, 1998).
2. Susan Glickman, *The Picturesque and the Sublime: A Poetics of the Canadian Landscape* (Montreal and Kingston: McGill-Queen's University Press, 1998), 10–11.
3. Anthony Trollope, *North America* (New York: Harper and Brothers Publishers, 1862), 68.
4. See Doug Paterson's essay "Place, Body, Memory – Placemaking in a Global World" in this volume for more on Parliament Hill.
5. Barbara Novak, *Nature and Culture: American Landscape and Painting 1825–1875* (New York, Toronto: Oxford University Press, 1995), 3.
6. Emerson's ideas are contained in his small book *Nature* that he published in 1836 (Boston, New York: James Munroe and Company, 1836).
7. Richard Morris, *Sinners, Lovers and Nature* (New York: State University of New York Press, 1997), 65.
8. Garry Wills, *Lincoln at Gettysburg: The Words that Remade America* (New York: Simon & Schuster, 1992), 63.
9. Wills, *Lincoln*, 64.
10. Wills, *Lincoln*, 70.
11. Wills, *Lincoln*, 29.
12. Samuel Hynes, *A War Imagined: The Great War and English Culture* (New York: Atheneum, 1991), 195–202.
13. Thomas Laqueur, "The Past's Past," *The London Review of Books* 18 (9 September, 1996), 3.
14. "Vimy Clippings," box 2, 5055, Allward Fonds (Queens University Archives).
15. William Lyon Mackenzie King, *Diaries*, 26 April 1922, Library and Archives Canada.
16. Terry Eagleton, *The Meaning of Life* (Oxford: Oxford University Press, 2007), 20.
17. Laqueur, "The Past's Past."
18. In 1832 The Rideau Canal was cut through the countryside to link the Great Lakes to the Ottawa River.
19. For a discussion on the interrelationship between landscape and the urban environment see: Spirn, *Language and Landscape*, especially her introduction.
20. See Julian Smith's essay "Cultural Landscapes – Architecture and Landscape in the 21st Century" in this volume for more on Confederation Square.
21. By the end of the First World War, the maple had become firmly associated with Canada's fallen servicemen. An early example of this occurred in 1921 at the unveiling of the Cross of Sacrifice in a cemetery near Vimy Ridge, when Prime Minister Arthur Meighen observed that: "Around and all over are being planted the Maples of Canada in the thought that her sons will rest better under the trees which they know so well." RG25, Vol. 325, *Liverpool Courier*, 4 July 1921, Library and Archives Canada.

What we see from particular nature-based practices in British Columbia is a kind of 'learning from landscape'—the formation of a sensibility to landscape that goes beyond scenic production. Emily Carr's SuperNatural would be a nature that is about emergence, multiplicity and open-endedness, where landscapes are continually made up of, and created by, multiple actors. The characteristics of this SuperNatural—that nature is entwined with culture, that it is embedded and multisensory, and that process and movement trump form—lend themselves to a strategy of emergence, where design springs from a direct relationship to site and all of its myriad cultural and ecological histories.

SuperNatural
The burden of wilderness

by Kelty McKinnon

In Vancouver, nature looms large. Snowcapped mountains form a dramatic backdrop to the city skyline, a thousand-acre temperate rainforest is located just blocks from the downtown core, and water surrounds the city on three sides in the form of bays, inlets and rivers. In the 1980s, the British Columbia Ministry of Small Business, Tourism and Culture developed the campaign 'Supernatural BC', promoting and defining the province by its spectacular and diverse Edenic scenery. The Supernatural campaign reinforced the primacy of nature over culture, placing wilderness at the fore of provincial and civic identity. Landscape architects working in this context have had to contend with the burden of wilderness, where 'landscape' has been forcibly equated to 'Nature'.

Vancouver's obsession with its natural environment is in keeping with a general Canadian preoccupation with wilderness. "Above all, (Canada) is a country in which nature makes a direct impression on the...mind,"[1] Northrop Frye writes,

> a country divided by...great stretches of wilderness, so that its frontier is a circumference rather than a boundary; a country with huge rivers and islands that most of its natives have never seen...this is the environment that (Canadians) have to grapple with, and many of the imaginative problems it presents have no counterpart in the United States, or anywhere else.[2]

In size, Canada is second only to Russia, yet its population, a mere 33 million (almost a tenth of the USA), largely huddles close to the American border. The general perception that north of this urban zone is a vast, rugged, unpeopled wilderness led Northrop Frye to identify the Canadian mentality as a 'garrison mind'[3] and Margaret Atwood to describe it as an 'obsession with survival'.[4] This myth of the great, unpeopled Canadian north was elaborated by the Group of Seven, whose collective manifesto was to capture in paint what they saw as a distinctly Canadian consciousness. Finding Old World approaches to painting ineffective in expressing the 'authentic' Canadian landscape, the group sought to paint what they saw as the 'essence' of the land through a grounded knowledge of particular, remote Northern landscapes.

While the Group of Seven's imagery reflected a predominant focus on Eastern and Northern Canada, the British Columbian painter Emily Carr, loosely affiliated with the Group, offered a divergent image of Canadian nature, one particular to the Pacific West Coast. Carr joined the Group's quest to express the nation's cultural identity by painting the coastal landscape, but her style and choice of subject matter redefined what landscape could be. While the archetypal Canadian landscape for the Group of Seven was one of pristine and rugged emptiness, Carr's was an active and intimate wilderness inhabited by people, where people and nature were closely intertwined.

Carr's writing at times seems old-fashioned in its fascination with transcendentalism and the sublime, but in her painting there is a persistent determination to articulate something beyond, and perhaps counter to these concepts. Her assertion that nature projects its own subjectivity, and that it is intertwined with culture, anticipated an alternate practice for landscape architects working through the myth of virginal Nature as the 'scenographic other'. Carr's writing and painting embody three related landscape characteristics that distinguish her conception of nature from her contemporaries and suggest alternative approaches to design.

First, Carr communicates a vision of nature that is not antithetical to culture. The Group of Seven, and indeed most North American landscape painters and photographers of the time including Ansel Adams, actively constructed images of virgin wilderness by cropping any signs of people or history from the frame. The aesthetic they sought was one of purity: an image of land before human occupation. Lawren Harris described this idealized space as, "a vast expanse of immensely varied, virgin land reaching into the remote north," and goes on to laud the purifying effects of nature: "Our whole country is cleansed by the pristine and replenishing air which sweeps out of that great hinterland."[5]

But while the British Columbian coast is exceptionally wild, it was also densely occupied for over 10,000 years by a number of cultural groups including the Haida, Tsimshian, Nuxalk, Northern Wakashan, Kwakwakw'wakw, Nuu-chah-nulth and the Coast Salish. By the time Emily Carr began to record these landscapes, an estimated 90% of the indigenous population had been decimated by smallpox and other

PAGE 242 Coal Harbour seawall with views of Burrard Inlet, North Vancouver and the Coast Mountains beyond. Vancouver, BC. THIS PAGE Rocky beach at Cates Park / Whey-ah-Wichen.

diseases introduced by Europeans. While many communities have thrived since that time, others were abandoned and gradually overtaken by forest. Carr painted both the imagery of everyday village life—children playing in front of cedar longhouses, canoes pulled up onto beaches—and the abandoned villages with their totems, welcome figures and longhouses overtaken by foliage. In both the peopled and unpeopled villages, there is an integration, indeed, a conflation of nature and culture.[6] The forest is seen as historical, occupied and mutable, and the products of settlement seem to grow out of it. As geographer Bruce Braun suggests,

> the natures we may seek...do not lie external to culture and history, but are themselves artifactual: objects made, materially and semiotically, by multiple actors (not all of them human), and through many different historical and spatial practices (ranging from landscape painting to the science of ecology).[7]

Carr's depiction of nature also included mined and forested landscapes.[8] But rather than depicting resource extraction as destructive, her landscapes were rendered with a "mood...not one of despair, but of renewal and regeneration."[9] Unlike the Group of Seven, Carr depicted landscapes as bound up with culture, and constantly changing.

Second, Emily Carr's work departs from a scenographic approach to landscape that addresses the land as a distanced, aestheticized object in favour of an embedded and embodied intimacy. In his essay 'Eidetic Operations and New Landscapes', James Corner contrasts these attitudes in his description of *landskip* versus *landschaft*.[10] The old English term *landskip*

> at first referred not to land but a picture of it, as in the later selectively framed representations of seventeenth century Dutch Landschaf paintings. Soon after the appearance of this genre of painting, the scenic concept was applied to the land itself in the form of large-scale rural vistas, designed estates, and ornamental garden art.

In contrast, the Old German term *landschaft* refers to "the environment of a working community, a setting comprising dwellings, pastures, meadows and fields and surrounded by unimproved forest or meadow." In other words, it was a relational amalgam of nature and culture requiring the situatedness of an insider versus the point of view of an outsider.

The distancing and detachment of traditional landscape painting was simply not possible in the rainforests of British Columbia. BC's coastal temperate rainforest is characterized in part by its numerous canopy layers, its wide range of tree sizes and ages, the abundance of epiphytes (plants living on the surface of other plants such as mosses, lichens and ferns), and its impenetrable understory of rapidly growing salal, salmonberry, alder and fern. Perhaps Carr's proclivities grew out of a reaction to the sheer bigness and density of things. Her forest interiors are cropped closely, stretched to the edge of the picture frame, "with no sky above and no anchoring earth below...."[11] In a letter to Eric Brown she writes, "Woods and skies out west are big. You can't pin them down."[12] Rather than lapsing into the folly of attempting to see and portray things in their totality, Carr layered numerous gradations of green to depict either an impenetrable, living wall or light, air and the space between branches. On positioning herself in these woods, she writes,

> You go, find a space wide enough to sit in and clear enough so that the undergrowth is not drowning you....Everything is green. Everything is waiting and still. Slowly things begin to move, to slip into their place....Nothing is still now. Life is sweeping through the spaces....You must be still in order to hear and see.[13]

Carr strove to paint a multisensory landscape, one that went beyond the visual to include sound, smell, touch and the kinesthetic; senses that require proximity and interaction. She was interested in synesthesia, where a secondary sensation accompanies an actual perception. In pondering this sensory overlap she wrote, "If the air is jam full of sounds which we can tune in with, why should it not also be full of feels and smells...."[14] Of course as a painter, she did not discard the visual, but attempted to communicate the sensual density of particular, intimate and relational environments.

Third, in Carr's later paintings, objects dissolve. Form gives way to process and movement. As she became more and more interested in capturing the dynamic landscape around her, the "well

LEFT Boardwalk through the woods at Cates Park / Whey-ah-Wichen. North Vancouver, BC. RIGHT Emily Carr, *Cedar*, 1942, oil on canvas. Collection of the Vancouver Art Gallery, Emily Carr Trust.

defined, contained and very tangible sculpted forms" of her painted trees, poles, rocks, leaves and skies "lost their defining edges, their particular substance...as they sway(ed) and merge(d) in a mutual life of movement."[15] Likewise, her earlier work positioned objects in the fore, middle and background as a device to express space and to frame a central object as the focus of the painting. As Carr concentrated more and more on expressing movement, these objects were discarded or merged together into one sweeping gesture of energy:

> Direction, that's what I'm after, everything moving together, relative movement, sympathetic movement, connected movement, flowing, liquid, universal movement, all directions summing up in one grand direction, leading the eye forward, and satisfying. So to control direction of movement that the whole structure sways, vibrates and rocks....[16]

Tree, earth and the spaces between were whorled dynamically together in the depiction of pure movement.

This particular characteristic grew out of an intimate familiarity with the rapid, dense growth of BC's coastal forests and the active relationship between air, sea, rain and vegetation. Carr's paintings depict ocean, beach, forest, sky and ground as a "living arena of processes and exchanges over time,"[17] and are pulled together into a portrayal of dynamic flux. In such an environment, "form is provisional and temporary, constantly on its way to becoming something else,"[18] impossible to pin down. In discussing contemporary landscape architecture, James Corner writes, "the discipline of ecology suggests that individual agents acting across a broad field of operation produce incremental and cumulative effects that continually evolve the shape of an environment over time."[19] Carr understood this notion of ecology at a time when nature was seen as constant and immutable. Beyond surficial effects, she attempted to communicate nonlinear processes and flows, and the emergent forces of nature. Carr describes the "unquenchable vitality of trees":

> There is nothing so strong as growing. Nothing can drown that force that splits rocks and pavements and spreads over the fields. To meet and check it one must fight and sweat, but it is never conquered.

Kelty McKinnon   SuperNatural

The city of Vancouver with its dramatic backdrop of forested mountains and snowcapped peaks.

Man may pattern it and change its variety and shape, but leave it for even a short time and off it goes back to its own, swamping and swallowing man's puny intentions. No killing nor stamping down can destroy it. Life is in the soil.[20]

Subjectivity shifts from a removed, external, sole author to a relational field of interacting subjects that is the landscape itself. Carr's paintings depict landscape as emerging from this "vibrating, coiling, cascading" movement

The Work of Phillips Farevaag Smallenberg

Immersed in the British Columbian landscape for nearly two decades, the firm of Phillips Farevaag Smallenberg (PFS) has innately absorbed these 'lessons of landscape': that nature and culture, particularly in a setting like Vancouver, are deeply intertwined; that landscape can be both scenic and embedded simultaneously; and that landscape is as much about process and metabolism as it is about form. The work of PFS doesn't assert any singular style or attitude; each project is developed individually, with a unique direction emerging from site conditions and collaborations. The following three local projects describe three different approaches to Vancouver's obsession with nature and the idea of nature in general: Coal Harbour Marina Neighbourhood Phase One Seawall, Langara College Library, and Cates Park / Whey-ah-Wichen Master Plan and Cultural Resources Interpretation Management Plan.

Cates Park / Whey-ah-Wichen

Langara College Library

Coal Harbour
Marina Neighbourhood

LEFT View from Stanley Park over Burrard Inlet to Coal Harbour's Harbour Green Park, the seawall and the city of Vancouver beyond. RIGHT Looking west along the seawall toward the Coal Harbour Community Centre and residential podium point towers above. Low tide reveals a rich marine ecology of mussels, starfish, barnacles, seaweed, crabs and fish.

Coal Harbour Marina Neighbourhood Phase One
Vancouver, BC

Vancouver is renowned for its seawall, a linear public space that literally circumnavigates the edge of the city. The vision of Park Board Superintendent W. S. Rawlings, the Stanley Park seawall was initiated in 1917 and took over sixty years to complete. It has since extended beyond the park, covering over 22 kilometres from Sunset Beach around False Creek to Kitsilano. With the completion of the Carrall Street Greenway that will link North False Creek with Burrard Inlet, the seawall will form a continuous loop around Vancouver's downtown peninsula.

The seawall is a key vantage point from which to appreciate views of the ocean and city against the dramatic backdrop of the Coast Mountains. It is rare in Vancouver to find a location where one's engagement with the city isn't tempered by the imposing presence of sea, forest or mountain. At the centre of the downtown core, one looks north to Burrard Inlet and the mountains, west to the forests of Stanley Park and south to the waters of False Creek. Such views are considered so intrinsic to civic identity that View Protection Guidelines were established by the City in 1989. Twenty-seven view cones were mapped to protect the most striking framed scenes of nature. Other codes and guidelines resulted in a building typology particular to Vancouver, the podium point tower. The narrow podium point tower model ensures ample spacing between buildings to maximize the view.

Because of this obsession with the outward view of nature and the city's peripheralized public spaces, Vancouver has been criticized for its perceived lack of urbanity.[21] This argument is based on the perception that the city stops at the water's edge. But between the seawall and the mountain view lies a stretch of water that is anything but an empty, unpeopled void. International cargo ships, cruise liners, tugboats, yachts, windsurfers, sailboats, kayaks, rowboats, public ferries, fishing boats and barges mix and mingle, adding to an already rich ecology of marine life and seabirds. The water is an intense zone of hybridized eco-urban activity that is, if anything, highly cosmopolitan.

The sea and seawall as prime public forum continues a lesser known urban tradition that is very much rooted in local culture. The first European explorers arriving on the coast of British Columbia commented profusely on two things: the density and impenetrability of the forest, and the relatively incoherent way that aboriginal canoeists traversed the water. Coastal First Nations public life played out primarily on water and beach. Longhouses faced out toward the sea; the forest was considered more dangerous, inaccessible and unpredictable than the open waters.[22] Historical European accounts of aboriginal navigation convey a frustration with the rarity of direct movement from one point to another. Canoes would meander in seemingly incoherent patterns. What was not clear to these European explorers was the fact that for native West Coasters, the sea was many things at once: front door to the community, market, fishing grounds, battleground, communication hub and civic plaza. Importantly, the sea was also intimately understood as a moving depth, not a planar undifferentiated surface. Seasonal and diurnal currents and underwater topography registered on the surface in all

THIS PAGE TOP The seawall affords views of Burrard Inlet activated with a bevy of seaplanes, freighters, cruise liners, yachts, kayakers, seals and cormorants. BOTTOM Bicycle and pedestrian pathways are separated by a slight grade change and a landscaped seating zone.
OPPOSITE PAGE TOP The promenade was scaled to accommodate pedestrians, joggers, cyclists and parents with baby strollers. The paving pattern reinforces the rhythm established by the seawall and railing details and subtly relates to the area's Art Deco heritage. BOTTOM LEFT The railing detailing is derived from historic remnants still existing in some areas along the Stanley Park seawall. BOTTOM RIGHT Looking down on the waterfront promenade and marina. City streets are connected visually and physically to the water and meet the seawall with a grand belvedere, wide set of steps and feature lights.

of its complexity. These rhythms, combined with knowledge of faunal behaviour and the daily tasks of trade, fishing and communication, registered First Nations navigation as erratic and nonsensical to the European mind.[23] Movement was a complex negotiation of ecological, cultural, political, economic and social forces, making for a much more intense sense of 'urbanism' than the European visitor was able to recognize. Today aquatic movement and interaction is no less complex and engaging, articulating diverse connections between city and water.

The Marina Neighbourhood was the first phase of Coal Harbour, a major waterfront megaproject on the former portlands between the Westin Bayshore and Canada Place. The concept plan was designed by Philips Wuori Long, and detailed design was then developed by PFS. Completed in 1997, the design for this portion of the seawall provides a 10.5 metre promenade for pedestrians, cyclists, rollerbladers and lingerers. Precast patterned concrete setts demarcate the various modes of movement and reference the historic quality of walkways in nearby Stanley Park. Public street end view corridors are protected to ensure direct views to the ocean and mountains beyond. At these intersections, the seawall widens generously, emphasizing the linkage of the promenade into the greater fabric of the city. The generous section allows for various means of movement and occupation. On any summer night, spontaneous activities abound—drumming circles, picnics and musical performances collect and disband amid the sounds of fog horns, the nine o'clock gun, herons squawking and seagulls dropping mussels to crack their shells on the pavement. Along the seawall, nature is urbane. The cult of the view doesn't detract from civic life; rather, it is part of the mélange. When the perceived wildness and unpredictability of nature butts up against the city, more unlikely forms of urbanism can occur.

Kelty McKinnon SuperNatural 253

OPPOSITE PAGE TOP Tiered seating zones and wall, curb and stair detailing provide a variety of ways for people to casually linger along the promenade. BOTTOM SERIES Activity along the promenade. THIS PAGE TOP Harbour Green Park. The undulating stone walls demarcate Coal Harbour's historic shoreline. PAGES 256–257 The Art Deco inspired precast concrete aprons shield the aquatic regeneration zone below the promenade while adding a level of placemaking detail to an otherwise engineered solution for extending the pedestrian deck out over the water.

Kelty McKinnon   SuperNatural   255

LEFT Southward view toward the library over the main water feature.
RIGHT Generative sketch of the urban character of the campus gardens.
PAGES 260–261 Dramatic evening reflection creates a dynamic landscape of water and layered planting.

Langara College Library
Vancouver, BC

The prevalence of water in Vancouver is exaggerated by the Coast Mountains that force warm Pacific winds upward, cooling the air and causing moisture condensation to fall as heavy winter rain. The first phase of the Langara College Master Plan, carried out by PFS in association with Teeple Architects and IBI/HB Architects, is both a celebration of water and an expression of nature's flows through the site. It includes Teeple Architects' new LEED® Gold library and classroom building and the collaborative redevelopment of the primary campus entrance sequence as the social spine of the campus.

The entire project, both architecture and landscape, captures the environmental flows that cross the site for energy and resources. The library's form is derived by modeling the erratic flow of local winds which are captured for passive cooling in five internal wind towers. The building also uses a geothermal system for heating and cooling water that passes through the building's concrete floors, ceilings and walls. Rather than using potable water for irrigation, both stormwater and greywater are collected in separate underground cisterns and reused on site. The abstract terracing of rectangular pools of water reasserts the historic northwest to southeast flow of two long-ago buried creeks that once crossed the site. A series of short terraced waterfalls makes visible the overall topographic drop. In all of these instances, dynamic environmental processes yield a very urban, decidedly modern form, emergent from site specific forces.

As a primary material of the garden, water is explored in all of its sensory delights. One is able to walk over water, sit on slabs set within the ponds, and study in the sun with one's feet cooling in the water. Water wells up, eddies, scrolls, boils, meanders, dribbles and cascades through the campus, disrupting discrete reflections of building, student and vegetation into an abstracted scattering of nature and culture.

In 2004 PFS, in association with Teeple Architects and IBI/HB Architects, prepared a master plan for Langara Campus that focused on simultaneously urbanizing and naturalizing the existing suburban campus plan that privileged parking over public space. The old campus plan turned its back to the street and surrounding neighbourhoods by placing immense parking lots between the campus and the street. The new plan effectively turns the campus inside out, putting parking underground and lining the streets with formal public gardens and gathering spaces. Nature plays multiple roles that contribute to the simultaneous urbanizing and naturalizing of the campus: nature as civic amenity, nature as organizing structure for campus circulation and gathering spaces, and in the case of stormwater infiltration ponds, nature as ecological metabolizer. Nature at Langara College is recognized as a source of visual beauty and delight, to be viewed from a distance, but also as a generator of flows and metabolisms to be occupied and interacted with. This "complex interweaving of natural ecologies with the social, cultural and infrastructural layers of the contemporary city"[24] brings us back to Emily Carr's depictions of nature as pure movement, her "coils, spurts and cascades of growth".

OPPOSITE PAGE TOP Fall colours celebrate the start of a new semester. BOTTOM Bridge crossing. THIS PAGE Careful detailing of concrete, water and planting result in a complementary contemporary landscape/building composition.

The poetics of landscape and architecture at play.

1. Dollarton Highway
2. Park Entrance
3. Roche Point
4. Inland Forest Zone
5. Nearshore Zone
6. Little Cates
7. Malcolm Lowry Trail
8. Anchor Trail
9. Beach Walk
10. Trail Link to Community
11. Foreshore Protection Zone
12. Enlarged Open Meadow
13. New Longhouse
14. New Feasthouse, Concession and Washroom
15. Canoe Shelter
16. Upgraded Boat Launch
17. New Floating Pier on Existing Dock
18. Reconfigured Mill Burner
19. Relocated and Upgraded Playground
20. Upgraded Tennis Courts
21. Upgraded Caretaker and Storage
22. Reconfigured Parking and Loop Road

Rendered master plan.

Cates Park / Whey-ah-Wichen Park
Master Plan and Cultural Resources Interpretation Management Plan
District of North Vancouver, BC

The Cates Park / Whey-ah-Wichen Park Master Plan and Cultural Resources Interpretation Management Plan is a comprehensive plan for a 22.3 hectare waterfront park in the District of North Vancouver. The park is located in the heart of traditional Tsleil-Waututh territory. The Tsleil-Waututh are Coast Salish people who historically were the only year-round residents of Burrard Inlet. Archaeological studies at the park show the presence of established villages, seasonal camps, burial sites and battle grounds from 3,500 years ago. Prior to European contact, the Tsleil-Waututh population was about 10,000. Today it is about 400. Today's Tsleil-Waututh First Nation is recognized as one of the most progressive aboriginal communities in Canada. Their expressed mandate is to establish a presence in all social, economic and political activities that impact their lands and waters; to regain ownership of sensitive wilderness areas; and to construct early childhood education and cultural centres from the revenue. The Tsleil-Waututh keep a strong presence in Whey-ah-Wichen and use the site for multiple activities including traditional canoe races, operating a food concession, co-sponsoring the annual Under the Volcano Festival, and using the park as a launching point for Takaya eco-tours which combine Coast Salish cultural interpretation with sea kayaking, canoeing and overnight camping.[25]

Cates Park / Whey-ah-Wichen's complex and layered cultural and ecological histories are revealed and capitalized on within the master plan. Burial grounds and middens are prevalent, although partially lost due to foreshore erosion from wave action, both natural and caused by motorized boats. A concrete cedar mill foundation and burner remnant remains from 1910, when a significant community was established around the logging industry. The majority of the park was logged at this time and some remnant stumps remain as nurse logs. Native subsistence was radically affected by the destruction of trees, understory and herbaceous plants. Most landbased animals disappeared along with their habitat, and shellfish and fish stocks declined due to pollution and the rise of commercial fishing. During the Depression, a squatter community was established at Roche Point at the south end of the park. Author Malcolm Lowry resided here while writing *Under the Volcano* and in 1944 Lowry and his wife built a shack on the shores of Roche Point where they lived until the squatter community was forced out in 1954. Only one of the shacks survived demolition and still exists today. The park was formally established in 1950, helping to protect its significant archaeological resources.

Much of the significance of the master plan has to do with its ongoing process rather than its finished form. The master plan takes an innovative approach to regional park planning by bringing a municipality and a First Nation together in a cooperative, collaborative visioning process that first addresses Coast Salish cultural identity and then identifies how to best accommodate Tsleil-Waututh cultural and eco-tourism interests within the park. Senior representatives of the District of North Vancouver and the Tsleil-Waututh First Nation formed a joint committee who then hired PFS and AldrichPears Associates to work with them to produce the Master Plan and Cultural Resources Interpretation Management Plan. Regular workshops were held with the project steering committee, and a series of open houses brought stakeholders and the public into the collaborative process.

The master plan emphasizes the quality of being embedded within the forest, while rhythmically choreographing scenic views out across the water. Historically, most of Vancouver and its surrounding suburbs were dense temperate rain forest, consisting of Douglas fir, western red cedar and western hemlock with occasional pockets of alder and maple. Today's second growth forest is overly mature, with very little understory or herbaceous growth. The District of North Vancouver community has identified the importance of forest to its sense of identity and aims to balance development with the protection of this natural resource.

For the Tsleil-Waututh, the forest provided much of the substance of everyday life. They extended a network of forest trails to hunt, gather and trade, and for spiritual and cultural activities. Berry producing shrubs and medicinal plants were actively maintained and protected while deer, elk, bear, mountain goats and beaver were hunted for hides, horns, wool, teeth and meat. Trees were paramount to everyday life. Not only were tools and other everyday items made from trees, the canoe, carved from a single western red cedar, enabled maritime culture to thrive.

TOP Filtered views across Indian Arm. BOTTOM Forest understory is being encouraged to grow back to add to the park's ecological complexity.

Tsleil-Waututh culture was predominantly marine oriented. Much of life was spent on the water for hunting, fishing, traveling, socializing, racing and engaging in or avoiding warfare. Flotillas of canoes moved across the water fishing for salmon and hunting seals, porpoises and migratory birds. There were many different types of canoes fabricated for different purposes. Some canoes carried up to fifteen people, while hunting and fishing canoes were lighter and easier to maneuver. The canoe was the vessel of life and death. In some coastal communities, babies were rocked to sleep in tiny canoes, and the dead were given treetop burials in canoes.[26]

The relationship between ocean and forest is reinforced in the master plan's attention to foreshore erosion control. It is estimated that between 18 and 25 metres of land has been lost off the foreshore in Cates Park / Whey-ah-Wichen in the last 50 years, including significant middens and burial sites. Shellfish, crabbing and fishing in the area have been affected by increased turbidity. By reinforcing the shoreline and riparian vegetation, habitat is restored for both wildlife and eco-tourism.

The master plan recognizes that ecological, cultural, social and economic concerns are strongly interrelated, and takes a long-term multifaceted approach to planning the park. A foreshore erosion protection plan and vegetation management strategy are outlined to re-establish native forest understory, wildlife corridors and healthy stormwater systems. Addressing the ecology of the site intensifies the spatial complexity and environmental experience, allowing Takaya Tours to enhance their eco-tourism program by adding educational and ceremonial programming. A LEED® certified feasthouse and longhouse are proposed that interpret traditional Coast Salish structures in contemporary materials to provide venues for celebrations, presentations, demonstrations and entertainment. A more strategic siting of parking, circulation, large and intimate gathering zones, playgrounds, the longhouse, the feasthouse and kayak and canoe storage facilities is proposed to protect remaining archaeological sites and sensitive riparian areas, improve the experiential qualities of the park and improve the connectivity of the park to greater regional circulation systems. New structures are to be placed in the footprints of existing roads and parking lots to minimize the chance of disturbing archaeological sites by using sites already excavated to the depth of the subgrade. The plan also enhances programmatic variety with improved access for all users from young children to scuba divers. Tsleil-Waututh field crews will also use the park, improved pier and boat launch as the starting point for eco-forestry, protected area management and salmon enhancement activities in greater Indian Arm. The wayfinding and interpretive strategies developed by AldrichPears Associates are carefully tied to the environmental experience of the park. Non-signage elements are used wherever possible to avoid becoming overly didactic.

Conclusion

What we see from particular nature-based practices in British Columbia is a kind of 'learning from landscape'—the formation of a sensibility to landscape that goes beyond scenic production. Emily Carr's SuperNatural would be a nature that is about emergence, multiplicity and open-endedness, where landscapes are continually made up of, and created by, multiple actors. The characteristics of this SuperNatural—that nature is entwined with culture, that it is embedded and multisensory, and that process and movement trump form—lend themselves to a strategy of emergence, where design springs from a direct relationship to site and all of its myriad cultural and ecological histories. As Emily Carr suggests, "Instead of trying to force our personality onto our subject we should be quite quiet and unassertive and let the subject swallow us and absorb us into it."[27] The projects discussed, while resulting in very different designs, all began with an extensive process of on- and off-site research and engagement that took into account the many ecological, cultural, economic and social realities of the site to bring to light invisible processes and relationships, accommodate overlapping program and, in the end, to create spaces that call attention to the phenomenal environment we live in.

Notes

1. Northrop Frye, *The Bush Garden: Essays on the Canadian Imagination* (Toronto: House of Anansi Press, 1971), 146.
2. Frye, *Bush Garden*, 164.
3. Frye, *Bush Garden*, 164.
4. Margaret Atwood, *Survival: A Thematic Guide to Canadian Literature* (Toronto: Anansi, 1972), 32.
5. Carl Berger, "The True North Strong and Free" in *Canadian Culture: An Introductory Reader*, Elspeth Cameron, ed., (Toronto: Canadian Scholars' Press, 1997), 96.
6. While Emily Carr has been criticized for continuing a colonialist tradition of cultural appropriation and the objectification of First Nations peoples, other writers, such as Gerta Moray in her 1998 essay "Wilderness, Modernity and Aboriginality in the Paintings of Emily Carr" in the *Journal of Canadian Studies*, Summer 1998, have countered these arguments: "Given her persistent acknowledgement of the continuing Native presence and her prediction that the moral force of aboriginal traditions would be revalued, it is my argument that Carr's late paintings with Native motifs can be seen as an extension of her earlier Modernist vision of mutual respect and communication."
7. Bruce Braun, *The Intemperate Rainforest: Nature, Culture and Power on Canada's West Coast* (Minneapolis: University of Minnesota Press, 2002), 3.
8. See Carr's paintings *Stumps and Sky* (1934), *Forest Clearing* (1939) and *Trees in the Sky* (1939).
9. Maria Tippett, *Emily Carr: A Biography* (Toronto: Stoddart, 1994), 167.
10. James Corner, ed., *Recovering Landscape: Essays in Contemporary Landscape Architecture* (Sparks, NV: Princeton Architectural Press, 1999), 153.
11. Doris Shadbolt, *Emily Carr* (Seattle: University of Washington Press, 1990), 211.
12. Carr to Eric Brown, March 4, 1937, National Gallery.
13. Emily Carr. *Hundreds and Thousands: The Journals of Emily Carr* (Toronto: Clarke and Irwin, 1966), 136.
14. Carr, *Hundreds*, 293.
15. Shadbolt, *Emily Carr*, 185.
16. Carr, *Hundreds*, 13.
17. James Corner, "Terra Fluxus," *The Landscape Urbanism Reader*, Charles Waldheim, ed., (NY: Princeton Architectural Press, 2006), 30.
18. Shadbolt, *Emily Carr*, 30.
19. Corner, "Terra Fluxus," 29.
20. Carr, *Hundreds*, 301.
21. See Lance Berelowitz's writings on Vancouver's public spaces in *Dream City: Vancouver and the Global Imagination* (Vancouver: Douglas & McIntyre, 2005).
22. See Jonathon Raban's description of Coastal First Nations' relationship to water in *Passage to Juneau: A Sea and its Meanings* (New York: Pantheon Books, 1999), 103–106.
23. Raban, *Passage to Juneau*, 99–103.
24. Charles Waldheim, *The Landscape Urbanism Reader* (New York, NY: Princeton Architectural Press, 2006), 48.
25. Much of the information gathered for this portion of the essay was obtained from the Cates Park / Whey-ah-Wichen Park Master Plan and Cultural Resources Interpretation Management Plan prepared by PFS and AldrichPears Associates.
26. Raban, *Passage to Juneau*.
27. Carr, *Hundreds*, 176.

Appendix

PFS Partners

Chris Phillips FCSLA BCSLA ASLA

A fellow of the Canadian Society of Landscape Architects, Chris Phillips is widely respected for his ability to create deeply memorable designs for a wide range of complex urban design and public open space projects. Over the past twenty years, he has created numerous significant public spaces both internationally and in Canada, and has been principal in charge of many award-winning urban development, community, waterfront, civic space and park projects. Chris is interested in the integration of regional context, metaphor and meaning and their collective contribution to the design of urban open space and the public realm. Central to his design philosophy is the importance of public open space as a locus of public life and an expression of democracy. His unique design process focuses on the creation of highly functional, aesthetic landscapes that are compelling, evocative and inclusive.

Chris has encouraged the inclusion of public art in his work, and is a past chair of the City of Vancouver Public Art Advisory Committee. He has brought his extensive professional experience and innovative design thinking to roles on the Vancouver City Planning Commission, the British Columbia Society of Landscape Architects (BCSLA), the Canadian Society of Landscape Architects (CSLA) and numerous art and design juries.

Marta Farevaag MCIP MPIBC

Marta Farevaag is an urban planner who has long been interested in the overlap between the fields of urban planning and landscape architecture, integrating it into both her master's studies at the UBC School of Community and Regional Planning and her professional work. She brings expertise in planning, project management and community process to PFS's large-scale urban design and heritage landscape projects including campus master plans, park management plans and downtown revitalization projects. She has been the author of many of the firm's reports, design guidelines and public consultation materials.

At UBC, Marta has taught sessional planning and urban design courses in both the School of Community and Regional Planning and the School of Architecture and Landscape Architecture. For many years she was a director of the Vancouver League, organizing free public lectures by internationally known designers. She was a commissioner on the Vancouver City Planning Commission and served as chair in her last year. Marta was also a member of the Vancouver Urban Design Panel and is currently a director of the Vancouver Heritage Foundation.

Greg Smallenberg FCSLA BCSLA OALA ASLA

Greg Smallenberg is a native of Vancouver, and has been a partner of PFS for most of his career. He holds an honours degree in landscape architecture from UBC. His primary focus has been on PFS's national and international portfolio, and establishing and directing project offices in both Ottawa and Shanghai. Greg is noted for his demonstrated success in leading highly visible, often complex projects for both the private and public sectors where he has worked with all levels of government. Commissions under his direction tend to be large-scale and multidisciplinary, ranging from contemporary built works to management plans for designated historic landscapes. He is interested in the intersections of culture, history and placemaking as they relate to landscape architecture and urban design.

Greg is recognized as a leader in Canadian landscape architecture. His process-based design approach, along with the respect he has garnered in diverse professional circles, has resulted in numerous invitations to present ideas at conferences and universities worldwide. He has served on several urban design juries in both Canada and Asia and has been a sessional lecturer at the University of British Columbia and a guest lecturer at several universities in China. He is a fellow of the CSLA where he served as a director. He has also served as director and president of the BCSLA and is currently a member of the Waterfront Toronto Design Panel.

Staff

PRINCIPALS

Ross Dixon CSLA BCSLA
Ross is a native of Alberta with a background in urban and regional planning, landscape architecture and CAD technology. For nearly two decades, Ross has focused on contract administration, cost control and site services for PFS's highest profile projects. He brings a strong understanding of construction, close attention to detail and a reputation of working closely with clients, consultants and contractors to all of the projects he helps realize.

Jennifer Nagai CSLA BCSLA OALA ASLA LEED® AP
Jennifer has worked extensively in both Toronto and Vancouver and has developed a diverse portfolio of high profile, contextually sensitive master planning and detailed design projects throughout Canada. Committed to high standards of execution in all aspects of design and project delivery, much of her work focuses on collaboration with artists where she specializes in articulating rich conceptual ideas through precise, expressive detailing. Jennifer is a LEED® Accredited Professional and brings innovative sustainable solutions to the many projects she directs for PFS.

Jeffrey Staates CSLA BCSLA OALA ASLA
With a diverse professional background in architecture, interiors, landscape and urban design, Jeffrey is committed to the creation of a meaningful and memorable public realm, and particularly enjoys projects that stress interdisciplinary collaboration. He is recognized for the innovative, high quality design and design detail he brings to many of PFS's signature projects. Jeffrey has extensive international experience and was design director of PFS Asia's Shanghai office.

SENIOR STAFF

Jim Breadon CSLA BCSLA LEED® AP
As a LEED® accredited professional, Jim is frequently involved in PFS's complex green building and site projects, emphasizing stormwater treatment, native plant associations and innovative sustainability strategies. Having been with PFS for nearly twenty years, Jim's extensive experience includes business parks and corporate headquarters, schools and colleges, research facilities, parks and open space systems.

Kelty McKinnon CSLA BCSLA
Kelty has a diverse background in environmental studies, public art and landscape architecture which she brings to all of the projects that she manages, researches and designs at PFS. She is also an adjunct professor in the Landscape Architecture Program at the University of British Columbia where she teaches design studios focusing on the production of emergent landscapes that engage environmental and cultural ecologies.

Chris Mramor CSLA BCSLA
Chris has been with PFS for nearly two decades, bringing his interest in creative conceptual design, integrated site planning, innovative construction detailing and heritage conservation to a diverse array of PFS's most significant local and international site planning and urban design projects. A native of Vancouver, Chris has a background in both forestry and landscape architecture.

Matthew Thomson
Matthew hails from Scotland and has a background in both fine arts and landscape architecture. He has been senior designer on many of PFS's key public and private projects, and specializes in illustrating conceptual ideas in renderings and perspective sketches. Matthew particularly enjoys working directly with the communities and individuals who ultimately inhabit the projects he designs.

CURRENT

Hanako Amaya
Nathan Brightbill
Jenna Buchko
Mike Derksen
Sarah Hall
Maureen Hetzler
Barbara Holmes
Alia Johnson
Kirsten Jones
Sara Kasaei
Matt Lang
Jia Li
Lin Lin
Anna Liu
Erika Mashig
Nastaran Moradinejad
Andrew Robertson
Nicole Taddune
Juliette Thomas
Cherie Xiao
Dan Yang

PAST

Cecelia Achiam
Rochelle Bacigalupo
Hugh Bitz
Sylvain Bombardier
Louise Boutin
Heather Braun
Donna Bridgeman
Dawn Brockington
Cathy Burke
Jessie Chou
Heidi Chung
Kate Clark
Clint Cuddington
Jeff Cutler
Susan Durieux
Mike Enns
Jamie Esko
Grace Fan
Doron Fishman
David Flanders
Joe Fry
Yvette Fynn
Bryce Gauthier
Farzaneh Ghassemi
Carsten Goehler
Roberta Greenwood
Blair Guppy
Neil Hadley
Susan Haid
Michelle Hayes
Michelle Hillier
Andrea Jeske
Chris Keatley
Marta Klaptocz
Keith Koroluk
Annika Korzeniewski
Kendra Kryszak

Ken Larsson
Derek Lee
Eva Lee
Jane Leroux
Eric Lott
Emma Lotto
Patty Lynes
Alison Maddaugh
Anson Main
Alexandre Man-Bourdon
Elizabeth McIntyre
Shona McLean
Allison McMahon
Carlos Mier Y Ponce Arzani
Oren Mizrahi
Marc Monette
Stacy Moriarty
Katie Murray
Ron Myers
Goya Ngan
Liz Nguyen
Cameron Owen
Christian Patterson
Kristina Patterson
Laura Phipps
Sarah Pickstone
Phillipe Poulin
Andrew Powers
Andria Preisse
Natalie Redlich
Stephanie Redlich
Sophie Robitaille
Sebastian Rost
Twyla Rusnak
Erin Ryan
Heather Sadler

Douglas Scott
Heather Scott
Xenia Semeniuk
Doug Shearer
Ying Shi
Maureen Smith
Steve Snider
Alexandra Steed
Anne Trumble
Wayne Turner
Alexa Uhrich
Bill Uhrich
Wojicek Walcynski
Jian Wang
Janet Webber
Derek Weckers
Clark Wilson
Michelle Wong
Zhiling (Shell) Xiao
Lu Xu
Qing Xu
Xu (Patrick) Yang
Yong Xu Yu

Contributors

Michael Van Valkenburgh FASLA FAAR
Michael Van Valkenburgh has been a practicing landscape architect for nearly thirty-five years and is the lead principal of Michael Van Valkenburgh Associates (MVVA), with offices in Cambridge, MA and Brooklyn. He has also taught landscape architecture at Harvard's Graduate School of Design since 1982 and is currently the Charles Eliot Professor in Practice of Landscape Architecture. MVVA's completed projects include Mill Race Park in Columbus, Indiana; Teardrop Park and Brooklyn Bridge Park in New York City; and landscape master plans for Princeton, Harvard, Wellesley College and Vassar College. MVVA is leading the multidisciplinary team responsible for recovering Toronto's Portlands, including the renaturalization of the mouth of the Don River. Michael holds degrees in landscape architecture from Cornell University and the University of Illinois at Urbana-Champaign.

Ken Greenberg FRAIC AIA
Former Director of Urban Design and Architecture for the City of Toronto, Architect and Urban Designer Ken Greenberg is principal of Greenberg Consultants, which focuses on campus master planning, regional growth management, new community planning and the rejuvenation of downtowns, waterfronts and neighborhoods. His projects are based internationally in such cities as Toronto, Amsterdam, Paris, Minneapolis, New York, Boston, Montreal, Washington and San Juan, Puerto Rico. He applies a holistic approach to city-building, crossing traditional boundaries and working in team settings to collaborate with professionals from a variety of disciplines. Ken has taught urban design at Harvard's Graduate School of Design, the University of Michigan, University of Toronto, University of Pennsylvania, University of Waterloo, Université de Montreal, UC Berkeley and the Chinese University in Hong Kong. He is a fellow of the Royal Canadian Institute of Architects, the Toronto Society of Architects and the Institute for Urban Design, and a frequent participant in the Mayors' Institute of City Design. His work has garnered awards from the Canadian Institute of Planners, the City of Toronto, American Planning Association and the journals *Progressive Architecture* and *Canadian Architect*.

Jacqueline Hucker
Jacqueline Hucker is an architectural historian. Associated with Parks Canada for more than twenty years, she specialized in the history of Canadian architecture, landscapes and cultural landscapes and for five years managed the Federal Heritage Buildings Review Office. Her primary interests have been First World War military commemoration and the preservation of Parliament Hill in Ottawa. Jacqueline served as the historian on the conservation team that restored Canada's National Memorial on Vimy Ridge, France, completed in 2007. She is joint author of *A Guide To Canadian Architectural Styles* (Peterborough, ON: Broadview Press, 2nd edition 2004) and has published a number of articles on Canadian architecture. She holds a BA from Queen's University and an MA from Carleton.

Dr. Eduard Koegel
Dr. Eduard Koegel is a Berlin-based urban planner, architect and author of several books on Chinese architecture. He is director of the Agency for Urban Development where he researches Chinese architectural and urban development. Funded by the German Research Foundation, his current research focuses on the work of Ernst Boerschmann at the Habitat Unit of the Technical University of Berlin. Eduard is also a Board Member of Stadtkultur International (SKI), a society focusing on cultural exchange between China and Germany. With SKI he has jointly organised many symposiums on architecture and urban development with the Heinrich-Boell-Foundation and the Architectural Society of China. In 2002 he founded the bilingual (German-Chinese) on-line magazine *IDAS* (Informationsdienst Architektur und Stadtentwicklung), where he is editor-in-chief. *IDAS* is dedicated to German and Chinese architecture and urban design. He also sits on the editorial board of Qinghua University's journal, *World Architecture*, in Beijing. Eduard received his doctorate at Bauhaus University in Weimar in 2007. From 1999 to 2004 he was Assistant Professor at the Technical University of Darmstadt in the Department of Planning and Architecture in Non-European Regions. Since 2008 he has lectured at the Institute for Philosophy, Science Theory, Science & Technical History at the Architectural Department of the Technical University Berlin.

Bruce Kuwabara OAA FRAIC AIA RIBA
Bruce Kuwabara is a founding partner of Kuwabara Payne McKenna Blumberg Architects (KPMB) in Toronto and has been recognized internationally as one of Canada's leading architects. His practice is committed to architectural excellence and the design of the public realm, and has earned distinction with 10 Governor General's Awards, Canada's highest architectural honour. In 2006 he was the recipient of the RAIC Gold Medal for Architecture. Bruce's projects have been published extensively both in Canada and internationally and are featured in a monograph, *The Architecture of Kuwabara Payne McKenna Blumberg Architects* (Basel: Birkhauser, 2005). Bruce has taught at the Faculty of Architecture, Landscape and Design at the University of Toronto (U of T) and at Harvard's Graduate School of Design. He is the honorary co-chair for fundraising responsible for establishing the Frank Gehry International Design Chair at the U of T, the first chair of the Waterfront Design Review Panel for Waterfront Toronto and a member of the board of directors of the Canadian Centre for Architecture. From 1986 to 1992, he was a member of the National Capital Commission Advisory Committee on Design. He continues to participate as a jury member, guest lecturer and critic on issues of architecture, urbanism and sustainable design.

Douglas Paterson FCSLA BCSLA
Douglas Paterson is professor emeritus and former director of the Landscape Architecture Program at the University of British Columbia. He is also past-president of the Canadian Society of Landscape Architects (CSLA), a fellow and past chair of the CSLA College of Fellows, and a past regional director of the North American Council of Educators in Landscape Architecture. He has served on the editorial advisory boards of *Landscape Architecture Magazine*, the *Journal of Landscape and Urban Planning*, and *Landscapes/Paysages*. Locally, Douglas has served as a member of the Vancouver Urban Design Panel, a member and chair of the Vancouver Planning Commission and the citizen-at-large representative on the Hastings Park Restoration Committee in Vancouver. He is currently a member of the national Vimy Memorial Restoration Advisory Committee.

Kelty McKinnon CSLA BCSLA
Kelty McKinnon is a senior landscape architect at Phillips Farevaag Smallenberg where she specializes in projects dealing with the public realm and public art both locally and internationally. Her project work includes the West Don Lands Public Realm Strategy, Lower Don Lands and the Harbourfront Competition in Toronto; Blue Mountain Central Park in Pudong; and Sun Palace Venus and Mercury in Beijing. Kelty is also an adjunct professor in the School of Architecture and Landscape Architecture at the University of British Columbia. She has written on diverse topics all related to landscape. Recent publications have dealt with issues ranging from hefted sheep and urban bestiaries to invasive plants in public policy and the contemporary restoration of historic Chinatown infrastructure. Her landscape architectural and artistic work has been exhibited in Vancouver, Montreal, Seattle, Minneapolis, New York, Berlin, Vienna, London and Walla Walla, Washington.

Julian Smith OAA ICOMOS
Past chief architect for Parks Canada's National Historic Sites program, Julian Smith is principal of Julian Smith & Associates, an architectural practice that combines his interests in historic conservation and contemporary design. His firm conducts planning, research, design and conservation work both nationally and internationally. Julian's projects include the restoration of Canada's Vimy Memorial in France, master planning for the Canadian embassy at the historic Villa Grazioli estate in Rome, an expansion plan and detailed design for an historic university campus in India, guidelines for a contemporary addition to the residence of the prime minister in Ottawa, and advisory services to Public Works Canada on contemporary additions to historic buildings within the Parliamentary Precinct. Julian started the graduate program in heritage conservation twenty years ago in the School of Canadian Studies at Carleton University, and continues his involvement there as an adjunct research professor. He has recently taken the position of executive director of the Willowbank School of Restoration Arts in Queenston.

Project Credits

ESSAYS

BELLEVUE CITY HALL 34–39
CLIENT City of Bellevue
PRIME CONSULTANT SRG Partnership Inc.
LANDSCAPE ARCHITECT Phillips Farevaag Smallenberg
Partner in Charge: Chris Phillips
Project Manager: Joseph Fry
CONSULTING DESIGN TEAM 4Culture • Abacus Engineering Corporation • Corson Studios – Dan Corson, Public Artist • Francis Krahe & Associates Inc. • Keen Engineering Inc. • Magnusson Klemencic Associates • Rod Turkington & Associates Ltd. • Alan Storey, Public Artist • Vincent Helton & Associates Ltd.

BLUE MOUNTAIN 182, 196–201
CLIENT Vanke Shanghai Co.
PRIME CONSULTANT Phillips Farevaag Smallenberg
Partner in Charge: Greg Smallenberg
Project Manager: Chris Mramor
Project Manager (Central Park): Kelty McKinnon

CANADIAN POLICE AND PEACE OFFICERS' MEMORIAL 232–235
CLIENT Public Works and Government Services Canada, Parliamentary Precinct Directorate
PRIME CONSULTANT Phillips Farevaag Smallenberg
Partner in Charge: Greg Smallenberg
Project Manager: Rochelle Bacigalupo
CONSULTANT DESIGN TEAM Intu Design Ltd. • Stantec Inc.

CANADIAN VETERANS' MEMORIAL 213, 236–240
CLIENT Ontario Realty Corporation
PRIME CONSULTANT Phillips Farevaag Smallenberg
Partner in Charge: Greg Smallenberg
Project Manager: Jennifer Nagai
ARTIST Allan Harding MacKay
CONSULTING LANDSCAPE ARCHITECT The Planning Partnership
CONSULTING DESIGN TEAM Alston Associates Inc. • Bruce Tree Expert Company Ltd. • Susan Coolen, Graphics • Jack Granatstein, Director General, Canadian War Museum • Julian Smith & Associates Architects • Martin Conboy Lighting Design Inc. • Quinn Dressel Associates • R.V. Anderson Associates Limited • Jane Urquhart, Writer

CATES PARK / WHEY-AH-WICHEN CULTURAL RESOURCE INTERPRETIVE AND PARK MASTER PLAN 246, 266–269
CLIENTS District of North Vancouver, Parks Department and the Tsleil-Waututh First Nation
PRIME CONSULTANT Phillips Farevaag Smallenberg in association with AldrichPears Associates
Partner in Charge: Marta Farevaag
Landscape Architecture Partner: Chris Phillips
CONSULTING DESIGN TEAM Alexander Heritage Consulting • Bunt and Associates • Jacques Whitford

CATHEDRAL PLACE 92–95
CLIENT Shon Group Realty
PRIME CONSULTANT Merrick Architecture
LANDSCAPE ARCHITECT
Phillips Farevaag Smallenberg in association with Cornelia Hahn Oberlander, Landscape Architect
Partner in Charge: Chris Phillips
Project Manager: Eva Lee

CENTRAL EXPERIMENTAL FARM MANAGEMENT PLAN 176–179
CLIENT Agriculture and Agri-Food Canada
PRIME CONSULTANT Phillips Farevaag Smallenberg in association with Julian Smith & Associates Architects and Contentworks Inc.
Partner in Charge: Greg Smallenberg
Planning Partner: Marta Farevaag
Project Manager: Blair Guppy
CONSULTING DESIGN TEAM The Corporate Research Group • Delcan • Spencer and Co.
SPECIAL ADVISORS Moura Quayle, Dean of Agriculture, UBC • Douglas Justice, Associate Director, UBC Botanical Garden • Brian Hall, Harvard Forest

CMHC SHANGHAI SUSTAINABLE COMMUNITY STANDARD 203
CLIENT Canadian Mortgage and Housing Corporation International
PRIME CONSULTANT Ramsay Worden Architects
LANDSCAPE ARCHITECT Phillips Farevaag Smallenberg
Partner in Charge: Greg Smallenberg
Project Manager: Grace Fan
CONSULTING DESIGN TEAM Archemy Consulting Ltd. • Coast Palisade Consulting Group Ltd. • Professor Patrick Condon SPECIAL ADVISORS Ian Theaker, Canada Green Building Council • Nils Larsson, Director, IISSBE (International Initiative for Sustainable Built Environment)

COAL HARBOUR MARINA NEIGHBOURHOOD PHASE ONE 242, 250–257
CLIENT Marathon Realty Corporation
PRIME CONSULTANTS Phillips Farevaag Smallenberg in association with Sandwell Engineering
Partner in Charge: Greg Smallenberg
Project Manager: Chris Mramor

CONFEDERATION SQUARE 156, 159, 162–167
CLIENTS National Capital Commission and Regional Municipality of Ottawa-Carlton
PRIME CONSULTANT, ENGINEER Stantec Inc.
PRIME CONSULTANT, LANDSCAPE ARCHITECT & URBAN DESIGNER Phillips Farevaag Smallenberg
Partner in Charge: Greg Smallenberg
Project Manager: Chris Mramor
CONSULTING DESIGN TEAM Birmingham & Wood Architects and Planners • Julian Smith & Associates Architects • Martin Conboy Lighting Design Inc. • Steve Torrance

EAST BAYFRONT PRECINCT PLAN PUBLIC REALM AND STREETSCAPE 69, 78–81
CLIENT Waterfront Toronto
PRIME CONSULTANT Koetter, Kim & Associates
PUBLIC REALM DESIGN LEAD Phillips Farevaag Smallenberg
Design Partner in Charge: Greg Smallenberg
Planning Partner: Marta Farevaag
Project Manager: Ken Larsson
CONSULTING DESIGN TEAM BA Consulting Group Ltd. • GHK International (Canada) Ltd. • Sustainable Edge Ltd.

GOLDEN OX MOUNTAIN 204–205
CLIENT Hunan Jingtou Enterprise Co. Ltd.
PRIME CONSULTANT Phillips Farevaag Smallenberg in association with Ramsay Worden Architects Ltd.
Partner in Charge: Greg Smallenberg
Project Manager: Ken Larsson

HASTINGS PARK RESTORATION PLAN 86, 114–121
CLIENT City of Vancouver, Board of Parks and Recreation
PRIME CONSULTANT Phillips Farevaag Smallenberg

Design Partner in Charge: Chris Phillips
Planning Partner in Charge: Marta Farevaag
Project Manager: Chris Mramor
CONSULTING DESIGN TEAM Archifolia • Birmingham & Wood Architects and Planners • Bush, Bohlman & Partners • Buzan Consultants Ltd. • Ken Clarke, Artist • Earth Tech • Rod Turkington & Associates Ltd. • Spectrum Skatepark Creations Ltd. • Vincent Helton & Associates Ltd.

HUI TIAN RAN CITYPARK MASTER PLAN 190–195
CLIENT Hu Nan Hui Tian Ran Investment and Development Ltd.
PRIME CONSULTANT Phillips Farevaag Smallenberg
Partner in Charge: Greg Smallenberg
Project Manager: Anna Liu

LANGARA COLLEGE MASTER PLAN AND LIBRARY 258–265
CLIENT Langara College
PRIME CONSULTANT Teeple Architects Inc. in association with Hancock Bruckner Eng + Wright Architects
LANDSCAPE ARCHITECT Phillips Farevaag Smallenberg
Partner in Charge: Chris Phillips
Project Managers: Doug Shearer and Heather Scott
CONSULTING DESIGN TEAM Altus Group Limited • Brook + Associates, Inc. • Bunt and Associates • Cobalt Engineering • EnerSys Analytics Inc. • Glotman-Simpson • Keen Engineering, Inc. • MKT Arkle Development Management Inc. • Morgan Stewart

METROPOLITAN APARTMENTS 202–203
CLIENT Chengdu Vanke Company
PRIME CONSULTANT Phillips Farevaag Smallenberg
Partner in Charge: Greg Smallenberg
Project Managers: Kelty McKinnon and Matthew Thomson

MOUNTAIN VIEW CEMETERY MASONIC AREA REDEVELOPMENT 104–113
CLIENT City of Vancouver
PRIME CONSULTANT Lees + Associates in collaboration with Phillips Farevaag Smallenberg
Partner in Charge: Chris Phillips
Project Manager: Chris Mramor
CONSULTING DESIGN TEAM Birmingham & Wood Architects and Planners • BTY Group • Bush, Bohlman & Partners • GeoPacific Consultants Ltd. • MMM Group • Perez Engineering Ltd. • Rod Turkington & Associates Ltd. • Vincent Helton & Associates Ltd.

PARLIAMENT HILL LANDSCAPE PLAN 122–127
CLIENT Public Works Government Services Canada, Parliamentary Precinct Directorate
PRIME CONSULTANT Phillips Farevaag Smallenberg
Partner in Charge: Greg Smallenberg
Project Manager: Chris Mramor
DESIGN TEAM Apropos Planning • James Clark, Landscape Architect • CSV Architects • EvB Communications • Intu Design Ltd. • Julian Smith & Associates Architects • Martin Conboy Lighting Design Inc. • Douglas Paterson, Landscape Architect • Stantec Inc.

RAVINE HOUSE NORTH GARDEN 58–63
CLIENT Private Client
PRIME CONSULTANT Kuwabara Payne McKenna Blumberg Architects
Principal in Charge: Bruce Kuwabara
Project Architect: Paolo Rocha
LANDSCAPE ARCHITECT Phillips Farevaag Smallenberg
Partner in Charge: Greg Smallenberg

RICHMOND CITY HALL 24–29, 286–287
CLIENT City of Richmond
PRIME CONSULTANT Kuwabara Payne McKenna Blumberg Architects in association with Hotson Bakker Boniface Haden
LANDSCAPE ARCHITECT Phillips Farevaag Smallenberg
Partner in Charge: Chris Phillips
Project Manager: Jeffrey Staates
CONSULTING DESIGN TEAM Arbortech • BKL Consultants Ltd. • Bush, Bohlman & Partners • DWT Stanley • G.F. Shymko & Associates Inc. • Locke MacKinnon Domingo Gibson & Associates Ltd. • Morris Specifications Inc. • R.A. Duff & Associates Inc. • Rod Turkington & Associates Ltd. • Vincent Helton & Associates Ltd. • Lynne Werker, Public Art Consultant

RIDEAU HALL LANDSCAPE DESIGN AND MANAGEMENT PLAN 168–171
CLIENT National Capital Commission
PRIME CONSULTANT Phillips Farevaag Smallenberg in association with Julian Smith & Associates Architects
Partner in Charge: Greg Smallenberg
Planning Partner: Marta Farevaag
Project Manager: Rochelle Bacigalupo
CONSULTING DESIGN TEAM Intu Design Ltd. • Mark Laird, Landscape Historian • Martin Conboy Lighting Design Inc. • Douglas Paterson, Landscape Architect • Edwinna von Baeyer, Landscape Historian

ROCKCLIFFE REDEVELOPMENT 66, 72–77
CLIENT Canada Lands Company Ltd.
PRIME CONSULTANT Kuwabara Payne McKenna Blumberg Architects in association with Greenberg Consultants Inc.
SUPPORTING URBAN DESIGN & LANDSCAPE ARCHITECTURE Phillips Farevaag Smallenberg
Partner in Charge: Greg Smallenberg
Project Manager: Jennifer Nagai
CONSULTING DESIGN TEAM Applied Ecological Services Inc. • Barry Padolsky Associates Inc. Architects • Delcan • DST Consulting Engineers Inc. • Halsall Associates Ltd. • IBI Group • Niblett Environmental Associates Inc. • L'OEUF Pearl Poddubiuk et Associés Architectes

SHERBOURNE PARK 9, 18, 21, 46–51
CLIENT Waterfront Toronto
PRIME CONSULTANT Phillips Farevaag Smallenberg
Partner in Charge: Greg Smallenberg
Project Manager: Jennifer Nagai
CONSULTING DESIGN TEAM Jill Anholt, Public Artist • The Planning Partnership, Consulting Landscape Architect • Teeple Architects Inc., Pavilion Architect • Cobalt Engineering • ERA Architects Inc. • The Municipal Infrastructure Group Ltd. • Quinn Dressel Associates • URS Corporation Canada Inc. • Vincent Helton & Associates

SHOUQIU SHAOHAO HISTORIC SITE 206–208
CLIENT City of Qufu
PRIME CONSULTANT Commonwealth Historic Resource Management Limited
LANDSCAPE ARCHITECT Phillips Farevaag Smallenberg
Partner in Charge: Marta Farevaag
Project Manager: Chris Mramor
ARCHITECT Ramsay Worden Architects
CONSULTING DESIGN TEAM
BDCL Design International Ltd. • EVS Environment Consultants • International Centre for Sustainable Cities

TOMB OF THE UNKNOWN SOLDIER 228–231
CLIENT Public Works Government Services Canada, Parliamentary Precinct Directorate
PRIME CONSULTANT Phillips Farevaag Smallenberg in association with Sauve-Boucher
Partner in Charge: Greg Smallenberg
Project Manager: Chris Mramor
CONSULTING DESIGN TEAM Maurice Joanisse, Artist • Mary-Ann Lui, Artist • Martin Conboy Lighting Design Inc. • Eleanor Milne, Art Advisor

TORONTO HARBOURFRONT COMPETITION 40–45
CLIENT City of Toronto
COMPETITION FINALIST Phillips Farevaag Smallenberg
Partner in Charge: Greg Smallenberg
Project Manager: Kelty McKinnon
CONSULTING DESIGN TEAM Fleisher Ridout Partnership Inc. • Julian Smith & Associates Architects • Kuwabara Payne McKenna Blumberg Architects

UNIVERSITY OF BRITISH COLUMBIA OKANAGAN (UBCO) MASTER PLAN 82–84
CLIENT University of British Columbia Okanagan
PRIME CONSULTANT Phillips Farevaag Smallenberg
Planning Partner in Charge: Marta Farevaag
Design Partner in Charge: Greg Smallenberg
Project Manager: Jennifer Nagai
CONSULTING DESIGN TEAM Kuwabara Payne McKenna Blumberg Architects • Stantec Inc.

VAUGHAN CITY HALL AND CIVIC PRECINCT 30–33
CLIENT City of Vaughan
PRIME CONSULTANT Kuwabara Payne McKenna Blumberg Architects
LANDSCAPE ARCHITECT Phillips Farevaag Smallenberg
Partner in Charge: Greg Smallenberg
Project Manager: Jeffrey Staates
CONSULTING DESIGN TEAM Bruce Tree Expert Company Ltd. • cm2r • Conestoga-Rovers and Associates • Dan Euser Water Architecture Inc. • Halcrow Yolles Partnership Inc. • LEA Consulting Ltd. • Leber | Rubes Inc. • Mulvey & Banani International Inc. • PMA Consultant LLC • Stantec Inc.

VILLA GRAZIOLI – CANADIAN EMBASSY 172–175
CLIENT Foreign Affairs and International Trade Canada
PRIME CONSULTANT Julian Smith & Associates Architects in association with Phillips Farevaag Smallenberg
Partner in Charge: Greg Smallenberg

VIMY MEMORIAL RESTORATION 210, 216–227
CLIENT Veterans Affairs Canada
PRIME CONSULTANT Cabinet Lefèvre Architects
LEAD CANADIAN ARCHITECT Julian Smith & Associates Architects
LANDSCAPE ARCHITECT Phillips Farevaag Smallenberg
Partner in Charge: Greg Smallenberg
Project Manager: Chris Mramor
CONSULTING DESIGN TEAM BET Louis Choulet • Bureau Michel Bancon • Cabinet Maurice Virtz • Coshytec • Jacqueline Hucker, Architectural Historian • Martin Conboy Lighting Design Inc. • Monument Vandekerckhove • Veritas

WASHINGTON MUTUAL CENTRE ROOF GARDEN 96–103
CLIENT Washington Mutual, Inc.
PRIME CONSULTANT NBBJ
LANDSCAPE ARCHITECT Phillips Farevaag Smallenberg
Partner in Charge: Chris Phillips
Project Manager: Joseph Fry
CONSULTING DESIGN TEAM Abacus Engineering Corp. • Birmingham & Wood Architects and Planners • Coffman Engineers • Coughlin Porter Lundeen • Magnusson Klemencic Associates • Rod Turkington & Associates Ltd.

WEST DON LANDS PUBLIC REALM PLAN 53–57
CLIENT Waterfront Toronto
PRIME CONSULTANT The Planning Partnership
URBAN DESIGN LEAD Sweeny Sterling Finlayson & Co. Architects Inc.
PUBLIC REALM LEAD Phillips Farevaag Smallenberg
Partner in Charge: Greg Smallenberg
Project Managers: Jeffrey Staates and Kelty McKinnon
CONSULTING DESIGN TEAM Jill Anholt, Public Artist • ERA Architects Inc. • Halsall Associates Ltd. • Martin Conboy Lighting Design Inc. • Studio-Lab Ltd. • Urban Tree and Soils

INTRODUCTION AND INTERVIEW

BRIDGEPOINT HEALTH COMPLEX 144–145
CLIENT Bridgepoint Health
PRIME CONSULTANT Stantec Inc. in association with Kuwabara Payne McKenna Blumberg Architects
LANDSCAPE ARCHITECT Phillips Farevaag Smallenberg
Partner in Charge: Greg Smallenberg
Project Manager: Jeffrey Staates

BURNABY CITY HALL 137, 142
CLIENT City of Burnaby
PRIME CONSULTANT Phillips Farevaag Smallenberg
Partner in Charge: Chris Phillips
Project Manager: Chris Keatley

CANOE LANDING PARK 130, 140, 143
CLIENT Concord Adex Inc.
PRIME CONSULTANT Phillips Farevaag Smallenberg in association with The Planning Partnership and Douglas Coupland, Artist
Partner in Charge: Greg Smallenberg
Project Managers: Jennifer Nagai and Jeffrey Staates

DAVENPORT – LASH MILLER COURTYARD 143
CLIENT Department of Chemistry, University of Toronto
PRIME CONSULTANT Phillips Farevaag Smallenberg
Partner in Charge: Greg Smallenberg
Project Manager: Doug Shearer

5th AND MADISON 10, 14, 144, 154
CLIENT Beacon Capital Partners Inc.
PRIME CONSULTANT Ruffcorn Mott Hinthorne Stine Architects
LANDSCAPE ARCHITECT Phillips Farevaag Smallenberg
Partner in Charge: Greg Smallenberg
Project Manager: Joseph Fry

GLENLYON BUSINESS PARK 6–7, 149, 154
CLIENT Canada Lands Company Ltd.
PRIME CONSULTANT CEI Architecture Planning Interiors in association with Phillips Farevaag Smallenberg
Partner in Charge: Greg Smallenberg
Project Manager: Jim Breadon

MANITOBA HYDRO HEADQUARTERS BUILDING 144
CLIENT Manitoba Hydro
PRIME CONSULTANT Kuwabara Payne McKenna Blumberg Architects in association with Smith Carter Architects

LANDSCAPE ARCHITECT DESIGN
Phillips Farevaag Smallenberg
Partner in Charge: Greg Smallenberg
Project Manager: Jeffrey Staates
LANDSCAPE ARCHITECT OF RECORD
Hilderman Thomas Frank Cram

NORTH VANCOUVER LIBRARY 12, 137
CLIENT City of North Vancouver
PRIME CONSULTANT Diamond and Schmitt Architects Inc. in association with CEI Architecture Planning Interiors
LANDSCAPE ARCHITECT Phillips Farevaag Smallenberg
Partner in Charge: Chris Phillips
Project Managers: Joseph Fry and Kirsten Jones

THE PALISADES 136, 137
CLIENT Westbank Projects Corp.
PRIME CONSULTANT James KM Cheng Architects Inc.
LANDSCAPE ARCHITECT Phillips Farevaag Smallenberg
Partner in Charge: Chris Phillips

THE RESIDENCES 137
CLIENT Westbank Projects Corp.
PRIME CONSULTANT James KM Cheng Architects Inc.
LANDSCAPE ARCHITECT Phillips Farevaag Smallenberg
Partner in Charge: Chris Phillips

RICHMOND OLYMPIC OVAL 13, 137
CLIENT City of Richmond
PRIME CONSULTANT Cannon Design in association with Hotson Bakker Boniface Haden
LANDSCAPE ARCHITECT Phillips Farevaag Smallenberg
Partner in Charge: Chris Phillips
Project Managers: Joseph Fry and Lin Lin

SAFECO ROOF GARDEN 150, 154
CLIENT Safeco Insurance Company of America
PRIME CONSULTANT Gensler
LANDSCAPE ARCHITECT Phillips Farevaag Smallenberg
Partner in Charge: Chris Phillips
Project Manager: Joseph Fry

SHANGRI-LA VANCOUVER 132, 135
CLIENT Westbank Projects Corp. in association with Peterson Investment Group Inc.
PRIME CONSULTANT James KM Cheng Architects Inc.

LANDSCAPE ARCHITECT Phillips Farevaag Smallenberg
Partner in Charge: Chris Phillips
Project Manager: Blair Guppy

SOUTHEAST FALSE CREEK PLAZA 135, 155
CLIENT City of Vancouver
PRIME CONSULTANT Phillips Farevaag Smallenberg in association with Hotson Bakker Boniface Haden
Partner in Charge: Chris Phillips
Project Manager: Blair Guppy

WALL CENTRE 4, 133, 135
CLIENT Wall Financial Corporation
PRIME CONSULTANT Bruno Freschi Architects • Hamilton Doyle Architects • Busby Perkins + Will
LANDSCAPE ARCHITECT Phillips Farevaag Smallenberg
Partners in Charge: Greg Smallenberg and Chris Phillips
Project Managers: Chris Mramor and Jeffrey Staates

WATERFRONT ESTATE 137, 139
CLIENT Private Client
PRIME CONSULTANT Arthur Erickson, Architect and Nick Milkovich Architects Inc.
LANDSCAPE ARCHITECT Phillips Farevaag Smallenberg
Partner in Charge: Chris Phillips
Project Manager: Chris Mramor

WOODWARD'S REDEVELOPMENT 135
CLIENT Westbank Projects Corp. in association with Peterson Investment Group Inc.
PRIME CONSULTANT Henriquez Partners Architects
LANDSCAPE ARCHITECT Phillips Farevaag Smallenberg
Partner in Charge: Greg Smallenberg
Project Manager: Jeffrey Staates

WYNDANSEA RESORT 152, 154
CLIENT Marine Drive Properties
PRIME CONSULTANT Folio Design, LLC
LANDSCAPE ARCHITECT Phillips Farevaag Smallenberg
Partner in Charge: Greg Smallenberg
Project Manager: Kelty McKinnon

Image Credits

This work is subject to copyright. All rights are reserved, whether the whole or part of the material is concerned, specifically the rights of translation, reprinting, re-use of illustrations, recitation, broadcasting, reproduction on microfilms or in other ways, and storage in data banks.

For any kind of use, permission of the copyright owner must be obtained. Every reasonable attempt has been made to identify the copyright owners of the pictures reproduced in this book. Errors or omissions will be corrected in subsequent reprints or new editions.

All photographs, drawings, renderings and models have been produced by Phillips Farevaag Smallenberg except for the following:

BELLEVUE CITY HALL
Lara Swimmer Photography: 34, 35 top, 36–37, 38 top, 38 bottom.

BLUE MOUNTAIN
OTOphOTO: 198 top, 201 top.

CANADIAN POLICE AND PEACE OFFICERS' MEMORIAL
Heawon Chun: 232, 234–235.

CANADIAN VETERANS' MEMORIAL
K. J. Bedford: 213, 237, 239.
Alan McKay Harding: 238 bottom left and right.
Christian Merrill: 240.

CATHEDRAL PLACE
SITE Photography, Scott Massey: 92 bottom, 94, 95.

CENTRAL EXPERIMENTAL FARM MANAGEMENT PLAN
Apollo Reverente: 177, 179 top and bottom.
Heawon Chun: 178 top and middle.

CANOE LANDING PARK
Courtesy of Concord ADEX: 130.

COAL HARBOUR MARINA NEIGHBOURHOOD PHASE ONE
SITE Photography, Scott Massey: 242, 250, 252 top and bottom, 254 top, 254–255 bottom series, 256–257.

CONFEDERATION SQUARE
Ewald Richter: 156.
Heawon Chun: 159, 165 top and bottom, 166–167.

EAST BAYFRONT PRECINCT PLAN – PUBLIC REALM AND STREETSCAPE
Urban Strategies, Courtesy of Waterfront Toronto: 69, 80.
Apollo Reverente: 78, 81 top and bottom.

5th AND MADISON
Benjamin Benschneider Photography: 10, 14, 144.

GLENLYON BUSINESS PARK
SITE Photography, Scott Massey: 149.

HASTINGS PARK
Pablo Mandel: 86.
Courtesy of the City of Vancouver: 115.

LANGARA COLLEGE LIBRARY
SITE Photography, Scott Massey: 258.
Shai Gil Photography: 260–261, 262 top, 263, 264–265.

MOUNTAIN VIEW CEMETERY – MASONIC AREA REDEVELOPMENT
Amanda Bullick Photography: 104, 106–107 top, 108 top and bottom, 109 top and bottom, 111, 112–113.

THE PALISADES
SITE Photography, Scott Massey: 136.

PARLIAMENT HILL LANDSCAPE PLAN
Courtesy of the Parlimentary Precinct Directorate: 123 top and bottom.

RAVINE HOUSE NORTH GARDEN
Tom Arban Photography: 58, 60–61, 62 top and bottom, 63 top and bottom.

RICHMOND CITY HALL
SITE Photography, Scott Massey: 24, 26 top, 29 bottom right.

RIDEAU HALL LANDSCAPE DESIGN AND MANAGEMENT PLAN
Canadian Aerial Photo Corporation: 169.
Heawon Chun: 170 top and bottom, 171.

ROCKCLIFFE REDEVELOPMENT
Canadian Aerial Photo Corporation: 72 bottom.
Kuwabara Payne McKenna Blumberg Architects with PFS: 75.

SAFECO ROOF GARDEN
Sam Van Fleet: 150.

SHERBOURNE PARK
Pro Modelbuilders (model construction), Walter La Daca Photography (photos): 49 right top to bottom.
Jill Anholt Studio: 51 top right.

Book Credits

SOUTHEAST FALSE CREEK PLAZA
Bob Matheson Photography: 155.

TOMB OF THE UNKNOWN SOLDIER
Heawon Chun: 230.

TORONTO HARBOURFRONT COMPETITION
Courtesy of the City of Toronto: 41 top.
Apollo Reverente: 41 bottom, 45 top left.
Courtesy of Kuwabara Payne McKenna Blumberg
Architects: 45 top right.

VAUGHAN CITY HALL AND CIVIC PRECINCT
Kuwabara Payne McKenna Blumberg Architects: 31,
33 bottom.

VILLA GRAZIOLI – CANADIAN EMBASSY
Giacomo Foti Fotografia: 172, 174, 175.

VIMY MEMORIAL RESTORATION
Blair Ketcheson Photography: 210, 216, 217, 218–219, 221,
222–223, 224, 225 top and bottom, 226–227.

WALL CENTRE PLAZA
SITE Photography, Scott Massey: 4, 134.

WASHINGTON MUTUAL CENTRE ROOF GARDEN
George White Photography: 98, 103.
Lara Swimmer Photography: 100 top and bottom,
102 bottom.

NON-PROJECT RELATED IMAGES:
Ramsay Worden Architects: 185 bottom.
Pablo Mandel: 246.
Emily Carr, *Cedar*, 1942, oil on canvas. Collection of
the Vancouver Art Gallery, Emily Carr Trust. (Photo:
Vancouver Art Gallery): 247.
SITE Photography, Scott Massey: 274 left and right, 275
left and right, 286–287.
www.istockphoto.com: 248.

BOOK DESIGN   Pablo Mandel / CircularStudio
DIGITAL IMAGE RETOUCHING   Doug McCaffry / Scanlab

TYPEFACE   In spite of—or perhaps because of—Helvetica's reputation for cold, calculated perfection, it has been the world's most popular Roman typeface for over four decades. Drawn by Max Medinger and introduced under the name Neue Haas Grotesk in 1957, its roots lie in much quirkier and personable material. Its earliest direct ancestor, known simply as Grotesk, was first introduced by the Schelter & Giesecke foundry in Leipzig around 1880. The Bauhaus, in nearby Dessau, chose this face as the main workhorse for their printing shop, and used it for the vast majority of their classic experiments in asymmetrical typography. In 1999 Erik Spiekermann asked type designer Christian Schwartz to consider drawing a revival of S&G's Grotesk, updating the family for contemporary typographic needs without rationalizing away the spirit and warmth of the original. The Regular, Medium and Bold are drawn directly from S&G sources, and the Super was added for situations where subtlety would be inappropriate. The family is released in 2002 under the name FF Bau, in homage to the most noted users of the original.
Source: www.fontfont.com

Richmond City Hall, Richmond, BC.

QTO SB 469.386 .C2 G76 2010

Grounded

Maryland Institute, College of Art
The Decker Library
1401 Mount Royal Avenue
Baltimore, MD 21217